The Bear
Went Over
the Mountain

For Theresa —
Enjoy the journey.
Keep the music playing.

Affectionately,
Carole

3/18

The Bear
Went Over
the Mountain

Finding America, Finding Myself

CARLL TUCKER

Mary Ann Liebert, Inc. publishers

Library of Congress Control Number 2007939788
ISBN: 978-0-913113-47-9 (cloth)
ISBN: 978-0-913113-43-1 (pbk)

Mary Ann Liebert, Inc., Publishers
140 Huguenot Street
New Rochelle, NY 10801

Printed in the United States of America.

For Peter, Becca, David –
without whom nothing

"I sha'n't be gone long, you come too."
—Robert Frost

Contents

Sunday Memorial Day weekend. 50. I buckle myself into an RV and flee to America.

I had never traveled in an RV, never been alone or anonymous, never fended for myself, never visited most states. I was counting on novelty to forestall despair.

My plan was to do something obvious no one had thought of. Why not visit the graves of the Presidents and Vice Presidents? Presidential grave-hopping is nothing new. But Vice Presidents? The Vice Presidents are fine company when you're feeling low. Except for the 14 who succeeded to the top job—and a few others noted for other achievements—these one-time titans have shriveled like popped balloons.

It would take about six months. Add the rest of the 48 contiguous states and the inevitable postcard sites and I'd be busy for nine—a resonant total.

Climate and map set my route. Home was Bedford, New York, a well-groomed suburb an hour north of Manhattan. From Bedford I'd drive south to Pennsylvania, west across the Appalachians, zigzag across the heartland to the Rockies, hug the Pacific from LA to Seattle, and return home via the Great Lakes, taking in New York and New England during their flamboyant fall. Home through Christmas, I'd return to the road in January, visiting the Southeast—west to Texas—for my winter leg.

The book I had in mind—well, I didn't really, just say what I saw. By looking, I've learned, you can see a lot. It's surprising how much.

1
A New Birth
of Freedom

i.

Embarking on a nine month meander of America—in a motor home—
elicits a variety of response, at least where I come from.

"You're what?"

"You're kidding, right?"

"Travels with Charley, eh?"

"On the Road."

"William—what's his name—Moon. Least-Heat Moon."

"That Frenchman, de something."

"Finding yourself?"

"Alone?"

"I've always wanted . . ."

"So what are you running away from?"

Reactions depict reactors. One or two pause. "I'm going to miss you."

Wherever we run is from. From here, yesterday.

Wherever we run is to.

My stated goal is to visit the graves and memorials of all our Presidents
and Vice Presidents and, for good measure, the 48 proximate American
states. That will keep me moving. My private motive is . . . who knows, as
mixed as dirt.

"I hear you're going to find yourself."

"I found myself years ago and was delighted with the discovery."

Where I come from, people do not volunteer to do strange things in their
middle years. It bespeaks failure. Appearances matter a lot and cost a lot.
Clipped climbing roses of exotic provenance and chintzes at God knows

what a yard. Lexuses and Mercedes our Chevys and Hondas. Perfect wives looming in their SUV's. "Expensive! Expensive!" each understated detail pulses like a motel vacancy light.

Net worth is worth. At the private elementary school of which I am a graduate, educators take pains to deny this. They teach "values." One value they do not teach is selling the sparkling vehicles in the parking lot, buying practical replacements, and remitting the residue to the poor.

I have lived here all my life. I learned to play tennis at "the Club" where whites-only is the rule both on the courts and the admissions committee. I have served my neighbors as editor and publisher of the local newspaper for 19 years, trustee of various charities, chairman of the hospital, cracker barrel pundit in my weekly column. We live in a nice house with a big field. Our three children grew up here. Our youngest is old enough to die in the army if not to order beer at a bar.

It is time for me to go.

Where to? Wherever. Itineraries silence inquiries. Going nowhere looks bad. Visiting the memorials of *all* our chief executives and their mostly forgotten understudies may be something to blab about. "Guess where Grover Cleveland's buried?" "Who was Schuyler Colfax?" Activity blinds us to our absence of significance. I'm busy, therefore I am.

I go not to stay. I go because I've been a somebody all my life, a small somebody, and now I want to be nobody. I go because last week, passing a house on "prestigious" Guard Hill (as the realtors style it), I realized I knew the names of its four previous owners, two now dead. I go because one life is too few.

ii.

Gray, gusty. Migrant shudders on the empty highway. We are new to each other.

Migrant is a Type C motor home, 23 feet long, 8-½ feet high, her white exterior, except for side door, windows, and retractable awning, identical to a box truck's. In theory, she can sleep five if you lower the eating table into a palette and spread a mattress on the ledge above the cab. My ledge is crammed with books, tapes, overflow from the closets. There are cartons—of more tapes and books—beneath my table. I want company no more than a turtle in its shell.

My decision still dazes me. My morning routine had been to wake early, write till I flagged, then drive to nearby Mount Kisco for a Starbucks. I'd order a Venti Frappacino or a Venti Mocha. That was how it was 30 days ago: Mayday. The cup was warm in my hand. Music was playing: Bach.

Guard Hill Road is unpaved. The houses cost millions. Their owners enjoy the illusion of an idyll 40 miles north of Manhattan. Maintaining dirt roads is more expensive than maintaining paved. You have to scrape and gutter them so they don't washboard or gully.

I know every house on this road. When I was a boy, we used to drive this way to "the Club." I wasn't very athletic, but I worked hard at my tennis because I knew my parents would be pleased. I got good grades at school for the same reason. Sometimes, we'd ride our horses on Guard Hill. On the straightaways we'd gallop, pebbles winging off hooves.

I had passed the Clock Tower, heading east. The Clock Tower is a Colonial style brick edifice in the middle of nowhere. The story, as I recall, involved a new husband anxious to console his unhappy bride. He'd moved her here from the City—this was before cars—and he thought it would soothe her to hear the gong of a clock.

Past the Clock Tower is where my son Peter, newly licensed, caught his right tire in the ditch and flipped clear over. There were no witnesses so I blamed the accident on myself. I dislike lying but the insurance company isn't a person. The cost of fixing the car would be the same no matter who'd been driving.

Beyond where the ditch used to be there's this white house. It's pretty and I like looking at it. That Mayday I looked at it and . . . something happened. This idea came to me—fully armed—like Athena out of Zeus's ear. The RV, the Presidents and Vice Presidents, it was all there. A minute before I'd been thinking about the novel I was working on and suddenly I was somebody else.

That night I told my wife. She was angry. Twenty-six years we've been married and always there's this writing between us like a slammed door. Even when I'm home I'm not home.

I could have asked her permission, I suppose, or broken it to her gently. But what could she have said? I told her the way you rip a band-aid. She turned rigid. Words rushed at her but she did not utter them. Why bother? I was going—nine months, maybe more, maybe forever. And that was that.

iii.

Garret Hobart is the first of my 65 dead white guys.[1]

Since our Presidents number 43 and our Vice Presidents 46, 65 seems a low tally, but then:

- one of our Presidents was a duplicate (Cleveland, our 22nd and 24th)
- nine Presidents and Vice Presidents were still above ground
- nine Vice Presidents succeeded to the office on the President's death or resignation and five won the job on their own.

Hunting down 65 graves carries me through 23 states and 226 years of history. It takes me places I would not otherwise dream of. Malone, New York, where William Wheeler is buried, is not a city to visit for any reason.

Presidential grave-hopping is not unusual. There are books that tell you how. At least two Americans have made their "search" for dead Presidents the basis for personal web sites. These sites feature snapshots of ample T-shirts leaning against, say, Fillmore's obelisk in Buffalo or the Adamses' cramped catacomb in Quincy.

Tracking Vice Presidents is trickier. The Internet helps. Findagrave.com records the posthumous whereabouts of millions of notables, at no charge. Why this site exists is a mystery. As with much on the web, it is pure gift, like a juggler on a street corner.

Migrant is not ideal for navigating cemeteries. She's wider than some archways. She's taller than cemetery branches, which are pruned hearse-high. Many the oak or spruce I've heard hideously clawing my roof.

I like cemeteries. They're quiet. Even when they're ugly they're pretty. Layout, architecture, and rhetoric recall residents' ways.

Mid-sized cities like Paterson, New Jersey, tend to contain one old ceme-tery, now located in a decrepit district. Beyond rusting wrought-iron fences, windows are boarded and trash whirls. Within, weeds encroach and paths rut as the cost of "perpetual care" exceeds donors' endowments. There are headstones askew, like bad teeth, and pediments resting where they top-pled. After 150 years, inscriptions fade to illegibility.

Garret Hobart sleeps in a mausoleum. Sundays there are no maintenance men about and the office is closed, so it isn't easy to find. Happily I have a

---

[1]That one, arguably two, weren't white I learned later.

printout, with a T-shirted grave-hopper by an iron door. Mausoleums be-came fashionable in the age of mansions. From 1870 to 1930 merit was measurable in marble. Cremation gained favor in an incinerating age.

Garret Hobart was William McKinley's first Vice President. He died in office, in 1899, of heart disease. He was 57. If he'd lived two years longer, 28-year-old Leon Czolgosz's second bullet would have created President Hobart, not President Roosevelt. There'd be no San Juan Hill in our mythology, no national park system perhaps, no Teddy bear.

iv.

Fla-Net Park and Netcong weren't on my itinerary. I'd never heard of Netcong, and it's not all that near where I wanted to go. My plan, after hunting down Hobart in Paterson, had been to overnight in the Delaware and Raritan Canal State Park. The only problem was, I hadn't called ahead. "You're calling Thursday," the girl laughed, "for Sunday Memorial Day Weekend!" I leafed through my Woodall's Campground Directory for North America, a 2,000-page tome detailing a world of which, until a month ago, I had lived in ignorance. The laughter was repeated by other pleasant voices—"Do you know what day it is?" asked one, who thought me kidding—until a chipper older lady said, yes, they had room at Fla-Net, for reasons I now discern.

Fla-Net has been plopped on one of those otherwise useless plots cre-ated when mammoth new shopping plazas are superimposed. A hill had been scalped, leaving darkened acres beneath the embankments of access roads. You couldn't locate even a self-storage facility here, or a warehouse, or a jail, and surely no one would choose to reside beneath the roar and grind of big-rigs. Perfect, then, for a seasonal RV campground whose pa-trons count pennies and object to almost nothing, as long as sewer and electric and water connect.

My slot is P-4. P stands for pull-through, a happy chance for one so un-skilled in reversing. How do you back up when you can't see behind? The side-mirrors try to peer around my van, craning their necks, but to fully re-flect the rear view is impossible. Truckers manage this all the time, with an ease I'd never honored.

My first business is to stow my last bags and the groceries. I take it slowly—what's the hurry? A tight space enforces attention. Pile things and you'll soon be tripping over them.

I choose Beethoven's string quartets Op. 59 #2 ("Rasumovsky") and Op. 74 ("The Harp") and play them loud. At home I can't do that. Past a certain hour music wakens—or signals my availability for conversation. My seclusion depends on keeping quiet. To play music loudly and refuse to open my study door would be insulting.

The music sounds fine. The red tomatoes and the uncooked steak on the counter—between the black three-burner range and the brushed stainless steel sink—look fine. As places are found for my clothes and books and jars and cans, my little realm looks fine—not pristine—that is not my nature—but orderly and serene. I pour myself a Jack Daniel's. It tastes fine. A bottle of Australian Miraz purchased at Shoprite promises future pleasure. I locate my saucepan and its lid and place the purple meat, red tomatoes, green lettuce, and two dill pickles to cook together. Then it is time for my first shower, which feels fine (if cramped).

Emerging clean, I wonder what to wear for dinner. Khaki shorts, a clean polo shirt, and sandals, I think, would be comfortable and seemly. But then I ask myself, Why wear anything? The shades are drawn, the door is locked, no one knows where I am, why not sit to dinner naked? This idea amuses me. It's not that I glory in my physique. I avoid mirrors. My body does not repel me but neither does it please. It just is, a necessary conveyance, with its share of maintenance problems. Sooner or later it will break down.

What amuses me is not the spectacle but the comedy. All my life I have "dressed for dinner." "Dress for dinner" is a phrase with exact connotations. And now, for the first time since infancy, I don't have to. I can be who I please.

Most people shy from freedom. They prefer enclosure—in relationships, obligations, associations, expectations. They want to have a name, neighbors, their particular pew. They do not want to ask, Who am I undressed?

I toast my new life—and Beethoven—and the steer sacrificed for my delectation—and the Australian vintner—and slip to sleep happy.

v.

My first full day on the job I . . . take off. Hey, it's Memorial Day: the whole country has today off!

Fact is, I'm beat. The consequences of my lurch are coming clear. Nine months from home is a long time.

8

Thankfully, I'm busy. One of the secret benefactions of an RV is its neediness. It demands to be filled, emptied, scrubbed, repaired. Many the retiree whose life's purpose is to putter.

I've scribbled a list. Towel hook for my shower, toilet paper holder, bungee cords to keep my books from sliding. Also a proper mop, and soap dish, and bug spray, and a doormat (rubber-backed, not to slide), and a trash pail small enough to stow behind the chair. Also dinner, and wine, and a hairbrush to scratch my back, and a bed-tray with legs where I can set books and water-bottle in the night and coffee and biscuits when I wake. And a flyswatter.

I am not a person who's ever bought such things. They were always there. Once, I mopped—when a water pipe burst and steam threatened the furniture.

I've never been in a Wal-Mart. I followed Sam Walton's story but felt no need to sample his wares. His formula, like so many big ideas, seems obvious in hindsight. Vast selection, cheap prices, courteous service—of course that's what shoppers want!

Two things surprise me about this Wal-Mart. First, there's no way out. I'm pretty good at directions, but here there's no sun or moon or Exit sign to steer by. You take a turn, then another, then another, and soon you are as lost as Hansel and Gretel. I could ask one of the beaming customer service associates, or whatever they're called, but not knowing the way out embarrasses me. Accelerating, I take a turn, then another, then a third—picking up one or two more items (which is what they intend)—until, panic mounting, I inquire.

My second surprise is the guys' faces. They're sad. Unshaved, in their twenties, with clinging shirts or a piratical earring, they've been dragged, this sunny Memorial Day, by the wife with tots in tow. The wives beam. They meet other wives and laugh and extol the finery of daughters. (One girl, she couldn't have been six, sported glittering eyeshadow and purple nails. She batted her eyes and posed her hands on her hips, like a cowboy-western madam.) The men grunt greetings, ashamed to be found here. Sons, tetchy, bolting, are rebuked for rambunctiousness.

I feel for the husbands. This is not where they should be—choosing this or that shower curtain on their day off. They should be in the open, banging a ball, buffing a truck, downing a convivial beer. Maleness used to be a big deal. But then something happened. Our strength wasn't needed any more—everything was push-button, including war. Our paychecks still came in handy—but the wife had a paycheck too. Even our seed wasn't needed: you could buy the missing ingredient at a sperm bank. A man's use now was to lug groceries—if he had any use at all.

vi.

Two miles out jogging. I hurry back. So many thoughts. I carry them as gingerly as eggs.

Item: The jollification of America. Front lawns and stoops regaled with flags, pennants, flowers, welcome signs and mats, wreaths, cutesy icons (mostly animals), statuary (religious and secular), birdbaths, benches, homey mottos, leftover Christmas tree lights. The validation of hospitality: I greet therefore I am. (Today's smiler: "You've seen the best, now visit the WURST!")

Item: Farm workers happier than mall shoppers. Leaner. Mental health means knowing we're meant.

Item: The dizzying perfume of honeysuckle, like a sudden dive into a boudoir. Buttercups, dandelions, white and purple thistles.

Item: A man mowing his lawn. Waves. Just another man. On Friendship Road.

Learning to attach my sewer hose, I get dowsed. *Item:* Why does waste disgust? To be discussed.

vii.

In the Princeton Cemetery, six graves attract. Two are on my itinerary. The other four snag my attention as I pass.

Grover Cleveland's modest monument makes no mention of the Presidency. Famously a scowler, is he scowling still?

Aaron Burr, Jr., Vice President and murderer of Alexander Hamilton, rests at the feet of his father's much larger marker. His dad was a Big Man—President of Princeton, son-in-law of the vaunted preacher Jonathan

10

Edwards. How much of the younger Aaron's wildness is attributable to desperation to reach his fathers' heights?

Paul Tulane (1801–1887) stands atop a tall pedestal. The benefactor of the university that bears his name, Tulane is portrayed as a craggy seer. His is the only statue in these decorous acres. No mention is made of his career as a dry-goods merchant. A bird has shat on his cheek and shoulder, too high to scrub.

The headstone of John O'Hara (1905–1970), a novelist never noted for humility, proclaims, "Better than anyone else, he told the truth of his time." Better than . . . T. S. Eliot? Faulkner? Frost? Williams? Hemingway? Fitzgerald? Auden? Nabokov? Warren? Welty? Better than—even—Ogden Nash?

An epitaph—for William H. Hahn, Jr. (1905–1980)—makes me sorry not to have known the man: "I told you I was sick."

The final tomb belongs to an unfamous couple, of which the husband is still living. On a long gray marble slab, their faces are amateurishly etched. Beneath names and dates and places of birth, they exchange connubial baby talk, indecipherable to the passerby. It's as if they'd left their bedroom door open. The effect is at once embarrassing and poignant, like desperate lovers clutching in a terminal, oblivious to the crowds.

viii.

The line for Independence Hall is an hour and a half. I find myself in the midst of a restless tenth-grade trip. They eye me curiously. A middle-aged guy with a backpack, who *chooses* to visit this stuff? What kind of dude is that!

My companions and the heat gloom me. I check my watch. I'd come to Philadelphia for George Dallas, Polk's neglected Vice President. Dallas's support for the annexation of Texas earned him the naming of a town, but who knows this, even in his eponymous metropolis? Who visits his cracked headstone, fading to illegibility in a parish graveyard?

I was in search of adventures, not your standard tourist sites. Independence Hall is one of those places, like Mount Rushmore or the Statue of Liberty, you've visited whether you have or not. If I left now, I'd beat rush hour—traffic is no treat in my van. A nice Sauvignon Blanc was chilling in my fridge—and fried chicken, and tomatoes, and plump peaches from a

11

farm stand. I could feel my skin after a shower—and the air conditioner—and Handel on the stereo, a flute sonata or concerto.

I almost bolt. But then the line shortens—what the hell, another 10 minutes, maybe 15. I lower my cap and try to doze standing.

Herded through the metal detector, I sit for the ranger's orientation. The more visited the site, the more banal the tour. The class-trippers snicker and smack gum. An earnest Asian-American translates loudly for her mother.

The Court Room is interesting enough, but now we are in the Assembly Chamber, where the Declaration of Independence was signed and the Constitution drafted. The ranger's voice fades with her kindergartenish Q-and-A. I imagine squat John Adams gesticulating forcefully, while lanky redheaded Jefferson sits silent, bemused, and Ben Franklin, chin lowered, seems to nap. John Hancock tilts back from his raised desk, as elegant and assured as Copley's portrait. It is warm—delegates fan themselves. The air quivers. Their assent to the document being debated could mean their necks in a noose.

Now it is 11 years later. Washington sits in the elevated chair, blank and stony as a pharaoh. Alexander Hamilton, another redhead, is talking, while skinny Jemmy Madison leans over a desk, explaining. Ben Franklin still seems to be napping. The fear is gone and in its place passionate divisions about the best shape for this new kind of nation. There is no debate, oddly enough, about this nation's unprecedented premise—that without king or aristocracy, free men could govern themselves.

Suddenly I am crying. The enormity of our fortune fills me like a cup past the brim. I pretend my eyes itch. To think of all we owe these men, mere men, for their courage and foresight. Before them, there had never been a nation like this. Two hundred twenty-six years later, this model would be the choice of most of those free to choose. The political engine manufactured in this room would power the spread of freedom to all races and conditions; an amassing and dispersion of wealth beyond imagining; and the fortification of freedom against oppression. There would be mistakes: slavery, genocide, foreign adventures. But where would our world be without what these men made? What would have become of Europe or ideas or innovation without American might? Even my paragraphs look to these men as fathers, for where there is no opportunity to express there is no enticement to reflect.

I wander the leafy brick streets of Society Hill, asking as the light fades: How can I thank them? How?

ix.

I wake with the sun. Over the hill's crest is a ribbon of shine. Rest makes me strong with hope. Spirits soar when we feel equal to our task.

One miracle of the road is concentration. I am enriched by all I *don't* have to do. Much of the audience no doubt smiles patronizingly when Porgy sings,

> I got plenty of nuthin'
> And nuthin's plenty for me;

"That plucky cripple—he's making the best of his rotten luck." Porgy is the wiser. Nuthin' *is* plenty—and more—for it restores to us the sun and the birds and the soft moment of waking, which busyness and business obscure.

We have more time than strength. Hours are not equal. For a few our heads and sinews flex; during the remainder, we lug our selves like a heavy pack. How many devote their best hours to their best use? Instead, we must shave and shower and dress and speed to the train to elbow into a seat to jostle with crowds to reach our desks. There's the newspaper and radio. But radio and newspapers are thin gruel for minds. They are to cerebration what golf is to exercise.

That was what I did for my most potent years—day after day, a martyr to some myth about "making it" and "keeping up." Earn more, buy more— for what? For more things to wheedle more time? To be envied for accomplishments I could not applaud?

This morning I wake. My window is six inches from my eyes. I stare into the unprecedented dawn. My toilet is two steps from my bed. I drain the night's accumulation, a sweet pleasure that most of us in our hurry overlook. I light my little kettle, spoon coffee into a beaker, arrange my bed tray, note the clock more from curiosity than compulsion, pour my coffee, flip open my laptop and I'm off, the freshness of the moment bellying my thought. No phones, no logistics, no niceties, just my work, which, to my shame, I waited a lifetime to accept.

"But you are lucky," I hear you object. "You sold your company. You can afford to loll!"

True, my criminal waste of years bought me something. But no honorable vocation really costs much. Thoreau did these calculations a century and a half ago. For six weeks' manual labor, he figured, he could buy 46 of freedom. The secret of economy is simple: spend less than you earn.

13

I have many fewer belongings in my van than I had at home, but I could do with fewer still. Things become our excuse for not being. Maybe the faces at Wal-Mart are sad because they're buying things they don't need, don't want, and can't afford.

X.

Woodward Hill Cemetery isn't easy to find. It's located on South Queen Street in Lancaster, Pennsylvania, which is now a barrio. Neighbors speak Spanish, laughing and arguing, calling from one porch to the other. A block away they have never heard of Woodward Hill—or James Buchanan. Maybe they didn't understand my question.

Lancaster could have been a contender. For a single day the Continental Congress met here—in 1777—as the delegates fled Philadelphia and the British. Lancaster was a candidate to become our national capital, beaten out by Washington, D.C. From 1799 to 1812, Lancaster was the capital of Pennsylvania, until that was moved to Harrisburg. The Conestoga wagon, which carried pioneers west, was manufactured in Lancaster. So was the Pennsylvania rifle (also called the Kentucky). F. W. Woolworth opened his first five-and-dime in Lancaster, changing forever America's—and the world's—shopping.

Today, Lancaster is a dilapidating shell, refilling with recent immigrants. It feels bewildered, like a stroke victim. It is alive, yes—it can lift its eyelids, gasp a few words, detect a pulse—but what is it supposed to *do*? It may learn to walk again, even thrive, but that's to be seen. Urban recoveries, like human, are hard to predict.

Climbing Woodward Hill a tombstone stops me. Its inscription reads:

CHARLES WINOWER

1865 –

CATHARINE J. WILL

HIS WIFE

1868 –1942

CORA E. DAUGHTER OF

CHARLES AND CARRIE E. WINOWER

1891 –1913

14

I snap a picture, to be sure. Where was Charles? If he were alive—age 137—we'd have heard of him. He seems to have outlived his second wife (Catharine J. Will and Carrie E. could not be the same person) and his daughter, who died at 22. But then what? Did he lose his mind? His money? Did he remarry—at 77—and take his repose beside a third bride? Did the carver forget to fill in the blank?

Buchanan lies alone as he lay—at least officially—all his days, our only bachelor President. The idea of a bachelor President troubles us, so we contrive an explanation—a youthful broken engagement, a grief-stricken fiancée who commits suicide, a disconsolate James who can never bring himself to wed. It makes a good story. Only months later will I stumble on a different explanation, which the docents at Wheatland, Buchanan's Lancaster estate, might hesitate to accept.

If only I could root for Buchanan. Lincoln and Washington and Jefferson and the Roosevelts don't need admirers. Neither do Jackson or Polk or Truman or Kennedy or Reagan or—any longer—thanks to a best-selling biography, grouchy John Adams. It's the ignored I want to boost. But Buchanan makes it hard.

No President was more preoccupied with appearances, not even Reagan. Buchanan was a dandy, tall, elegant, precise, diplomatic to a fault. He kept track of his every penny in script as flawless as a schoolmistress's. The tail of his initial J coils thrice like a snake—it must have taken him a minute to execute his autograph. Through the front entrance of Wheatland, which he described as "the beau ideal of a statesman's abode," he welcomed Southerners; through the rear, Northerners. Why? Because the front boasts a white portico, reminiscent of a plantation, while the rear is more restrained and New Englandish.

Buchanan spent much of his career as a diplomat.[2] Diplomacy makes a poor training ground for leaders. Easy duplicity and an impulse to appease ill become an establisher of policy and enforcer of the law. In the four years before the Civil War, when he might have used his authority to force a reconciliation between north and south, Buchanan sat and hoped—and drank. After Lincoln was elected, he quit trying.

Buchanan said to his successor at his inauguration, "My dear sir, if you are as happy in entering the White House as I shall feel on returning to Wheatland, you are a happy man indeed."

---

[2]Buchanan was an ambassador twice—to Russia, under President Jackson, and to England, under President Pierce. In between he was Secretary of State to President Polk.

xi.

"Have you done Gettysburg yet?"

Gettysburg is one of those places Americans "do." Niagara Falls, Disney World, Mount Rushmore, Hearst Castle, the Statue of Liberty, Grand Ole Opry, Grand Canyon, the Alamo, Independence Hall, we check them off. Lesser-known landmarks we may discover, but these must-sees we surrender to: buy our ticket, get in line, and see what we are shown.

I grit my teeth. I want to experience Gettysburg; I don't want "the Gettysburg experience." I am an explorer. If I dress like a tourist and snap pictures and grin on cue, it is only because I go disguised. It scares me to become another click through the turnstile.

"Destination attractions," as the travel industry dubs them, bob in a sea of crud. T-shirts, mugs, wax museums, halls of fame, perfumed candles, plush toys—there's no end to what we'll shell out for. We're suckers for cute. Ye-olde's and costumed waitresses and "authentic olde-style tavernes" (for some reason we favor extra e's) make us feel at home.

The standard Gettysburg tour begins where the battle did, so unexpectedly, that July morning. The quiet took me by surprise. Gone now are the honky-tonk and jarring jokes ("If at first you don't secede . . ."). Except for a passing jet and occasional distant car, the gentle hills look much as they did when eager Harry Heth's Union infantry met hard-driving John Buford's Confederate cavalry and the fight was joined. Soon corps after corps were pouring into one another—ten thousand dead or wounded on that day alone. It is quiet enough to hear the "bullets hissing, humming and whistling everywhere; cannon roaring; all crash on crash and peal on peal, smoke, blood, wreck and carnage incomparable," as one young gunner recalled.

Monuments proliferate—hundreds, in all shapes and sizes. Here at such an hour this regiment made a stand and there a general fell and there a corps, despite grievous casualties, recombined to attack, and to the memory of these gallant soldiers the good citizens of Vermont—or North Carolina—or Rhode Island—or Cayuga County—have erected this memorial. Atop Seminary and Cemetery Ridges, so many pillars and obelisks and statues and slabs stand sentinel it seems as if that terrible hour of 1:00 p.m., July 3, 1863, were about to toll anew.

I'm not one for military history. Flanks and feints and ordinance and corps and brigades flummox me. Perhaps because I've never been a soldier, my imagination struggles to reconstruct battles. Shut my eyes and all about me is clash and stench.

16

The wonder of Gettysburg National Park is how clearly the complicated events of those three days lay out. Squint and you can almost discern the troops arrayed or the sharpshooter crouched on the rock. You can feel Lee's quandary (Without a victory here, could the South forestall defeat?), his frustrations (Where was Jeb Stuart when he needed him? Why, in God's name, didn't Longstreet or Ewell move?) and his grim resolve (They had to win here, had to, or else). Curiously, participants sensed Gettysburg's decisive character, though it fell in the middle of the war. If Stonewall Jackson hadn't been killed two months earlier, at Chancellorsville; if Colonel Joshua Chamberlain had been driven off Little Round Top; if the charge that history credits to Pickett had succeeded; if one of a dozen other misses and near-misses and misdirections hadn't occurred, the course of the battle, of the war, of all history, might have been changed.

Historians frown on what-ifs. What happened, they insist, is what concerns us, not what might have happened. The truth is murky enough; don't cloud it with maybes!

Their skittishness is understandable. Still, unless we play what-if, unless we speculate on alternative outcomes, we will never feel the urgency of the past. If we don't play what-if, we are likely to shrug so-what. So what that thirty thousand young lives were snuffed those three days? That was then. What difference can it make to me today?

On Cemetery Ridge, we feel the difference. It's dizzying. If one young bluecoat had flinched, if fear of death had mastered his fear of disgrace, if the sudden memory of a fiancée or newborn had caused him to turn tail, the contagion of panic might have taken hold, the Union line been broken, the British been convinced to enter the War for the Confederacy, the will of the North buckled, and the future of our continent been marred by the contest between two nations. What might our modern world have looked like without a strong United States? One can almost see Hitler rubbing his soft hands at the prospect.

Most deaths don't mean much. These meant more than we can imagine. That's what Lincoln told us, in the "few appropriate remarks" he delivered at the dedication of the Gettysburg National Cemetery five months later. If you ever doubt the power of speech, mark how these simple sentences echo down the years. Nowhere are the pain and majesty and urgency of the American experiment more powerfully set forth. Nowhere do we realize so vividly, viscerally, that what we've been making in America is not just a nation but a notion. Most patriotic rhetoric is twaddle, as persuasive as red-white-and-blue whirligigs. Here, pure as the purest cocaine, is the essence of our ideal, the most ennobling since man first sensed he needed some system to survive.

America has suffered three births: two in Independence Hall, when we declared our freedom and created our government; and a third at Gettysburg, when we cured our creation of its fatal defect. As Lincoln observed, America could not survive "half slave, half free." On the hills of Gettysburg, in a riot of horror and glory, we became one.

xii.

I linger a day in Gettysburg to take stock.

For 50 years, I have never been alone. There were always family, fellow workers, friends, schoolmates, teammates. My solitude was circumscribed—an hour or two before daybreak or at night; a Sunday afternoon. I played the role I'd been cast in: publisher, husband, father, son, pooh-bah. If I strained at my leash, it was only now and then, scribbling poems in secret. I fantasized escaping—who doesn't?—but never in earnest. I took pride in being reliable.

Obligation is the salvation of mankind: I'm expected, therefore I am. We dare not inquire who we'd be without our appointments. We feign martyrdom: "I can't believe I have to spend an evening with Esther Cramm!" We envision ourselves as heroes, sore oppressed. Leave the cell unlocked, though, and we stay put.

A writer's work is portable, my laptop as importunate as any boss. I was on vocation, not vacation. Still, I wondered how, on my own, I would behave. Would I be a sloth, a recluse, a rake? Would I be glad in the night? Would I gorge myself on ice cream or turn sickly? How much liquor would I glug?

After eight days, patterns were emerging. I was happy in the morning. Words and ideas were ample company: the time to play with them, bliss. I was more responsible than I'd have predicted. I shelved, stowed, mopped, laundered, repaired. Migrant was not neat but neither was she a college dorm. I could lay my hands on (almost) any tool.

My days I'd tamped into routine. I woke with the sun, lit the kettle, straightened my sheets, plumped pillows, and returned to bed with coffee, biscuit, and laptop. A day unelectrified (when somehow even my generator wasn't powering the sockets) caused alarm.

I wrote as long as I could—two, three, four hours at most. My cell phone off, nothing could interrupt. Once (this was later, in Minnesota) someone knocked and my heart sprang like a coil.

After writing, I ran—two, three miles—as fast as I could. I hate running. But I hate not running more. The day I failed to run I despised myself. Hypochondria spiked. I deserved to die.

After running, I'd stand at my table, dripping, savoring plum or peach, studying maps. I'd measure the distance to my day's destination, invariably underestimating, then turn on my phone. The right number of voice mail messages was four. More became burdensome. Fewer meant abandonment.

Itinerary set, I'd shower and sometimes shave. It's a shame men's tonsorial fashions have become so iffy, because now we have to decide. On the one hand, shaving is a waste of time with no image to maintain. On the other hand, I did not want to look scruffy.

My mufti was polo shirt, khaki shorts, sandals. In sun, I wore an un-logo'd baseball cap. My sartorial aim is to vanish—by dressing like everyone else.

Scrubbed and combed, I swept, swabbed, unplugged, drained and filled Migrant, then settled into my throne. For the first half hour on the road, I'd listen to music. I'd brought along several hundred CDs, sleeved alphabetically, from Bach to Wagner. These times were glorious, whatever the weather. When seeing is your goal, every view is vivid.

Sight sated, I went to school. Having exhausted the American history lectures offered by The Teaching Company, I played audio-books. I am blessed with ignorance. I have so much to learn I am never bored.

Most days I took in a site or two, and by five or so, having eaten little, I'd be stalking a supermarket. I shopped for dinner daily—usually a T-bone, with tomatoes from a farm stand; sometimes chicken or sausage; sometimes zucchini; seldom dessert or bread (they were banned from my van); and always wine. Once or twice a week, I drank too much, and woke in the night with a headache. How could I have been so stupid! After that first giddy meal at Fla-Net, I dined clothed.

As I ate, I either read or watched a movie. Producer Ken Burns and my old friends Philip and Peter Kunhardt have herded history into prime time with their PBS documentaries. Film is limiting: events must be narrowed into dramas, ambiguities simplified. The viewer is invited to accept, not debate. Still, the pictures, the music, the restless motion of the camera make yesterday entertaining, opening a path to future study.

19

Sleepy by eight, I went to bed. There is scant society in RV parks beyond what you bring. Where campers visit for weeks, acquaintances develop, as in any resort. In some of the more luxurious parks you'll find recreation centers and planned activities. I was a transient, seldom staying longer than two nights. In nine months, I encountered three other RVers traveling solo, all of whom struck me as strange.

I am pleased with myself that Monday morning in Gettysburg. The sky is blue. The grass is green. I've survived my first week. I can cope. I can work. I can enjoy. I think of that magical moment in *Amahl and the Night Visitors* when the crippled shepherd boy, blessed by the Christ child, lays down his crutch. "Look, mother!" the boy exults, "I can walk, I can dance, I can run!"

2
Ohio

i.

Westward to the mother lode of Presidents.

From William Henry Harrison's election in 1840 to Warren Harding's in 1920, eight of our 21 Presidents resided or were born in Ohio.[3] Eliminate the five Presidents during that period who succeeded to the office and one finds that Americans, over eight decades, voted for Ohioans half the time.

Half! The only comparable dominance of our national life was in the beginning, when four of our six Presidents hailed from Virginia and the rest from Massachusetts. These men, though, were Founding Fathers or their heirs, members of what we recognized as a ruling class. With Andrew Jackson's election in 1828, we booted aristocrats, permitting their return only as anti-elitists. The Roosevelts, Kennedy, and the Bushes, while high-born, took pains not to act it.

Ohioans like to claim there's something Presidential about their stock. So do lottery winners explain why they deserve the jackpot. Truth is, in our far-flung democracy, geography is destiny. In theory, any little boy or girl can grow up to be President. In practice, Alaskans, Mississippians, Rhode Islanders need not apply.[4]

Ohioans suited us because of their "normalcy" (an Ohioan's coinage). New Yorkers, Bostonians, Philadelphians back then floated in a higher sphere. Easterners were richer, better educated. They talked funny—through their noses—in grammatical periods. When they traveled, it was

---

[3]William Henry Harrison (1841), Grant (1869–1877), Hayes (1877–1881), Garfield (1881), Benjamin Harrison (1889–1893), McKinley (1897–1901), Taft (1909–1913), Harding (1921–1923).

[4]Official designations may mislead. Dick Cheney, for example, hails less from Nebraska, where he was born, or Wyoming, where he technically resides, than from Washington, D.C., where he's spent most of his career. Generals, likewise, derive less from their home states than from the battlefields where they gained their fame.

eastward, by boat. No one, in their view, ever *chose* to go west. No, deary, you *fled* across the Appalachians—because you were indigent or criminal or foreign.

The lengthy roster of Ohio Presidents is notable for personal modesty. True, William Henry Harrison was raised on a Virginia plantation before moving west. But he made his name butchering Indians—what could be more American than that? His grandson, Benjamin Harrison, is the only grump of the lot—co-winner, with John Adams, John Tyler, and Richard Nixon, of the Grumpiest President award. Ben, however, transplanted to Indiana as a young man: his sulks wouldn't have done in hearty Ohio. It's hard to imagine a more equable bunch than Grant, Hayes, Garfield, McKinley, Taft, and Harding—drinking buddies all (though Hayes would have had to sneak out past his beloved "Lemonade Lucy," a devout teetotaler).

Equable too, heading west from Gettysburg on Route 30, are the climate and terrain. Comfortable circumstances produce comfortable characters. Where the soil is generous, the weather temperate, the population well-fed, edginess and shrewdness are less likely to root. We prefer to think our personalities fixed—that I would be "I" no matter where. Travel suggests that selves are accidents. We are where we have lived.

Roadside billboards show the difference between places. Here they shout, "ADULT VIDEOS. NUDE GIRLS—FREE FOOD." The looming face of a "hostess" winks me to a "GENTLEMAN'S CLUB." Back home, we're coyer about horniness, preferring to ignore its ubiquity. Here they're less prim, maybe because they're getting cows and hens and goats to go to it daily.

I stop at a farm stand. It is strawberry season and I'm savoring a pint a day. Supermarket strawberries are consistent, but dull. They come from California, where agri-scientists in white coats tweak them for color, flavor, durance. Local strawberries surprise, whether by sweetness or tartness hardly matters. The suspense wakens senses like a reveille.

Winding up a mountain, even a small old mountain, after a straight flat drive, is a pleasure. Superhighways do not wind up mountains. They burrow under or flatten or slice. Nowadays you can span a great river and not know it.

Tuscarora Summit is part of the Appalachian Ridge. There's a roadside restaurant at the crest called The Mountain House. I seldom stop at restaurants, but somehow today I feel the need. I am seeing too much.

The gravel parking area is nearly empty, but maybe there's a waitress to talk to.

The Mountain House looks like every other working man's bar in America. The air is fetid with old smoke. Windows are shaded. There are neon beer signs, a pinball machine in the corner, a juke box. The TV is on. Bright plastic tap knobs glisten.

I order the Mountain House special—a double hamburger with lettuce and tomato and onions, chips on the side—and a Bud. A guy who orders a Bud is less suspect. Here, as in all such establishments, one detects an undercurrent of wariness. What kind of guy arrives at The Mountain House past one on a weekday, driving a motor home *alone*?

I hurry onto the deck where I sip my beer—from the bottle—and bask and think. The deck is festooned with parti-colored plastic pinwheels and pennants that crinkle in the breeze. I don't even know what I'm thinking about or if I'm thinking at all. A pair of bikers has parked and is peering over the precipice, holding their helmets. The words of a nursery song return to me:

> The bear went over the mountain
> The bear went over the mountain
> The bear went over the mountain
> To see what he could see.

The woman behind the counter, Joanne I think her name is, brings my burger. I ask the name of the mountains in the distance. She's not sure, she's from the eastern side, she'll get somebody. Out comes a nice-looking man named Holler, in his mid-thirties I guess, who says he's pretty sure the nearer rise is Scrub Ridge and beyond that Sidling Hill. Holler has only recently moved out of his parents' home into his own—an RV on two acres—and no, his mother wasn't too sad when he left, not as much as he'd expected, glad more likely he got his own place finally and besides he still sees them plenty. I am curious about his life in his motor home, why he hasn't married. There's no asking, though. Decent folk only take from others what they're willing to give.

Twenty minutes down the road, behind schedule, I remember with a wince I forgot to leave a tip. I could go back, but that would be strange too. I can hear Holler and Joanne, in the smokiness. "He seemed like an OK guy," one shrugs, "but—" The other finishes the sentence, "You never know."

ii.

Our four murdered Presidents—a wound that won't heal. Their memorials are defiant—fists of granite and marble, an eternal flame. (Only Grant's matches them in grandeur, where we buried our national nightmare.) Again and again gunshots crack. The potential of each man shimmers like a lost Eden.

Anger rises from fear. That four punks could hurt us—Booth, Guiteau, Czolgosz, Oswald! We feel violated, threatened.

William McKinley rests atop a man-made mountain. Its phallic resemblance is undeniable. From the summit you can see all Canton, McKinley's lifelong home. Canton's other draw, the Football Hall of Fame, attracts more visitors.

McKinley had a genius for niceness. He comes down to us as one of the most irresistibly amiable souls to hold office. He refused requests so sympathetically that those he disappointed felt sorry for him. A Congressman who'd stormed into the President's office emerged, shrugging, "I don't know a blamed word he said, but it's all right, boys." House Speaker Tom ("Czar") Reed grumbled enviously, "My opponents in Congress go at me tooth and nail, but they always apologize to William when they are going to call him names."

We poke his reputation incredulously. There must be something more, some hidden streak of calculation or malice. His devotion to his invalid wife was the talk of Washington. McKinley would have Ida seated beside him at White House dinners so he could veil her face with a napkin when she suffered an epileptic seizure. Each afternoon, at precisely three, McKinley would step to his office window and wave a handkerchief toward his childhood sweetheart, who was waiting in the Presidential quarters. McKinley's first words after being shot were for his assassin, "Don't let them hurt him." His next were for Ida: "My wife, be careful, Cortelyou, how you tell her—oh, be careful."

We distrust niceness. Newspaper editor William Allen White groused that McKinley "used too many hackneyed phrases, too many stereotyped forms. He shook hands with exactly the amount of cordiality and with precisely the lack of intimacy that deceived men into thinking well of him, too well of him." Similar complaints were lodged against Reagan. Perfect appearances peeve us. Nobody, we insist, could be that pleasant.

McKinley's prodigious popularity resulted in part from a war he never wanted to wage. Into every other American war, we were led by our

President. Into the Spanish-American war, our President was led. It's troubling how a citizenry that prides itself on goodness could have been hustled into a shameless land-grab by a belligerent Assistant Secretary of the Navy (Theodore Roosevelt) and a scheming press. Publisher William Randolph Hearst's infamous cable to his artist in Cuba still rankles: "Please remain. You furnish the pictures and I'll furnish the war." Little was gained by the fighting but Puerto Rico and Guam—and the Philippines, which cost us a fortune and our reputation as freedom-lovers.

Historians and critics favor exciting Presidents: it gives them more to talk about. McKinley, by their standard, bores. Yet across the years, we feel his beneficent presence, like a smiling Buddha. Niceness is power: it radiates, persuades, reassures, reduces the rancor between men. A President who loves his wife, turns away anger with soft words, and quiets political strife is not a treacly embarrassment but a credit to those who trusted him.

My snapshot of McKinley's memorial includes a beefy bronzed bicyclist resting at the base of the long marble stair. Shirtless, he has a clipped beard and tattooed biceps. He is listening to music through headphones. For him, the monument is not about the President or Ida, only a place to pause. He fills out the picture somehow.

iii.

This dawn's landscape is angry, bitter, my first such. I peer out my window before turning on a light to see if anyone's looking.

I am here by accident. Any of us is anywhere by accident, but some accidents are planned. Garfield's tomb closes at four, not five-thirty, as the brochure advised, so I decided to overnight in Cleveland to avoid extra driving.

This camp is located in a soggy, buggy crotch of land under a train and highway bridge. The roar of metal and rubber wheels is incessant, bone-jarring. Underfoot is muddy, littered, rank. The air feels malarial, like the swamps risked by America's settlers. My neighbors are not comfortable suburbanites, vacationing or retired. They live here. Their rusting vans are circled with litter—old tires, broken furniture, tots' toys. You watch where you step.

People live here because it's cheap. You don't have to work long to sustain yourself. Native garb is torn undershirts, five-day beards. Voices, too loud, are graveled with tobacco. There is no aspiration here, no neat little flowerpots or deck chairs, no fluttering flags. People live here because they've got to live somewhere.

Last night, for the first time, I wished I'd brought a gun, as more than one friend urged. Guns spook me; I've only shot one once—but I could feel dread tickling. How easy it would be to vanish here, to be swallowed in this muck. My absence might take days to discover. No one would know where to look!

By the time I pulled in it had been too late to find another campground and I haven't the guts to squat in a mall parking lot. What you buy at a brand-name campground for 25 or 30 bucks, as much as water, electric, and sewer hookups, is a presumption of protection. In this camp I didn't feel protected. I drew my shades, locked my three doors, and turned on the TV. I didn't want to be listening for footsteps.

I woke thinking of James Garfield. Garfield is among our most accomplished Presidents, yet all most of us remember about him is that he was shot. A poor kid from the wilderness, Garfield rose because his widowed mother pushed him. He clung to education not to drown. God smote him and made him a preacher. He became a professor—of Latin, Greek, mathematics, whatever needed to be taught. He became a college President. He became a state senator. When the Civil War broke, he insisted on enlisting. He recruited a brigade. He studied war as he studied everything. At the Battle of Chickamauga, he refused to retreat after his commanding officer had fled. His coolness forestalled a Union rout. He studied law and became a lawyer. He bought a farm and studied farming. Elected to Congress, he studied finance and administration. He worked and worked, not exulting in his humble origins but hating them. He did not mean to run for President in 1880, and grew agitated, the record suggests, when at the deadlocked Republican convention, he was nominated without his say-so. All his life he was wracked with doubts, which he confided to articulate journals. His industry was desperate. He was among the best prepared of our Presidents, the most experienced and deeply read. Teacher, preacher, lawyer, soldier, politician, farmer, father, he never stopped studying. Then, eight weeks into his term, a deranged office-seeker shot him. Modern medicine could have saved him. If he'd received no medical care, doctors now think, he might have pulled through. The treatment he received was the best of its time and the worst for his condition. After eighty days of surgeries to extract the elusive bullet[5] he died and the nation, which had held vigil, was convulsed with grief. He was 49.

Contrast Garfield, the striver, with the denizens of this camp. These are freedom's flotsam. No hope brightens their landscape, only a grim determination not to drift lower. Why did these souls end up here while penniless Garfield scaled the heights? Why is one man's obstacle another's hurdle? What gives us the courage to dream?

iv.

It is 3:30 a.m. in Bayshore Estates Campground, Sandusky; quiet, except for the trees. A fresh cool breeze makes it feel autumnish, though it's scarcely June.

I wake brimming. This is my gladdest hour—guarded by silence, fortified by sleep. Anything seems possible before phones and voices and traffic.

Bayshore Estates is my pleasantest campground so far. It's big—more than six hundred sites. It's located in a resort town, where hospitality is gospel. And it's quiet. The peace of Sandusky, "the sixth nicest small town in America," as its literature boasts, isn't mauled by planes and big-rigs and garbage trucks chomping and beeping and thudding in your dreams. The periodic train makes a racket (trains are long here in the prairie) but it's comforting, like the bong of a clock.

Much thought is given—in government, business, society, housing, our lives—to the question of optimal scale. What's too big, what's too small, and what's, in Goldilocks's formulation, "just right."

In RV campgrounds, bigger is better. The desk is more likely to be manned 24/7. Attendants know the answers to more questions, having been asked more often. Sites tend to be uniform and maintained; you don't have to grope in the grass for a seeping sewage pipe. You can buy a bag of ice or a carton of juice or a missing gizmo at the store. You're less likely to be stared at quizzically when you ask to hook up your laptop.

Smaller or bigger is a question for tombs, too. In Princeton Cemetery, I admired the modesty of Grover Cleveland and smiled at the ostentation of

---

[5]Embedded bullets need not be fatal. Andrew Jackson carried one near his heart most of his adult life.

Paul Tulane. Princeton Cemetery, like any, takes its tone from its founders. For the colonists of the eighteenth century, luxury and display were repugnant. Republican Roman virtues were extolled. There was too much work to do—building God's kingdom and this New World—to waste energy on vanity.

When Cleveland's Lake View Cemetery opened for business a century and a half later, aspirations had changed. God's kingdom had been established—here in America. We were rich, we were mighty, almost as mighty as England, and we wanted to crow. In Cleveland, they had a further reason for crowing—to show themselves the equal in wealth and culture of those lah-dee-dahs in Boston and New York.

James Garfield's tomb, which rises 180 feet from atop Lake View's highest hill, is a fantastic castle, by far the most ornate Presidential tomb. In a frowning Colonial spirit, I was prepared to be appalled: "All this for a President who served only 200 days, for eighty of which he lay dying? Harrumph!" Instead, I was dazzled. The gleaming mosaics, the stained glass windows, the extravagant marbles, the exuberant eclecticism of the "high Victorian" décor, the turrets, the friezes, the inscriptions, the heroic white marble statue of the man make this a worthy rival of the royal tombs of Europe. Here is America the stud, shirt off, flaunting our pecs, strutting our stuff. "We're good, man, every bit as good as you Brits or New Yorkers. We can out-wrestle you, out-peacock you, out-anything you! Take that! (Golden mosaics.) And that! (Exquisite stained glass.) And that! (180 vertical feet of sandstone.)"

Youthful pride can be both vainglorious and glorious at once. Sure, it's obtuse, this flaunting obliviousness to decay. Yet how splendid, once, even for an hour, to have been so convinced, potent, proud!

But for *Garfield*? This was not a Lincoln or Washington or even a McKinley, whose achievements were unarguable. Before he became President—by accident—Garfield was a worthy man with a thick résumé, but a pol, one of dozens. As President he did little more than die.

The grief sparked by Garfield's death in 1881 resembles, in our own day, the reaction to the deaths of JFK or Princess Di. The recent introduction of the telegraph, which could dispatch hourly bulletins of the President's condition far and wide, made Garfield's last eighty days our nation's first media event. The longer he lingered, the more our hagiographic impulse made him seem a saint. We got sadder and sadder; by the time death finally released him, the light, it seemed, had gone out of the world.

Grief is not rational. Nor is its cause always what we suppose. A big death may hit us hard not because we revered the dead person but because it reminds us of Death itself. It isn't Garfield's or JFK's or Princess Di's deaths we mourn but our own. We strive—and then what? Does anything really matter?

Garfield's tomb brings him to life. Without its durable glory—and the emotion it recalls—he'd have dwindled into a footnote. We think of him today because in his time he was so much thought of. Ostentation *can* defy oblivion—at least for a while.

There are other notable graves in Lake View. John D. Rockefeller's is an obelisk, taller than anyone else's. Visitors leave coins on it hoping.

Jephtha Wade's Memorial Chapel is also featured. "Who," you may ask, "was Jephtha Wade?" As it happens, he was founder of Western Union, a titan in his times. But today Jephtha Wade endures only as the resident of a sublime space designed by Louis Tiffany. He endures as Pope Julius II endures, because a great artist was hired to adorn his tomb.

v.

A sunny summer morning, a little after seven. I'm lying in bed, my laptop atop my thighs, a soothing, familiar weight. The coffee cup on my bed tray steams invitingly. Beside it stands a nippled plastic water bottle, whose contents quiver. I suppose my fingers on the keyboard, or even my breathing, are enough to disturb its calm.

I am still in Bayshore Estates, on the shore of Lake Erie. Actually it's on Sandusky Bay, which is on Lake Erie—that's what the map says. The water doesn't recognize any distinction between Lake and Bay and would be surprised to hear of it.

My itinerary places me this morning in Cincinnati, 240 miles south of here. The next three days I am supposed to visit Hayes in Fremont, Harding in Marion, Taft's home in Cincinnati and the tomb of William Henry Harrison in North Bend. My itinerary prods me. I balk. That my itinerary is my creation does not diminish its authority. We all need a boss, whose approval we depend on.

I'd like my itinerary to pat me on the back, but its demands are unreasonable. So I'm rebelling, giving myself the day off. "The day off!" I see your eyebrows arch. "What is this whole crazy excursion of yours, Carll, but days, months, even a lifetime 'off'?"

29

Private visions are problematic. One traveler sees an oasis where his fellows see a mirage. "Look there!" the traveler insists. His companions, squinting, shake their heads.

I have an idea for this adventure. It is big in me, and vague, and thrilling, and sometimes I wonder if I'm mad. How can you research a book if you don't know what it's about? "America? *All* the Presidents and Vice Presidents? All 48 proximate states? That's insane!"

Maybe. The odds are long anything will come of this. But then, aren't the odds long for any of us? Most of our lives don't amount to much: kids, a bank balance, a friend or two if we're blessed, maybe a gold watch. A paltry return, come to think of it, for all our exertion. Why not, in view of our doom, live our joy?

I have stalled in Sandusky—told my boss, in so many words, I'd be taking this time off, and if he didn't like it, he knew where he could stick it— because the amount I'm experiencing exceeds my ability to fathom it. Hobart, Cleveland, Burr, Dallas, Buchanan, McKinley, Garfield, Gettysburg, Independence Hall, van life, road life, the Football Hall of Fame, the "news" I'm not reading (though isn't it all news?)—it's beyond me. I never expected to become "expert" on these topics and the endless others that ramify but I wanted, needed, to *understand*. "Understanding" is a subjective, not an objective, measure. One man's understanding is another's puzzlement. The purpose of my journey is to make something of my time, and to make anything of your time you need to give yourself time. Whiz by too fast and it's as if you've never been. We must see with our eyes *and* our hearts to have seen at all. That's the wisdom of the bear: he did not wander over that mountain willy-nilly, because he was bored or lonely, he went for a purpose: "to see what he could see." And he succeeded—as much as any of us can hope to: "He saw the other side."

Life and perception refuse infuriatingly to keep pace. Sometimes activity lifts and crashes us like a wave: we have no thoughts; all we can do is hold tight. At other times, our days flow torpidly; we are restless and dull and feel life's passing us by.

The impossible object of a perfected life is to balance living and seeing: to eat that strawberry slowly enough to savor it, but not so slowly that you taste little else. The corollary to Socrates' famous dictum, "The unexamined life is not worth living," is "The unlived life is not worth examining." The contest between these imperatives is daily, personal, exhausting, and invigorating. How do you know if you've made the most of your time?

You know.

vi.

Foot-tall yellow letters on a plate glass storefront. It is mid-morning in Fremont, one of those prairie cities produced by the confluence of river, railroad, and turnpike, once proud with farmers in their wagons, now crumbling, bypassed. Places, unlike people, do not die when their time is done. They persist, aggrieved that a past does not guarantee a future. Banners droop from streetlamps: "Historic Downtown District." But there is little to be found here. Sidewalks are cracked. No one comes.

My reflection in the glass startles. I'd expected someone younger. I am in my uniform—polo shirt (pine green), khaki shorts, sandals. Beside me is a robin's-egg-blue Ford, not old enough to be antique. I have hurried to snap this picture, looking up and down the street. I worry that my interest in this storefront will seem mocking. I'd hate to insult any citizen of Fremont. They have troubles enough.

The letters read:

CHEAP TOBACCO

- CIGARETTES
- DIP • CHEW
- TWIST
- PREMIUM CIGARS • PIPE TOBACCO

Beneath the glass an empty wooden window box is propped on concrete blocks.

I am far from home. In Mount Kisco, such a store would have a name and quaint logo. It would be called a "tobacconist," or some such. There'd be come-ons, specials, a cigar store Indian. Dip, chew, and twist would not be offered.

Cheap would not be uttered, much less shouted. It's too frank, like that roadside billboard announcing "NUDE WOMEN—FREE FOOD." Sophisticates buy "bargains," "discounts," "clearance," "half-off," "seconds," "manufacturers' close-outs," not "cheap." Cheap conjures shoddy.

I am in Fremont to visit Spiegel Grove, the home and grave of Rutherford Hayes. Later, I'll head for Marion and Harding.

Ohio is proud of its Presidents. It is their license-plate boast. Eight—think of it! Or, rather, don't think of it. Of the eight, four died in office—two by

31

disease, two by bullet. The rest left the job discouraged or disgraced. The best of the lot—McKinley—historians rate as middling. Grant and Harding—in today's polls—bring up the rear.

Any loyal buckeye must scorn such results as accident. Who knows what William Henry Harrison or Garfield or even Harding might have accomplished had they lived. McKinley, flushed with the success of the Spanish-American War, might have been barreling to greatness. Taft, none nicer, got done in by his patron and predecessor, Teddy Roosevelt, who couldn't abide his loss of limelight. True, Hayes and Benjamin Harrison didn't accomplish much—and Grant and Harding, too credulous, coddled crooks—but, hey, it's not easy being President!

Ohio is a pleasant state. Mountains shield it from the winds of change that race across oceans. Any settler in Ohio was committed to this continent. He had come a long way. He could not gaze across the waves and dream of home.

Pleasant states produce pleasant people. But the traits that made Ohioans attractive candidates—modesty, amiability, candor, trust—disadvantaged them in office. Great Presidents are seldom pleasant. They are sly, ruthless, wary, full of themselves. They drive, they do not saunter. They know where they mean to steer and will not be brooked. Their determination makes them daunting. They will pay any price to achieve their vision, including the loss of friends.

Every President we remember as effective we also remember as inscrutable. Washington, Jefferson, Jackson, Polk, Lincoln, the Roosevelts, Wilson, Truman, Kennedy, Reagan will keep observers debating forever. There seems, always, a gap between the public actor and the private plotter, a gap we can never quite bridge. I can never get comfortable in their company. I feel them sizing me up.

I'd much rather hang with the Ohioans. All but cantankerous Ben Harrison feel like fun. They take me at my word. They don't push too hard.

Americans repeatedly make the mistake of electing Presidents we like. We seek a companion-in-chief. We discount intellect, experience, ideas. Especially in our up-close-and-personal TV epoch, we opt for the cuddly.

Visiting the upholstered homes of Garfield, Hayes, Harding, and Taft, it is hard to imagine a nation where much goes wrong. I'm sure the Harrison farm in North Bend was comfortable too, where young Ben grew up, and the McKinley home that Canton permitted to be razed. Here was a world where souls were well-meaning and straightforward, there were no angry

gaps between classes or races, you did your duty and told the truth, and
cheap tobacco could be "cheap tobacco."

Would it were so.

vii.

A word more about Hayes.

If there's something everybody knows about Hayes it's that he "stole"
the Election of 1876. Samuel Tilden, the reforming Democratic Governor
of New York, won the popular vote (51 percent to 48 percent) and, as a
result of political finagling by the dominant Republicans and a shady deal,
was robbed of his victory. Tilden's lead in the electoral college stood at
184 to 165. But there were 20 electoral votes in dispute—in South Carolina, Louisiana, and Florida. These "natural" Democratic states were still
ruled by reconstructing Republicans. The Democrats figured since Tilden
won the popular vote he should be declared winner. The Republicans referred the dispute to a 15-member commission, made up of eight Republicans and seven Democrats. The commission found for the Republicans
in each state—voting eight to seven. The House was divided but the Senate, where the Republicans held a majority, concurred, so Hayes was
elected.

The shady deal, to placate the Democrats, was to "end Reconstruction,"
removing Federal forces from the South, thus exposing the freed Negro to
generations of subjection by supremacist whites.

It was horrible, a nadir in our national fortunes, an indelible blot. Hayes,
whatever his virtues, had played a shameful role. It was a moment which,
blushing, we should draw the curtain on.

Or was it? Yesterday I finished reading Hans Trefousse's biography of
Hayes in the American Presidents series and now I am confused. These
hundred-page accounts are Godsends to the time traveler who can't spend
a month with every President. Biographies used to be brief. They told stories listeners might have time for. Twentieth-century scholarship favors
tomes. These weighty volumes are feats—invaluable—but how many readers
can devote so much time to one person?

Trefousse convinced me my vision of the 1876 election was—at least,
might be—wrong, not just in detail, but in its consequence. Rutherford
might not be "Ruther-FRAUD," as the Democratic newspapers dubbed him.
He might even be a hero.

My doubts began with the man. Hayes is our dullest President, rivaled only by Gerald Ford. What makes him dull is his decency. He is always doing right and he's always happy about it. His lifelong diary shows a soul untroubled by remorse, anguish, power-lust, vindictiveness, or any deadly sin. When he's sad, it's when he should be—when one of his children or his wife Lucy or a friend dies. Otherwise, he's sunny—so sunny you find yourself yearning for storm.

Hayes would not have been party to a bargain he thought shady. He says as much and we believe him. You or I might find our morals melting as we approached the Presidency. Not Ruddy. He'd have been satisfied losing to Tilden, if that's what happened. He *was* satisfied—for the few hours on Election Night he thought he'd been beaten. He slept soundly. But fresh facts persuaded him that something unsavory was afoot. White Southerners, by threats and violence, had kept freed slaves from voting, then misplaced the ballots of those brave enough to cast them. In light of what we know about Southern politics for the next 80 years, Hayes's interpretation seems plausible. He'd have won, he was sure—if his voters had been allowed to vote.

Then there's that shady deal. Granted, Hayes withdrew the army from the South when he took office. But that's what he'd promised to do in his letter accepting nomination. His agents simply assured the Southern Democrats that Hayes would do as he promised, which was what Hayes always did. Was Hayes then a secret Southern sympathizer, an enemy to the Negro? Far from it. He devoted much of his post-Presidential career to Negro education—our first President to promote humanitarian causes after leaving office, as Jimmy Carter and Bill Clinton would do a century later. Hayes removed the troops because he saw what most Americans saw: that Reconstruction had failed. Lincoln died and Thaddeus Stevens and Charles Sumner and Andrew Johnson and Ulysses Grant and plenty of others botched it. The thirteenth, fourteenth, and fifteenth amendments weren't enforced in the south until the 1950s and '60s. It took Eisenhower, Kennedy, and a second President Johnson to complete Emancipation.

Hayes saw there could be no knitting of the nation until the army of occupation was removed. He also believed that Southerners would fulfill their promises to obey the law. That was naïve—but so? Almost any President at that moment would have done what Hayes did, because that's what the majority wanted. Americans were sick of the Civil War. The intractability of the colored problem was annoying. We the voters wanted to move on.

Is Trefousse correct? I'm not sure. Facts are buried beneath mudslides of myth. Such messy outcomes unsettle. Those of us who lived through the 2000 election debate will go to our graves insisting on our version. Hanging chads will hang forever.

That's what spoils my sleep. What we call knowledge is belief. We can see George Washington chopping down that cherry tree—but it never happened. We can hear Patrick Henry declaiming, "Give me liberty or give me death!"—only he never said it. We know that the Election of 1876 was a "legalized fraud"—but it wasn't—at least, may not have been. What else that we're sure of is fiction? Can we know anything really?

viii.

And then there's Harding.

Calling on Harding in Marion is awkward, like a hospital visit. The prognosis is bleak:

> Warren G. Harding occupies an unenviable position in the pantheon of United States presidents. He has been voted the worst chief executive in every presidential poll ever conducted. . . . Participants in the Ridings-McIver Presidential poll agree overwhelmingly that Harding deserves low marks for his poor performance in every category. His best rating, for the Political Skill category, apparently for his impressive election margin, was only thirty-eighth. He was ranked our worst president in the Leadership and Appointments category and next to last in the Accomplishments and Crisis Management and the Character and Integrity categories. Descriptive comments include such remarks as "out of his depth" and "over his head."
>
> The revelations that surfaced after his death destroyed Harding's reputation, leaving him the most disgraced president in the country's history up to that time. The presidency demands a person versed in and interested in the great domestic and foreign issues of the time. Alas, Harding was interested mainly in poker, bootleg bourbon, and willing women. He was, sadly, just a small-town politician, an average man in a job that demanded far more than an average man could deliver, or as poll participants describe him, "an amiable fool, incompetent, inept, corrupt, immoral."
>
> (*Rating the Presidents*)

Lurid badness thrills. The Texas Book Depository, from which Lee Harvey Oswald shot President Kennedy; the site of the Murrah Federal Building in Oklahoma City, blown up by Timothy McVeigh; the graves of John

Dillinger, Jr., and Al Capone draw crowds. These villains were big-time. We ogle them, pretending not to.

But Harding?

I'm alone on my tour of his cozy Victorian on Mt. Vernon Street, nodding politely as the docent tells me how the President enjoyed his waffles with creamed chipped beef. She's ready for questions about his infidelities, his impounded love letters (due to be released in 2008), his hectoring wife (whom he called "The Duchess"), his alleged bastard (or was Harding sterile?), his poker games and bootlegged bourbon, his losing stock speculations, his legacy of scandals, his rumored suicide (or was it murder—by his humiliated wife?), but why ask? I can read it in books.

His memorial, too, reeks of failure. A grieving nation wanted something grand for Harding, whom, alive, they'd loved. But when it came time to dedicate the gleaming marble colonnade three years later, President Coolidge found himself too busy. It took four more years until a President was willing. By June 1931, thanks to the Depression, Herbert Hoover was almost as vilified as the predecessor he eulogized.

Sad, too, seems Harding's awareness of his inadequacy. He's forever sighing.

The only thing I really worry about is that I might be nominated.

I am just beginning to realize what a job I have taken over. God help me, for I need it.

I listen to one side and they seem right and—God!—I talk to the other side and they seem just as right! I can't make a damn thing out of this problem.

I am not fit for this office and should never have been here.

My God, this is a hell of a job. I have no trouble with my enemies. But my damn friends . . . my goddamn friends. . . . They're the ones that keep me walking the floor nights!

He ridiculed his own oratory as "bloviating." H. L. Mencken lampooned him, as one of the "booboisie." Sinclair Lewis's *Babbitt*, published in 1922, seemed to embody the natty dummy in the White House.

I hurry away. It's unpleasant thinking of lowlifes in high places. I'll say something about Harding—but what? Maybe a meditation on mediocrity. Or a reflection on small-town newspaper publishing, an experience we share.

Paul Johnson jostles my coffee.

My method, such as it is, is to study as I travel, fast as I can. I'm an explorer, not a scholar. There's no way I can develop a near acquaintance with all of the 65 dead Presidents and Vice Presidents I'll be visiting. There is no end of knowing but there is an end of time. I rely on the consensus—what choice do I have? "The worst chief executive in every presidential poll ever conducted": 900 historians must be right.

Johnson's *A History of the American People* is, to my taste, our most engaging general history. His erudition dazzles. His wit lofts. He says what he sees.

I reread his Harding assessment, to be sure:

In all essentials Hardy had been an honest and shrewd president, prevented by his early death from overwork from becoming, perhaps, a great one.

Honest? Shrewd? Diligent? Near-great?

Footnotes point me to *The Strange Deaths of President Harding*, published in 1996. Its author, a Professor Ferrell, has tracked down the accusations heaped onto Harding—the illegitimate daughter, the White House hanky-panky, the booze, the poker, the graft, his suspicious death—and found them mostly slanders. The best-selling exposé by Harding's self-proclaimed mistress, Nan Britton, published after his death, is so riddled with lies it's impossible to assess its assertions. A popular novel that described a guilt-ridden President poisoning himself was pure scurrility. Characterizations of the White House as a seedy speakeasy were fostered by Harding's opponents.

Yes, there were scandals that began to emerge before Harding's death (by heart attack) and continued for years after. Two of Harding's cabinet were crooks. But lots of Presidents had dealt with mischief-makers in their Administrations and emerged admired. Harding, in the popular mind, is credited with nothing—not the disarmament treaties of 1921, or pardoning Eugene Debs and other "Red Scare" prisoners, or appointing the first Jew to a high government office, or delivering the first civil rights speech by a

President in the former Confederacy, or reversing Wilson's policy of excluding blacks from federal posts, or creating a federal budgeting office (forerunner of the Office of Management and Budget), or appointing notables like Charles Evans Hughes (Secretary of State), Andrew Mellon (Secretary of the Treasury), Herbert Hoover (Secretary of Commerce), and William Howard Taft (Chief Justice), or convincing the steel industry to shorten the 12-hour workday or for the economic recovery he presided over or the huge majority he was elected by or the deep esteem he was held in when he died. Nothing endures of his Administration, in the popular mind, but ineptitude and slime.

Here, thanks to Johnson and Ferrell, was a different Harding, victim rather than villain; competent, not inept; a man of decency and self-doubt (sometimes in that office we could do with more self-doubt); a man who'd made his country more prosperous and less prejudiced and his world safer; no Lincoln, but far from our worst.

Even his maligned rhetoric rang: "America's present need," said Harding,

> is not heroics, but healing; not nostrums, but normalcy; not revolution, but restoration; not agitation, but adjustment; not surgery, but serenity; not the dramatic, but the dispassionate; not experiment, but equipoise; not submergence in internationality, but sustainment in triumphant nationality.

We can debate his prescription, but there is music here.

History takes time. But surely the work of Johnson and Ferrell would begin to hoist poor Harding out of the reputational basement.

We cling to our myths. Harding's our worst because everyone says he is. Harold Evans, in his best-selling *The American Century*, published in 2000, repeats Nan Britton's calumny as gospel. He cites Paul Johnson (though not Ferrell) in his bibliography. Did he read Johnson? Or did the smear make better copy?

Harding's bastard daughter is reported as fact in two other popular surveys that appeared in 2000—*To the Best of My Ability* and *The Reader's Companion to the American Presidency*—again without a caution. Blurbs laud these editors as distinguished historians.

I shudder. How many lies have I swallowed without knowing? How many slurs have I repeated? How many have I slighted who deserve regard?

ix.

I am *still* in Sandusky. But I know now it won't be forever. I'll move on because, well, I have a job to do, albeit of no known use. I'll move on because to stay would be too terrible.

But first, just one more day off. Sunday.

I decide to visit an amusement park—Cedar Point on Lake Erie—one of the nation's first.

I only visit amusement parks alone. In company you have to cheer and clap on cue. There is no worse torture than having to have "a good time."

An amusement park alone is an observer's bonanza. People come here to be seen. The midway is a parade. You are meant to gaze.

I had gorged on one such spectacle already—Hersheypark in Hershey, Pennsylvania.

Hersheypark is an entrapment devised by the famous manufacturer of chocolate. The idea is to tease you in with a free show—about the wonders of chocolate—and a free sample (which costs them less than a penny)—then to herd you, salivating, into a vast chocolate emporium, so you can overspend on "souvenirs"—"Daddy, Daddy, please get me this Bullwinkle full of Kisses—pleeease!"—then, crazed by sugar and pressed by the crowd, to whoosh you into the amusement park (for 40 bucks) where you can spend more money on . . . fattening food—what else?—and T-shirts and baseball caps and plush animals and gimcrack.

Where I come from, people are slim, especially the women. The rich in any epoch want to look the opposite of the poor. Our poor nowadays are fat.

I'm unused to seeing fat people. Here it was hard to find one svelte. Thighs and upper arms bulged; breasts and bellies sagged; jowls jiggled. Our national gait had become a waddle.

The phenomenon interested me—The Sickening Thickening of America. I snapped pictures. It felt a little mean-spirited, but I had to make sure I wasn't dreaming.

A long flat sandy ribbon that crooks into Sandusky Bay, Cedar Point began its park life after the Civil War, as the new prosperous leisure class sought shore breezes for their summer ease. A big old porched hotel and parasols and oom-pah-pah bands characterized its early years; then came a carousel, a primitive roller coaster, arcade games; and gradually, by natural evolution, the proliferation of thrill rides and shopping pods and restaurants and amphitheaters and eye-popping displays that today's amusement park patrons expect.

The fat problem is as bad here as at Hersheypark. Flesh strains out of skimpy garments. It's not just the huffing middle-aged tourists, limping on bloated ankles. It's the nubile and adolescents and small children—stuffed as turkeys. Fat parents dandle fat babies. Ice cream and cakes and cotton candy and French fries and fried chicken and chocolate bars are being gobbled, licked, slurped.

It seems counterintuitive—that in this best of all times in the best of all nations we're committing mass suicide by gluttony. Why?

Partly it's our sedentary habits: no one farms; few exercise. Fitness is the province of jocks and the rich. Most of our nation sits—at a desk, behind the wheel, in front of the TV, on the beach, by the pool, in a bleacher.

Partly it's the aggressive abundance of food. New supermarkets with their bright aisles and gleaming displays make food a drug. The more we eat, the more we want to. And what we like to eat, what advertisers tempt us with, is fats and sweets.

Partly we're bored. Eating is activity. Half the conversations I overhear concern recipes and restaurants. On the bench beside me, four adults, relaxing from their jollity, spend half an hour discussing last night's dinner. One had the lamb, another the veal—breaded, with apple sauce—while a third thought the wine particularly nice—what was it called? People who have other interests don't talk much about food (unless they're chefs). Food is boring. But the weakening of community leaves food one of our few common topics.

Mostly, though—and this is the shock of my trip so far—we're sad. America—the triumphant—is not smiling—not in Wal-Mart, not in line for Independence Hall, not diving our noses into cotton candy. Having been deprived of our natural physical occupations by the genius of technology, we pine for some challenge to be fit for. How those blobby teenage girls must despise themselves! How, I wonder, can that ballooning young husband and wife endure one another undressed?

I wait at the gate for the shuttle to my RV park. Throngs of schoolchildren jostle toward buses. Many of these children are from inner-city schools, brimming with life and cursed with ignorance. Some boys are so fleshy it's doubtful they'll live through their twenties; our hearts aren't built for such a load. And what are they doing? Packing their distended cheeks with fried sugared cakes. It's all I can do not to waylay one of the children and inveigh: How much health, son, are you forfeiting on "amusement"? How many dollars are you wasting? Where is your future if you toss away health? Where is your common sense?

x.

A Demotic Poetry Sampler

On a T-shirt, stretched across an ample teenage bosom:

> *I*
> *am not*
> *like Oth-*
> *er girls*

On gift-store placards:

> *My Wife Says*
> *I Never Listen*
> *To Her*
> *At Least I Think*
> *That's what She said*

> *   *   *

> *Every man's*
> *Got to*
> *BELIEVE IN*
> *SOMETHING*

> *I BELIEVE*
> *I'LL HAVE*
> *ANOTHER*
> *Beer*

> *   *   *

> *I Can only Please*
> *One Person a Day*
> *and Today*
> *Ain't Your Day!*

Tomorrow
Ain't Lookin
Too Good
Either!

* * *

I asked Jesus
"How much do
You love me?"
"This Much,"
He answered
Then He stretched
out his arms
and died

* * *

I'm in Shape!
Round is a shape
Isn't it?

This letter may surprise you after how we parted. It will surprise me if I mail it.

You'd have smiled at me the other day, maybe even fondly.

I was driving to William Henry Harrison's tomb. (How's that for a conversation stopper!) The site is not much visited. If Harrison's remembered at all it's for the brevity of his term (31 days) and a campaign slogan, "Tippecanoe and Tyler too." Harrison's was the first bullshit campaign. His handlers had remade their aristocratic candidate into a second Andy Jackson—log-cabin-born tough guy. Harrison's claim to fame was as military governor of the Indiana Territory (as far west as we went then), he defeated Tecumseh at the Battle of Tippecanoe.

Tecumseh, best I can tell, was a valiant tribal leader, one of a long string who tried to prevent his people's extinction. He began by trusting the white men's promises. Only after realizing how forked these tongues were did he take to arms.

The Battle of Tippecanoe wasn't a fair fight. Native Americans, while not averse to killing, had little gift for systematic slaughter. They lacked the European genius for inventing lethal weapons and marshalling troops.

The campaign of 1840 barreled Martin van Buren out of office. Van Buren, like Hoover 92 years later, was made a goat by an economic depression he couldn't have forestalled. Harrison, our oldest President (until Reagan), neglected to wear an overcoat to his Inauguration, delivered the longest Inaugural address in history (100 minutes, but it feels longer), caught cold, and died.

His tomb is in North Bend, Ohio, high on a bluff overlooking the Ohio River. It's at the end of a leafy suburban street barely two cars wide. Poor Migrant was a tank here. People stared.

Having snapped the tomb—don't ask me why, but a photo of a grave makes my visit real—I was heading back along the narrow street when this knocking started. You know my solution to mysterious noises—wait until they stop.

It worked—the knocking stopped. But then it started again—louder. There were flashing lights and a siren.

I pulled over—onto someone's lawn.

The policeman was polite. "Do you realize, sir, you are dropping parts all over the road?"

"Parts?"

"From your rig."

I swung out to inspect. My awning was dangling like a broken wing.

"Thank you, officer. I'll take care of it."

"No problem," he smiled.

Now it's one thing to say you'll take care of a busted hundred pound, fifteen foot awning falling off your van, and another thing to do it. Where was I going to put this ship's mast once I removed it? It wouldn't fit through any of my doors, I couldn't abandon it and I couldn't lug it anywhere. It was too heavy.

At home I'd have known what to do: call somebody. Here, I suppose, I could have called Good Sam. (Short for Good Samaritan, Good Sam is the RVers' equivalent of Triple A.) But how long would Good Sam take to show up? Besides, bumping off an awning was embarrassing.

Finally, I figured it out. I clambered up my ladder and levered the leaden length onto the roof, securing it with bungee cords. Two boys on bikes stopped to watch.

Back on the road, I felt unexpectedly smug. At home if something breaks—when we don't call someone—we carry it to the attic. Here I had no choice. So I fixed it.

I'm writing you—I'm not sure why. An RV park isn't lonely when I'm rested. But at night sometimes it's hard.

I probably won't mail this with how things stand. Maybe some day.

3
Indiana

i.

The flatness of the prairie. Horizons straight as a ruler, roads straight, telephone poles as regular as inch-marks. Trees the only mountains, removable. Houses straight; barns, silos, straight; tractors steering straight— for miles—with their road-wide cultivators and man-high wheels. Eternity will come before it's crowded here.

Bob Bolyard is scrubbed and beaming. He has helped me lift my broken awning off my van and now we are talking in the sun.

The Bolyard Family are Christian entertainers. Bob, his wife Brenda, his blind 84-year-old mother-in-law, who plays keyboard, and his daughters, when they're available, travel around the country in their RV performing Gospel music and praying in churches that will invite them. When there's time between gigs, they perform for prison inmates. Their compensation is the offering collected during the service. Sometimes it's enough to cover fuel costs; sometimes it's "more than we'd ever expected." "So do you make an OK living?" I ask. "Oh, no," Bob laughs, "but God takes care of us." Bob has two bad hips from his decades as a coal miner and they live off his disability pension. He asks me about my religion. "I was raised Episcopalian," I fumble, suddenly awkward, "but now I'm not much of . . ." "Don't you worry," he hands me his none-too-crisp card. "God has his plan for each of us."

The four children in "the Bill Witek family" range in age from the teenage daughter, who does homework while minding the front desk, to her littlest brother, who can't be more than six. All the Witek children are blonde and cheerful and respectful. Each has his task—steering guests, weeding, raking, collecting trash, feeding the goats—assisting their pleasant, industrious parents in the management of this impeccable campground. The earnestness with which the littlest fulfills his duties makes me smile.

God is the center of the Bill Witek family's life. The posted Christian sayings attest to it (mostly, Sermon on the Mount). On Sunday morning, the office is closed as the Witeks conduct "Worship Services for Kampers in Recreation Hall."

In December 1888, a month after he'd been elected President, Benjamin Harrison was visited at his Indianapolis home by the Republican National Committee Chairman Matt Quay. The election had been scummy, even by the standards of the time. The Republicans had won by colluding with New York's Tammany machine, who found President Cleveland's reforming zeal annoying. Votes were purchased systematically; political operatives received written instructions. The Republicans, as usual, had more money to disperse, thanks to the largesse of department store magnate John Wanamaker, who received a cabinet post.

The President-elect greeted Quay with the words: "Providence has given us the victory."

Quay held his tongue, but later remarked: "Think of the man! He ought to know that Providence hadn't a damn thing to do with it."

God is busy in Indiana. Where I come from God is mostly an accessory, like a handbag. People go to church or temple because that's what people do. Discussions of God are deemed indiscreet. If a neighbor quizzed me about the role of God in my life, I'd think him, well, a little, you know. . . .

Bob Bolyard and the Bill Witek family compare favorably to my neighbors back home. They may not be sprightly conversationalists. They may not know much about the ballet or what's wrong in Israel. They probably haven't traveled to Europe. But they know why they're here. They are glad, grateful, serene.

The Witek children, especially, strike me as luckier than the overprogrammed children of privilege. They have something to do—something important—which they do with their parents daily. "The Bill Witek family" is an essential unit, a corps in the army of God, and there's a war on. Necessity is a blessing; superfluity a curse. The Bill Witek family has neither time nor money for learning specialists or psychiatrists or sleep-away camp or boredom. When they have a problem, they pray, then get on with their work, which never ends.

God isn't a cure-all. But purpose is. The price of national prosperity is loss of purpose. Too many Americans lack an exciting reason to get up in the morning, to quit kvetching and gorging on pizza, candy, cocaine. It is hard to improvise a life, to occupy empty hours.

God, of course, can be a blind. Was Ben Harrison deceiving or deceived? When weepy Bill Clinton visited the preacher after contaminating his office, were his tears penitent? Was God really involved in 9/11?

It is easy enough to disprove God and scoff at true believers. The harder question is, What gladdens the human heart?

The American prescription for distress is Buy Something. That's because our stores have a lot to sell and they need us to cooperate.

Possessions can quiet a soul for a while. The problem is, the relief doesn't last. We develop resistance to the cure and have to consume larger doses.

The greatest gift a parent can give his child is purpose, and parents should be measured against that mark. The child who knows why he was born, why his existence matters, what his job is, is happier, stronger, saner, more productive. The child without useful work will be less happy, secure, productive, and more likely to be entrapped by joy-peddlers.

When our children were young, I ignored this obligation. We were lavish with things, activities, but not a creed. I am sorry now.

ii.

Rain threatens. This is how I will remember Indianapolis—with a sullen sky.

Crown Hill Cemetery is a trove. Within a few yards, three Vice Presidents and a President. The next most abundant cemeteries—the National Cemetery in Arlington, Hollywood Cemetery in Richmond, and Princeton—contain two Presidents or Vice Presidents each.[6]

Indiana's glory seems incredible today, more startling even than Ohio's. From 1868 to 1925, an Indianan or Ohioan occupied the Vice Presidency or Presidency half the time. During that period there were only four years when at least one of our top jobs wasn't supposed to be occupied by

---

[6]If you count Jefferson Davis, President of the Confederacy, as an American President, Hollywood Cemetery holds three.

either a Buckeye or a Hoosier (Garfield and McKinley foiled the voters' plans by getting murdered; Thomas Hendricks and Harding died in office). In the eighty years since 1925, we've drawn from those states only once— Dan Quayle, of Indiana.

Where leaders live point to who we are. For our first four decades it was all Easterners—Virginia, Massachusetts, and New York men. In 1828 came Andrew Jackson, the first President from a state without a seacoast. For the next four decades, southern states contributed their share of chiefs; after the Civil War, it was 67 years before we recruited from the old Confederacy (John Nance Garner, Franklin Roosevelt's first Vice President, was a Texan). With roads and railroads and the telegraph, what we called the West crept westward—from Ohio to Indiana to Illinois. Not until 1928, with the election of Hoover, did we jump the Mississippi. Airplanes made the Midwest vanish. We flew from city to city. Indiana became nowhere.

Crown Hill Cemetery, one of the country's largest, recalls Indiana's pride. The slopes bristle with obelisks. (The funerary obelisk became fashionable after 1878, when Egypt's Ismail Pasha gave "Cleopatra's Needle" to America.) Eli Lilly of Eli Lilly is buried here, and Richard Gatling, inventor of the machine gun; Booth Tarkington, the once-popular novelist and playwright; and high on the hill, under an exuberant arcade, James Whitcomb Riley, "the Hoosier Poet." (When was the last time Americans boasted of a poet?)

Five Indianans were President or Vice President from 1868 to 1920: Schuyler Colfax, Benjamin Harrison, Thomas Hendricks, Charles Fairbanks, and Thomas Marshall. Four are buried in Crown Hill. (Colfax can be found—if you look hard—in South Bend.) Three of them were Republicans, two Democrats. That's another reason Hoosiers kept getting nominated. Candidates are preferred from states where the electoral cache is rich and the contest close. In the 1916 election, *both* the Republican and Democrat Vice Presidential candidates were Indianans. In the 1920 election, both Presidential candidates were Ohioans.

Maybe it's the weather, but the obscurity of these dead leaders saddens me. Who remembers Thomas Hendricks? From 1868 to 1884, Hendricks kept almost being nominated for President. In 1876, he was almost elected Vice President on the Tilden ticket. In 1885, Hendricks became Vice President—under Grover Cleveland—only to die 10 months later. Hendricks appears to have been more interested in running for offices than filling them. He would "fearlessly refuse to commit himself on any question until after his party has taken a position on it," in the words of one opponent. Still, he was a big man in his moment and now even my brother-in-law who knows everything about American history can't place him.

The same would be true of Charles Fairbanks if the citizens of Alaska, grateful for his support during boundary negotiations with Canada, hadn't named a city in his honor. Fairbanks had the misfortune of serving under Teddy Roosevelt, who loathed him. Not until 1960 did nominees pick their running-mates. Relationships in those forced marriages were often frosty.

Wilson's understudy, Thomas Marshall, may have been the funniest man to hold the job. It was he who told the story of the fellow who had two sons, one of whom drowned at sea, the other of whom became Vice President. "The poor father died of a broken heart," said Marshall. "He never heard of either one afterward." As presiding officer of the Senate, Marshall was overheard quipping, while some blowhard blew, "What this country needs is a really good five-cent cigar." If the twenty-fifth amendment had been in force, Marshall would have become Acting President in 1919. Instead he acquiesced to Edith Wilson's "stewardship," as she called it, when for a year and a half she kept her stricken husband hidden and ran the country in his stead.

If fame is measured by Internet presence, Crown Hill's—and Indiana's—most famous son is neither President nor Vice President nor playwright nor poet nor pharmaceutical magnate. It's a gangster. As tidily as if he had been tucked into bed, John Dillinger, Jr., rests beside his mother and father and sister. His small stone is the same as theirs, just a name and dates—1903–1934. No mention is made of his career.

iii.

I have left Indiana but the memory of her only President dogs me.

It is easy to ridicule Ben Harrison. He was an "iceberg," whose handshake was likened to "a wilted petunia." At 5'6" he was our second shortest President (only Madison, who stood 5'4", was shorter). In his official cabinet photograph, Harrison sits on an elevated chair—on a pillow—to surmount the rest. (I can't help thinking of the phone books placed beneath us, as children, to lift our faces over the supper table.) He had a high squeaky voice. Methodical as a typewriter, he exhibited no passion. His program of rewarding Union war veterans and sheltering industry with high tariffs depleted the surplus he inherited and debilitated the economy.

He was succeeded by the President he'd defeated four years earlier, Grover Cleveland—a stinging repudiation.

Few besides Hoosiers have nice things to say about Harrison, and they don't have an easy time of it. Yet visiting his home on North Delaware Street in Indianapolis, feeling the rooms he built and inhabited nearly half his life, standing in the rain by his conservative grave, a sympathy sneaks up on me. We Americans are a harsh, dismissive people. We know—as if it were fact—who our "great" Presidents were, our "near-great," our "average," and our duds.

Ben Harrison deserves better. No, he's no Lincoln, Washington, Jefferson, Jackson, Roosevelt, Roosevelt, or Truman. He had no lasting triumphs prior to his Presidency—as did, say, John Adams or Madison or Grant or Ike—to assure his place in our pantheon. His reputation wasn't buoyed by the tears of a nation, as were those of our murdered Presidents and those who died in office. Neither his personality, nor accomplishments, nor his era, nor his words, nor the accidents of his tenure raise him in our regard.

I'm sure I wouldn't have cottoned to President Harrison had he greeted me at the pompous home he built with his earnings as a lawyer (he was the most successful Indiana attorney of his day). Ben Harrison didn't much like people—strangers, anyway. He was shy and impatient. He was wary of our derision. He knew we were comparing him with his Presidential grandfather, the revered William Henry Harrison (who stood six inches taller than his grandson). We may have been seeing in this Benjamin a decline from an earlier Benjamin, his great-grandfather, a signer of the Declaration. We would have known that Ben's Civil War career, while creditable, was not glorious. We certainly would have deprecated his social graces compared to his handsome wife's. (Caroline Harrison, whom young Ben had wooed hard, was a surprisingly gifted china painter and watercolorist, as well as an able musician. She had a sense of history and style, inaugurating the White House china collection and the first White House Christmas tree. When she died, two weeks before her husband was trounced in his bid for a second term, the light went out of Harrison's life. "After the heavy blow of the death of my wife," he wrote, "I do not think I could have stood re-election.")

Hell, everybody was better in some way than Ben Harrison. That's how Ben would have seen it. But Ben had brains and determination and he was not afraid to work, no sir, work harder than anyone else, from dawn to dusk, if that's what it took. The jut of his jaw and his hard stare declare his stubborn resolve to live up to his oppressive heritage. "I will show all," he once wrote privately, that my "family name is . . . safe in my keeping." If he was dry and shy and humorless, so be it; charm was Caroline's department. His was business. "I do the same things every day," he wrote, "—eat three meals, sleep six hours, and read dusty old books the rest of the time. My life is about as barren of anything funny as the Great Desert is of grass."

And not only was he a worker. Once elected President—by whatever means—and that, in those days, was the business of the political handlers— Ben was fiercely upright—to a fault. He would do what he thought right, dammit, whether it was politic or popular.

Such a lonely, pent-up soul—we feel him in his house—every day a slight, a lampoon, a rebuff, and a renewal of his determination, by tireless effort, to make it right. His wife, as she had been from those early courting years when his assiduity earned him the label of "that tireless midnight dude," was his soul; he wept himself red-eyed as she lay dying in the White House. Then, returning home to Indianapolis, beaten, his loneliness became intolerable and he remarried—to a widow 25 years his junior, a niece of his late wife's. His two grown children did not attend his wedding and never spoke to their father again. "It is natural that a man's former children should not be pleased . . . with a second marriage," he wrote. "But . . . a home life is essential to me."

Benjamin Harrison was not a good President. He was not a pleasant man, to all but a few. His manner, because he was shy, could be obnoxious or grandiose. He had no popular touch, none of the flexibility and instinct the Presidency requires. He deserves his low ranking. But he was a good man, who worked hard, and stuck by his values, no matter the cost.

Acting Attorney General William Howard Taft, who would become one of our most lovable Presidents, wrote of Harrison in 1890, halfway through his troublous term: "The President is not popular with the members of either house. His manner of treating them is not at all fortunate, and when they have an interview with him they generally come away mad. . . . I think this is exceedingly unfortunate, because I am sure we have never had a man in the White House who was more conscientiously seeking to do his duty."

There are worse epitaphs.

4

Kentucky, Tennessee, Kentucky

i.

Fueling Migrant takes 10 minutes. If I'm lucky the nozzle will lock so I can do chores. It's surprising how much you can get done in 10 minutes: rinse a dish, fold a towel, swab a windshield, scan a map. It's pleasant making use of empty time. I listen for the pump's beep.

Sometimes, for reasons unfathomable, the nozzle's lock has been removed and I must stand in the stench, fingers aching, watching the gallon dial tick toward 50. Some people can wait equably anywhere. I envy their calm: why resist? My zeal is always to be making—a phrase, a smile, camp. Thwarted, I fuss.

This Interstate exit feels memorized: the same chain motels, vying for favor; the same ever-loftier canopies shading a parade of gas pumps; the same McDonald's and Kentucky Fried Chicken and Taco Bell and Burger King with their automatic cheer. Busier junctures sport malls, with Wal-Mart and Staples and Home Depot and Circuit City and Bed, Bath, and Beyond or the equivalent; and always, everywhere, the encroaching concrete barriers and crusted belching steam shovels and trucks wrecking and raking roads "to serve you better."

Monotony disheartens by making the world feel small. We travel thousands of miles to nowhere. Novelty invigorates by widening our sights. How can we render a negative verdict on life with so much unseen?

Smaller roads rescue our humanity. Here we find characters, not cogs; local businesses, not faceless corporations. Exuberant flower gardens or flaking stoops tell stories. Two nearly identical farmer's markets half a mile from each other on the same sparse stretch make economic rivalry real. (McDonald's or Burger King—who cares?)

52

ii.

Kentucky Horse Park is a vast extent of fields, rings, arenas, and barns. Before engines, horses were our locomotion. Life, death, prosperity might be decided by a man's skill in the saddle. Today horse riding is an ornament. Somewhere near here is Churchill Downs. Saudi princes shift in their sleep, dreaming of roses.

The rich haul horses in trailers. They pay trainers, vets, grooms, equine shrinks—shamans and astrologers, for all I know. They spend on their horses, to show they can. They form horse associations and elect officers and squabble over rules. They imagine their squabbles matter.

The RV crowd can't afford horses. They keep dogs instead. Wide worried women walk tyrannical pooches on retractable leashes. When Fido yaps or snarls, his owner beseeches tolerance with a hapless smile. At my last stop the RV beside mine contained three pleasant-looking mutts, which, during the day, their owner roped outdoors. Whenever anybody approached, these sentries barked, bringing the owner out of her van to scold them fondly. "I just don't know what's wrong with them today," she would declare. This woman was not unattractive, fortyish, I guessed, with a healthy hoyden complexion. There didn't seem to be a man in her van, or children. Her dogs explained her.

I love dogs. I love horses. All my boyhood I rode—around the ring, over fences, to hounds, to agreeable applause. I rode because we were supposed to—why else keep a stable? I tried to ride better than my siblings— or anyone else—to be loved more.

My dogs have mattered more to me than most humans. When my black Labrador, Paddle, died three years ago, I sobbed. I thought I could never cherish another dog, but then my heart pined and I accepted Hercules. Hercules is also a Labrador, brown. I left him home in my son's care. I thought of bringing him. But then this story would be of a man and his dog. I needed to be free to see.

iii.

Hurry. The day after tomorrow I am due in Knoxville, to visit a friend. That means three dead guys in three cities in two days.

* * *

Zachary Taylor is one of two Presidents for whom we have no memorial. No museum, no library, no ancestral home, no birth cottage, nothing, only a modest tomb. (John Tyler is the other. His plantation, now privately owned, is closed to visitors.) Taylor's tomb may be found in a small national cemetery in Louisville. Anonymity is a strange fate for the hero of Buena Vista, a President so popular that after his death—of cholera—16 months into his term, the funeral procession stretched nearly two miles, with tens of thousands of mourners lining the route.

Old Rough-and-Ready had not wanted to be President. He was a soldier. He hardly combed his hair. His clothes look dusty. Warriors find politics distasteful. Their worlds are simpler—friend or foe, life or death, right or wrong—none of this mincing and nuance. Taylor saw the looming split between slave-owners and northerners and he knew what to do about it. If the South tried to secede, he swore to lead the Army to suppress their rebellion. Would Taylor's hard line have avoided the Civil War or shrunk it into a skirmish? Taylor's three successors—Fillmore, Pierce, and Buchanan—were politicians, who believed they could purchase peace with talk. Fear of war led to war more fearful. One yearns—on behalf of the 600,000 soon-to-be war casualties just then climbing trees and playing barefoot—to call across the divide: "Don't eat those uncooked vegetables and fruits, General! Don't drink that milk! It will make you—and the country—sick!" But the circuits to the past are busy. General Taylor *will* take his refreshment, sir, it's a hot Fourth of July and he feels like it. And those boys, a decade later, will die.

Richard Mentor Johnson's clothes seem dusty too. It's something about Kentucky—a hardihood, an indifference. The timber is tougher this side of the mountains. Maybe it's those years of Indian fighting. Or the rocky ground. Or distance from the sea.

When Richard was a sleeping infant, his older sister tugged a flaming arrow out of his cradle. Indians, always Indians. We grimace now at the fighting, knowing the outcome. Genocide—in hindsight. At the time, the contest felt matched. Scalps and war-whoops were facts. Savagery seemed justified.

Nicknamed for the Shawnee chief he purportedly slew,[7] "Tecumseh" Johnson was rough, as Andy Jackson, his mentor, was rough. They both

---

[7]Both William Henry Harrison ("Tippecanoe") and Richard Mentor Johnson took credit for eliminating the reviled Tecumseh.

carried wounds and bullets. They swore. They didn't give a damn. Johnson's family had amassed almost ducal holdings in Kentucky, a county's worth. In those days, there was no secret ballot: decisions were made by "voice vote," and no sane voice in Scott County would oppose the Johnsons. Johnson's common-law wife was a slave, Julia Chinn. He loved her, educated her and their two daughters, treated her with respect. Such arrangements were acceptable in the early days. But then the South turned polite. It wasn't the miscegenation they objected to but Johnson's openness about it. "If Col. Johnson had the decency and decorum to seek to hide his ignominy from the world," sniffed the *Louisville Journal,* "we would refrain from lifting the curtain. His chief sin is the publicity and barefacedness of his conduct, he scorns all secrecy, all concealment, all disguise."

Johnson was a Man of the West. From 1803, when Jefferson's Louisiana Purchase gave America a West to go to, until 1846, when the Mexican War colored in our map from sea to sea, the Man of the West was America's pride.

Our Founders had been European in garment, habit, attitude. They wore knee-britches and read Latin. America to them was an ennobling idea. To the Man of the West, America was hard-won fact, chancy civilization hacked out of murderous wilderness. With stone and timber to clear and bobcat and natives to defend against, who had the leisure for debate or even "eddication"? You worked, that's what you did, and seized and brawled and killed and drank and got by. To the Men of the West—the Daniel Boones and Andy Jacksons and Davy Crocketts and Tecumseh Johnsons—the refined lawyerly Easterners seemed stuck-up sissies. Real men didn't quote Montesquieu. Christ, you couldn't even say his name.

The Man of the West was an indigenous species, hardy and original, no European clone. But with civilization comes the itch for sophistication. Unlettered forbears, with their homespun ways, turn embarrassment. A disheveled (albeit amiable) drawler, who campaigned on the slogan, "Rumpsey, Dumpsey, who shot Tecumseh," was not the sort a knowing nation wanted for its President. And to think the man never married, yet had two daughters by a *Negro* and treated them as *equals!* To Southern whites, whose increasingly desperate defense of slavery was deepening their certainty about racial superiority, such tolerance was unthinkable.

Tecumseh Johnson was Andrew Jackson's natural successor. Jackson loved him. Johnson had his sort of background, his sort of enemies, had stood by him through hell. But Martin Van Buren, the "red fox" of Kinderhook, New York, was more useful in a sly town like Washington.

Johnson tried to do right, in his blunt honest manner, but Van Buren, inventor of the political machine, *got things done*. Getting things done is more useful than doing right. When Jackson fell out with his Vice President, John C. Calhoun, it was Van Buren, not Johnson, he invited to join his ticket. Four years later, in 1836, it was Van Buren, not Johnson, he anointed as his successor, offering Johnson the Vice Presidency as consolation.

Van Buren and Johnson were both "self-made" (a phrase that originated at the time). But one was cut to a sophisticated Eastern pattern, the other to the rambunctious West's. Frontiersmen would continue to appeal to Americans (Paducah, Kentucky's, Alben Barkley, Vice President from 1949 to 1953, was our last log-cabin leader). We would have two more Western soldier-Presidents (Generals William Henry Harrison and Zachary Taylor). But more and more, it would be the Van Burens, lawyers and operatives, who would master America's politics.

The Van Buren–Johnson ticket was whupped in 1840, in the midst of an economic panic. They didn't even carry Kentucky. Johnson spent his final decade setting up schools. His Choctaw Academy educated hundreds of young men from various tribes. He'd killed Indians, sure—but he didn't hate them. Didn't hate Negroes either—loved his wife and daughters more than life itself. Didn't see the point of hate. In the wilderness, folks were folks. You needed one another to survive.

John C. Breckinridge is the last of the old Kentuckians. Handsome, passionate, and brave, Breckinridge, at 36, remains our youngest Vice President. Another man who got things done, he served as second to a petty posturer who did nothing. President Buchanan wouldn't even permit Breckinridge to call on him, cowed, one suspects, by his Vice President's vigor. When Breckinridge was finally summoned to the White House, three years into Buchanan's term, it was to discuss the President's strategy for saving the dividing nation. What was Buchanan's plan? To proclaim a day of humiliation and prayer. Breckinridge did his best to be polite.

Breckinridge may have doomed his beloved Union by running for President in 1860. He knew his candidacy was a "forlorn hope," but he couldn't bring himself to support his old ally, Illinois Senator Stephen Douglas, now his adversary. Was it vanity, pride, the deepening nihilism of the hour that swayed him? If the Democrats had held together, they might have forestalled Lincoln's being elected with less than 40 percent of the popular vote and thus, secession.

Breckinridge, recalled Ulysses Grant, "was one of the last to go over to the south and was rather dragged into that position." At the end of his term as Vice President, Breckinridge fled to the Confederacy, to escape arrest as a traitor. The ablest of the political generals, he served memorably at Baton Rouge, Murfreesboro, Chickamauga, Chattanooga, New Market, Cold Harbor, and Shenandoah. Named Secretary of War for the Confederacy in February 1865, he counseled surrender in April. "This has been a magnificent epic," he said; "in God's name let it not terminate in farce."

Again to escape hanging,[8] Breckinridge fled to Cuba via Florida, thence to England. Broke and broken he returned to Kentucky in 1868. Seven years later, he was dead from the effects of wounds received at Cold Harbor. His small stone in the Lexington Cemetery is lichen-mottled and hard to find. "John C. Breckinridge," it says. "Born Jan. 16th, 1821. Died May 17th, 1875." That is all.

iv.

In my dream I hear the beating of a bird's wings, a small bird, trapped, frantic. An instant ago the sky was its world and now there are walls. Its panic is poignant—and dangerous. It could hurt itself—or me—in its escape.

I open my eyes. It is not a dream. A latch has slipped in the night and my door is open. Soon the little bird has found its way out. We are both glad.

It is dawn. I am in Greeneville, Tennessee, stony, steep terrain that two centuries ago made its settlers hardy. Geography is destiny. The farmer with flat alluvial fields and an encouraging climate sees God in one light; the fierce clearer of flinty slopes sees Him in another.

Yesterday I spent in Knoxville, with my friend Steve. Steve guides a large department store chain. We live near each other at home and where we vacation. Steve was in Knoxville, visiting one of his divisions. I flexed my schedule to meet him there.

The department store was invented in the nineteenth century. The French like to take credit, but even if Bon Marché, in Paris, was first, the evolution of the form, like most commercial innovations of the last 150 years, was an

---

[8]Until President Andrew Johnson's "Christmas Amnesty" in 1868, the fate of the Confederacy's leaders was uncertain. Many in the North, including influential voices in Congress, wanted them tried and executed.

American accomplishment. The commercial genius of America—welcome or not—is among the wonders of planetary time: how we've infected ourselves with an appetite to buy what we don't need.

My friend Steve is a good businessman. He is smart, sensible, amiable. He works hard. He likes to win. Commerce, like war, is a game, and those who play it best are those for whom the game is all, who hone their lives like an arrow toward its mark.

The leader of this division, headquartered in Knoxville, is a forceful woman named Toni. If Steve reminds me, in his imperturbable equanimity, of General Eisenhower, Toni conjures Patton. Command is her compulsion. She needs to shape her troops to her purpose. All that opposes her is Satan. Resistance excites her: obstacles make the game more fun.

Conviction is charismatic. Urgent, soul-certain faith attracts like a magnet. Most humans suffer a deficiency of belief. They hanker for an assurance that eludes them. Creeds rescue us from questions too painful to pose: Why are we here? Where do we end?

Lacking our own conviction, we glom, if we're fortunate, onto another's. The specifics of a creed hardly matter. Whether the purpose of our corps is to crush a pesky competitor or Beelzebub, what difference? Enemies are all imaginary. They exist only if you believe in them.

Toni and her dedicated lieutenants take Steve on a tour of two stores, with Steve's pal Carll tagging along. I observe, enthralled. I'm susceptible to games—they suck me in with their innumerable puzzles. What's the objective, strategy? What are the tactics? How do you deploy your players? What's your opponent up to? What are his strengths and vulnerabilities? Do you have enough ammunition? Are your battle orders sound? How solid is your intelligence? Which of your troops can you trust? Which can you *really* trust? Do you attack head-on, or flank, or feint? At dawn or in the dark? What tricks can you contrive that none will suspect? When is boldness folly or caution prudence?

The game creates its own logic and its own language. Acronyms, abbreviations abound. I strain to understand, as if they were not speaking English. "Moderates," "separates," "explode," "coach," "market," "price point," "key items"—the words are familiar, but not their sense.

Retailing is seduction. The serpent in the garden was the first retailer. The stores Toni commands do it well. The attendants are attractive and agreeable. Floors and shelves shine. (Courtesy and cleanliness are the first indices of retailing competence.) Displays of merchandise flirt without coercing. Customers seem glad.

The clatter of commerce lofts us like music. "How can I help you?" "Might I interest you in . . ." "How are you today?" "You look great in that!" "That's you to a T." I have forsworn things—they distract, delude; I inveigh against them; I have no room for them—yet I find myself hankering to buy. A small insanity takes hold. I think, "Yes, that would suit me nicely."

I end my day—with only a few superfluous purchases—stupefied by abundance. So many good souls striving! And to good effect.

"So what do you think?" Steve asks. I wonder. I do not know. Part of me recoils from the greed of our age. We should do with less, respect what we have. "Better things for better living"—the old General Electric slogan—is a bear-trap. Buried beneath things, the bear will never go over the mountain. He will never leave home.

Yet purpose is splendid. The arrayed corps of cadets, standing stiffly, shoes gleaming, bayonets upright, eyes forward, stirs even the pacifist's heart. A deed may or may not be worth doing—opinions differ—but who can deny the glory of a deed well done?

v.

John Jones, Jr., stands on the rooftop verandah of the General Morgan Hotel in Greeneville. It is a clear, temperate night. John, the editor of the *Greeneville Sun,* points up and down Main Street, exuberant about the efforts being made to restore the depleted center of his rural Appalachian town. Business, in Greeneville, as in almost every other mid-sized American town, has been sucked onto the commercial strip, a cluttered flat stretch of highway dominated by—Wal-Mart—who else?—and a dozen other stores, restaurants, and gas stations with familiar logos.

Greeneville, the county seat of Greene County, Tennessee (pop. 60,000), got its start when travelers across the mountains paused to refresh themselves at a deep clear-water spring (still extant, behind the library, but polluted). One of those travelers, in 1826, was a 16-year-old illiterate apprentice who was fleeing his master. The young man was prepared to keep moving, but Greeneville, he was told, needed a tailor, so he stayed.

It is hard to conceive of the courage of Andrew Johnson. We can still see him sitting cross-legged on his tailor's table, shearing and stitching and ironing, while listening to the reader he'd hired to tutor him while he worked. (The cabin in which Johnson lived and worked in those early years is elegantly preserved.) At 20, the loquacious and industrious Johnson was elected alderman; then mayor; then state legislator; and at age 35, a member of Congress. Charles Dickens, visiting America, found Johnson's dark-eyed appearance "remarkable . . . indicating courage, watchfulness, and certainly strength of purpose."

Johnson's working-class origins were an easy target for his detractors. Angered by his resistance to increased appropriations for West Point, Congressman Jefferson Davis sneered: "Can a blacksmith or tailor construct . . . bastioned field-works . . . ?" "Sir," Johnson once responded to another such slight, "I do not forget that I am a mechanic. . . . Neither do I forget that Adam was a tailor and sewed fig leaves, or that our Savior was the son of a carpenter."

Greeneville was hell during the Civil War. The farmers in these hills, who worked their own land, felt little sympathy with slave-holders, yet were subjected to incessant combat. Johnson, denounced by many Tennesseans as a traitor, risked his life to keep his state from seceding. When he failed, he—alone of all the Senators from the Confederate states—remained in Washington. His family was turned out of their home, Johnson was hung in effigy, but he didn't budge. In 1862, he accepted the job of military governor of his home state—a role certain to earn him enemies. In 1864, in recognition of his services to the Union and to present a Unity ticket, Lincoln picked Johnson, a Democrat, to replace Maine's Hannibal Hamlin as Vice President. Forty-one days after the Inauguration, Lincoln was killed.

Popular history, sometimes cruelly capricious, recalls two details about Johnson's career, both of which seem shameful: he was, until recently, our only President who had been impeached; and he was drunk at his inauguration.

He *was* drunk—but he was not a drunk. Exhausted and not feeling well, he accepted a brandy—from the embittered outgoing Hamlin—while waiting for the Inaugural ceremonies to begin. Then he accepted another. Called upon to speak, he improvised the sort of speech you give when you've had a glass too many—sounds good to you!—earning himself the nickname "Andy the Sot." Evidence indicates that Johnson rarely, if ever, drank to intoxication. He may not have been clear what he was drinking, may even have been slipped a mickey. But that's politics.

Johnson's impeachment, unlike Clinton's, is a badge of honor. He refused to be rolled by a presumptuous Congress. Johnson, like Lincoln, believed that charity, not malice, toward the defeated rebels was the way to knit the union. The radical Republicans wanted the South to pay—and pay—for their sins. The dark glare of Pennsylvania's Thaddeus Stevens, the Radical leader in the House, even now proclaims their policy: add sickle and hood to his photograph and he could pass for the Grim Reaper.

The Radicals thought they had, in Johnson, a willing tool. A man of such humble origins—and a Democrat and Southerner, to boot—would never defy them. Like Jefferson Davis, like just about every high-toned college-educated grandee Johnson had met in his stubborn rise, the Radicals mistook their man. To level Johnson they'd have to chop him down; he would not bend.

The Senate wanted to force Johnson to retain Edwin Stanton as Secretary of War. Johnson refused, seeing this as a violation of his Presidential prerogative.[9] He knew he would be impeached. A single brave vote—of Senator Edmund G. Ross of Kansas—stood between Johnson and conviction. Johnson's refusal to truckle—and his acquittal—while it did not save the South from ineffectual and divisive Reconstruction—protected future Presidents from arbitrary removal. "High crimes and misdemeanors" has to mean more than "I hate your politics."

Historians differ widely in their assessment of Johnson. Some rate him near great; others call his term a flat-out "failure." Why the gap?

Partly, it's the man. Johnson was tough, disdainful of the privileged, proud of his origins, private, suspicious, and uncongenial. His contempt was fiery. "If I should happen to die," he said, "I would bequeath the last dollar to some negro to take my dirty, stinking carcass out on some mountain-peak to be devoured by the vultures or make a fire that it might pass in smoke and ride upon the wind in triumph over the godforsaken and hell-deserving, money-loving, hypocritical, back-biting, Sunday-praying scoundrels." Such a voice either thrills you with its daring or repels with its intemperance: there is no middle ground.

Partly it's his policies. Johnson, like Lincoln, wanted to restore the South to the Union, not reconstruct it. He knew that to treat the Confederate states like conquered colonies, confiscate what was left of the rebels' property, deny them a voice in their future, and make their former slaves their superiors, would result in rancor and resistance. Whether Johnson's (or Lincoln's) coaxing would have worked better than the Radicals' cudgeling is anybody's guess—what-if is the quicksand of history—but it could hardly have worked worse. The Radicals' policy fostered the Ku Klux Klan

---

[9]The Tenure of Office Act, designed to keep Stanton in office, was finally declared unconstitutional in 1926.

and doomed the freed Negro, after a dozen years of federal protection, to an oppression as dire as slavery.

Johnson's achievements as President were meager. Except during his first eight months in office, before Congress convened, he got little done. Most of his vetoes were overridden. Never before or since has Congress been so dominant or the President so impotent. The imponderable remains: Could any successor to Lincoln have done better? Could any man have stood against the Radicals' revenge?

Standing on the rooftop verandah of the General Morgan Hotel, listening to John Jones's articulate affection for his town, I feel how place gives us strength. Andrew Johnson knew where he stood because he knew where he came from. He came from Greeneville: from a mud-wattled tailor's shop on Depot Street and later, from the handsome (though by present standards, modest) brick home he built for himself on North Main. He knew himself from his neighbors—those wary, independent farmers and merchants who'd come to his shop to talk politics and who elected him alderman, mayor, assemblyman, representative, Senator. He knew in his own heart the anguish of his town as Confederate and Yankee troops took and retook it 23 different times in the war's course. Politics was not just a "career path" for this tailor who'd never graced a classroom; right and wrong were not iffy propositions, easily compromised. Right and wrong were visceral, organic, homegrown. Politics was not a choice: it was all a man could do.

John Jones, Jr., shares that sense of place. He edits a newspaper that his grandmother started 86 years ago. That enterprising lady knew nothing about newspapering or business, only that she had two young children to feed and a ne'er-do-well husband ("if a rabbit has to climb a tree," she'd later explain, "he'll climb a tree"). John edits a newspaper of which his father, John Sr., is publisher, a younger brother co-publisher, another brother the former editor, his mother a popular columnist, and in which other relatives fill other jobs; a newspaper so woven into the fabric of Greene County it is hard to imagine life here without it.

Family newspapers are a dying breed. I published one myself—and sold it, to the country's biggest publisher—to be free. Big newspaper publishers can publish newspapers more efficiently than local owners. They can buy newsprint cheaper and offer combination advertising rates to major advertisers. They have cost-control and accountability systems they've developed to maximize return. Their local editors are unlikely to violate a budget out of allegiance to the community. It's the corporation that promotes editors, not the town. This town is where they're assigned today. Tomorrow it will be somewhere else.

I hope the Jones family clings to the *Greeneville Sun* forever, but that would be a miracle. Sooner or later, families disperse. Money—ease—freedom tempt. A place is just a place, after all—Greeneville's sort of a hick town, when you think of it—up there in the hills—not where the action is, really. We move on.

That's not what John Jones feels. Or what Andy Johnson felt. For them, Greeneville was the world. No place was more important.

Nowadays, increasingly, we don't come from anywhere. Or know who we are.

vi.

Nashville. Quarter of ten home time, quarter of nine here. A new time zone—the phrase resonates. A new time zone.

Dave and Daphne are performing tonight in the theater shed. Sunday night gospel hour.

No one chooses an RV camp for religious elevation. Dave and Daphne are entertainment. A few dozen gray-hairs slouch slack-jawed in folding chairs. A beribboned basket for "love offerings" begs at the door.

I wander in. Wandering is what I do. I prefer being nobody. For the past three days, visiting friends, I have been somebody—with a name—and it wearies me. If I am "Carll Tucker" with a history, relations, shared acquaintances, I must act the part. That it's a part I've written does not lessen the theatrical requirement.

Now I am anonymous again—in Emerson's uncomfortable formulation, "a transparent eyeball." Being seen alters what you see. A leading man must see "in character." Invisibility is the ideal condition for an observer. Strolling by, in khakis, T-shirt, slip-ons (the adjustable rubber kind), I can think what I like.

Dave and Daphne give me the creeps. Their every sigh and eyelash-flutter is a cliché. They are desperate: no thriving entertainer would be drawn to such a gig. They can say they're doing the Lord's work—to us, maybe even to themselves—but they fool no one. We are here in the shadow of Grand Ole Opry, the Vatican of Country Music. Dave and Daphne strain toward that heaven, not the one they croon about. But the years accumulate. They are not talented. They play for the pittance in the basket.

63

Only fools debate creeds. One can, however, examine the efficacy of faiths, how they add or subtract. A worthwhile religion improves its adherents: makes them saner, kinder, gladder, humbler, more helpful to their neighbors and themselves. A good God whips us into shape, like a good father. A bad God pampers or deludes.

The God of Dave and Daphne is worse than none at all. He is the ultimate permissive parent. He loves us—does he ever! This claim is tirelessly asserted—but his love never troubles us, never demands reform or oblation, never swells in fury or directs us to sacrifice. Their God has been to the same hospitality school attended by the desk clerks of hotel chains. His smile is painted. He hopes we'll have a real nice visit and come back again real soon.

"Jesus will fix it all." Dave-and-Daphne's refrain sets some gray-hairs nodding like dashboard dolls. For a toddler, perhaps, such specious comfort is permissible—Mommy and Daddy will kiss every boo-boo and make it better—but for an adult to swallow such pap makes me fume. Life hurts, dammit! It is rife with disappointments. No one knew that better than Jesus—"My God, my God, why have you forsaken me?" Can Jesus—or Allah—or Buddha—or any swami—help reconcile us to the facts? Perhaps: but not by pretending they aren't there!

An innocuous, feel-good religion hardly differs from cocaine. It transports us for a while into a pain-free cloud where all seems possible, agreeable, then redeposits us into a world that mocks such fatuity. "Begin from where you are," the poem suggests, "or you are lost." Any God worth worshipping begins from where we are—our unpretty predicament—then helps us to accept, understand, even rejoice. A God worth worshipping is not always glad to see us, but He is sometimes glad when we have done Him proud. A God worth worshipping does not pat us on the back if we've sloughed off, but demands we make the most of our time.

I did not leave a love offering. I might have, if I had any change, just to brighten their day. But my money was back in my van, and besides, I really didn't want to encourage them. A full basket might suggest their message was gaining.

vii.

Andrew Jackson was a storm of a man. We still shudder at his roar. Ferocity was his nature, his temper hair-trigger. He carried in his tall slender body saber wounds and bullets—not from enemy fire, but from duels and brawls he provoked.

We approach even his memory with trepidation. He's the sort that wakes with a start, his alert glance assessing, "Friend or foe?" If friend, then loyalty is expected, and will be returned. If foe, beware. Jackson was an indomitable hater. "When Jackson begins to talk about hanging," said his one-time enemy and later friend, Senator Thomas Hart Benton, "they can begin to look for the ropes."

No man was less suited to the office. "Do they think I am such a damned fool as to think myself fit for President of the United States?" he growled. "No, sir; I know what I am fit for. I can command a body of men in a rough way; but I am not fit to be President."

Yet no man was more suited—and he knew that too. The Presidency, through its first six occupants, had been the province of the genteel: gentlemen; believers in civility and the superiority of a few. "Republic" and "democracy" descend to us as synonyms—Roman and Greek for the same idea—but our Founders saw a difference. In a republic, the power of the people (that is, white male property owners) was vested in its representatives, who were drawn from an unofficial elite, an aristocracy of wealth and education, if not titles. In a democracy, a representative was the people's servant, elected to do its bidding; eligibility to vote was less exclusive; and no segment of the electorate was presumed superior. "Democracy" meant mobocracy to our Founders. It conjured guillotines and sansculottes.

Jackson sprouted from the mob. No property, no pedigree, no parents, no politesse, no diploma, he rose by brawling, killing, brute will. At age 13 he enlisted in the Revolutionary army; captured, he defied a British officer, who slashed him with his saber, gashing his head and almost severing his arm. His mother died of plague some months later, leaving Jackson his family's sole survivor and, as he recalled, "utterly alone." He went to the Western district of North Carolina (which he would help shape into Tennessee); made himself a lawyer, prosecutor, judge, militia captain; took a bullet near his heart in a duel of honor (it lodged there till he died: Jackson fired his shot coolly after having been hit, fatally wounding his opponent in the groin); set out to horsewhip Thomas Hart Benton in a private quarrel and nearly lost his arm again; in the Creek War killed Indians, lots of them, then cheated them by treaty; humiliated the invincible British army in the Battle of New Orleans. Far from President Madison's sight or hearing, Jackson ignored his military orders, carrying on unauthorized campaigns of conquest. (Later Jackson-esque generals, Patton and MacArthur, would be relieved for less flagrant insubordination.) No national hero had loomed this large since Washington and none, including Washington, had been so beloved by the little guy. Denied his first election as President in 1824 (which Henry Clay tipped to John Quincy Adams, in return, Jackson partisans claimed, for his appointment as Secretary of State), Jackson drubbed his opponents the next time around. (One boyhood schoolmate remembered that while skinny Andy might be "throwed in three fights out of four . . . he would never *stay* throwed.")

Jackson's Inaugural Day marked the transformation of America from a republic to a democracy. Jackson opened the doors of the White House and a horde of his supporters jostled in, making a mess. The polite folk shuttered their windows or left town. (John Quincy Adams, a sore loser, fled Washington the night before.) Old Hickory not only rattled the teacups of the American aristocracy, he smashed them. From now on the common man would be king. If a high-born ran for office, he'd have to scuff up his past, make himself poorer and scruffier, don cowboy boots and a twang. "In the United States," noted Alexis de Tocqueville in 1831, "the people have no hatred toward the higher classes of society; but they have little goodwill toward them and are careful to keep them from power." That is the Jackson effect.

Jackson was in many ways an inept President. He plunged the nation into gratuitous crisis by defending the honor of a woman who had none (that Peggy Eaton was married to his friend, Secretary of War John Eaton, was all Jackson needed to know; that Peggy Eaton had ascended to prominence on her back he didn't want to know).[10] His hatred for the Bank of the United States was pathological—and, in the view of most later economists, a mistake.[11] He brandished the Constitution when it suited him and ignored it if inconvenient ("Mr. [Chief Justice] Marshall has made his ruling," he once sneered. "Now let him enforce it"). His murderous abuse of the Creek, Choctaw, and Cherokee still makes us wince. His slashing political style

---

[10]Not unlike the brouhaha over Monica Lewinsky during Clinton's Presidency, the Eaton—or Petticoat—Affair divided and distracted Washington, bringing other public business to a standstill. Whether the vivacious Mrs. Eaton's infidelity to her former husband had brought about his suicide, which Jackson insisted was a "damned lie," hardly merited the attention of the entire government.

[11]A central bank, Jackson believed, would serve the interests of snooty Eastern capitalists, not the little guy. By deregulating the national currency, he made credit easier to come by, which led to the devastating Panic of 1837.

established a vituperative tradition that endures. Where our first six Presidents wanted to abolish slavery, Jackson saw no problem with it. John Quincy Adams wanted to educate Americans; Jackson preferred them illiterate (and passionate in their loyalty to him).

Jackson was a nightmare—and a Godsend. More than any other leader, even Lincoln, he opened America to Americans. He "throwed" the American elite so it would "stay throwed." He made the average guy proud of his averageness. His story—hardscrabble orphan boy with no eddication makes good by grit and whups the highfalutin big-shots—became our essential myth. Davy Crockett, "Tecumseh" Johnson, James K. Polk, Andrew Johnson, Huck Finn, Walt Whitman, Wyatt Earp, Herman Melville, Winslow Homer, Ty Cobb, Charles Ives, John Dillinger, Jr., Jack Kerouac, Jackson Pollack are all his intrepid children.

I shy from his glance. I am the sort of hothouse orchid Jackson loathes. I am John Quincy Adams, trained in the best schools, oppressed by lineage, my pink cheeks painted by Copley. I am soft, a man of mind, who's only once shot a gun and that at skeet. In the aggressively grand rooms of "The Hermitage," Jackson's proud proof of having made it, I can feel his clenched jaw as he'd "lay bare his arm, bandage it, take his penknife from his pocket, call a servant to hold the bowl, and bleed himself freely"—I who call my cardiologist at a twinge.

The period-petticoated docents at The Hermitage insist that reports of Jackson's dueling are exaggerated. They want to tame him, make him nice. They are wrong—in fact and intent. Jackson's brilliance was his hardness. This, not the wallpaper and plantings, is what we've come to experience.

Jackson's tomb may be the saddest of all our Presidents. Beneath a pretty cupola he rests beside his wife, who'd suddenly sickened on the eve of her husband's Presidency—slain, Jackson was certain, by slander. He composed her epitaph: "Here lie the remains of Mrs. RACHEL JACKSON, wife of PRESIDENT JACKSON, who died the 22nd Decr 1828—Aged 61. Her face was fair, her person pleasing; her temper amiable, and her heart kind; she delighted in relieving the wants of her fellow creatures, and cultivated that divine pleasure by the most liberal and unpretending methods; to the poor she was a benefactor; to the rich, an example; to the wretched a comforter, to the prosperous an ornament, her piety went hand in hand with her benevolence, and she thanked her creator for being permitted to do good. A being so gentle, and yet so virtuous, slander

67

might wound, but it could not dishonor; Even death, when he tore her from the armes of her husband, could but transport her to the bosom of God."

His own epitaph reads: "General ANDREW JACKSON. Born March 16, 1767, Died June 8, 1845." Neither husband, father, son, President, only General: embattled, defiant, "utterly alone."

viii.

Dolly Parton, not Andrew Jackson, has made Nashville a tourist Mecca. Adjacent to this large RV camp are two others, of like size, two RV dealerships, and a Camping World, where RV's are serviced and supplied. My 23-footer is a dinghy next to most of these land-yachts. My neighbor's is a burnished bronze bus as big as Manhattan Transit's. A similar model—with décor one might characterize as Sixties Bordello—is being offered in the parking lot for a million-two.

Tourism is mega-business and the way you lure multitudes is with a "unique theme." History or topography make some sites "naturals"— Washington, D.C., for instance, or the Grand Canyon—but most "unique themes" have to be contrived. The theme may be an entertainer—Dollyland, say, named for Dolly Parton—or a sports star, or a cartoon character, or even a food item (for example, Hersheypark). New "unique themes" are unlikely to be historical. "Heritage tourism," as it's called, represents a scant fraction of the whole. Andrew Jackson interests Americans less than Yogi Bear.

Nashville got lucky with Grand Ole Opry. Country-western music is big, and Nashville is its capital. From that seed have sprouted hotels, restaurants, RV parks, gay-nineties boat rides, mini-museums (Waxworks of the Stars, Cars of the Stars, Willie Nelson and Friends, etc.). Miniature golf is available for outdoor exercise. And then, of course, there's the Mall.

The Opryland Mall is vast and new. Its architecture is cute-crazy— irregularly angling walls and rooflines splashed with whimsical graphics— to pretend it's not a big box. Inside, it resembles other malls: high ceilings, a curving central corridor of brand-name stores, a bustling food court, benches for the footsore, and no windows to remind you of the hour. Colliding musics generate a jarring cacophony. Then there's that invariable mall-smell—of new clothes and cooking grease and perfumes and recycled air.

I loathe malls, but I go—to buy, yes, but mostly to watch. Our insatiable appetite for superfluities amazes me. Shopping is America's preferred recreational activity. This is how we spend the time we've saved.

I wonder what the Pilgrims or the Founding Fathers or Andy Jackson or honest Abe would have made of this. Here is the America they risked everything for. Would they be proud?

The life of a nation resembles the life of a man. Numberless details compose a few chapters that seem obvious in retrospect. America began when the Europeans got here. For a century and a half they cleared the land—of rocks and trees and natives. Then they formed their own nation, which they fought to defend. Then they fell to fighting among themselves—over slavery. The victory of the North consolidated the union. For the next hundred years or so we devoted our energy and ingenuity to getting rich. We went to war to advance our interests. We won; it was fun; one after another, our adversaries toppled, till there were none left. At home, we improved ourselves by securing rights—for workers, women, blacks, seniors, homosexuals, the disabled, children. We eliminated most poverty and many diseases. We established government programs to care for our old and young. We were interested in America, excited by it. Then that interest and excitement began to wane. A bad war and lying politicians soured us on government. Our lives made easy by prosperity, we turned our attention to diverting ourselves. Restaurants, TV, movies, theme parks, video games, stadiums, malls, Internet chat—we became wizards at filling empty hours. Having nothing to do we did it beautifully.

We also developed the diseases of the underemployed: hypochondria, finickiness, fickleness, dyspepsia, depression, obesity, indolence, addiction, fad-ism, recklessness, selfishness. We chased the next new thing, in the forlorn hope that it would rescue us from futility. We were well cared for, sure, but why were we here at all?

ix.

Leaving my campground in Opryland I crossed the Cumberland again—in Nashville you are always crossing the Cumberland—to visit Polk's grave at the capitol. I almost crashed, running a confusing stop sign. On the Interstate, I kept glancing for twirling lights.

The Tennessee statehouse is an elegant, lofting building, built before the war—which here means the Civil War—perched atop Nashville's highest hill. With its cupola and pillars and porticoes, this statehouse was a proclamation of parity—Tennessee's as good as any of you! Sad to think one of its first occupants was Tennessee's *military* Governor—Andrew Johnson, in 1862—before Lincoln tapped him as Vice President.

A honking, hollering, anti-tax protest on the street had the capitol cordoned off with that chilling yellow tape used by police. One of the protesters had brought her malformed child in a wheelchair to dramatize her point, which was, I guess, she couldn't afford no income tax, with all her bills. I'd have thought her crippled son—he was 10 or so—pointed to an opposite conclusion: that *needing* government sometimes, we should fund it.

I walked past the cordon, feeling like a scab. I set off the metal detector twice—with my camera, then my keys—causing some visiting bluehairs to frown.

Both houses of the legislature were in session so the corridors were crowded with lobbyists. What a life, waiting for some lawmaker to emerge from his chamber so you can sweet-talk him for two minutes. Legislators pretend to hate being pestered, but really they enjoy it. We all want to have something other people want. What lawmakers have—which puffs them up—is their vote.

I made my way to the gallery of the Assembly because nobody stopped me. All but one desk in the well was full. On that one lay a bouquet.

The legislators were honoring a fallen colleague. "You know I'm not one who says much in this chamber, but . . ." "I'll get through this if I don't look over in that direction . . ." (pointing toward the flowers). "I didn't know——well, but sitting listening, I felt I had to say something. . . ." Politicians, in my experience, *always* feel they have to say something.

I tried piecing together the story from the eulogies. This grief was fresh. The man had died yesterday. And suddenly—he'd been at his desk in the morning. And shockingly, perhaps not from natural causes. There were all sorts of references to the inscrutable wisdom of the Almighty and "we were there for him" and peace at the last. I looked around for someone to ask about it, but they all seemed so solemn—balling handkerchiefs and such—I thought I'd wait till I could find a newspaper.

It turned out the departed was a suicide—bullet through the head—because the cops were about to collar him for exposure—to teenage girls. He was a Republican running unopposed, which probably meant he was from a rural God-fearing district. He'd served in the legislature 10 years.

Making my way out of the cool cavernous corridors into the bright midday, I couldn't help wondering what makes a man—a man of some local luster—expose his unspectacular equipment to strangers. What madness gripped him, spurred him to exploits he must have known were fatal?

I felt a sneaking kinship with the poor guy. Exposure isn't my disease—of genitals, anyhow—but we all have our secret insanities, don't we, our caged demons who shame us, whom we hate yet prize? Consider: is there anything about yourself you wouldn't confess to anyone—not to your best friend, your priest, even your God? It may be no big deal really—a habit, an appetite, an opinion—but it shames you, and you want to be rid of it, purified, forgiven—part of you does—yet part of you clings to it, like a tress in a locket.

All longing, when you think of it, is crazy—whether to be President, or write a book, or shock some unsuspecting maidens with a flash of flesh—the expression of a recurrent ache that nothing quiets for long. Respecting convention, the acquaintances of the late legislator will say he "snapped," went crazy; but we know, whether we admit it, the craziness is there—in each of us. Jostle us just so and you unlatch the cage.

Perhaps the most eloquent commentary on this episode was offered by a fellow legislator, an older heavy-set tobacco-chewer, who splayed himself in his chair, gazing upward, wearied by all this jawing. Maybe he'd never liked the deceased. In any event, no use going on about it. "We came here to work," I could hear him thinking, "not flap our traps. This damn budget is still out of balance—so what's your pleasure, gentlemen (and gentle ladies)? An income tax? A state lottery? Cuts in services? Let's get on with it."

X.

Horse Cave, Kentucky. I awake. The light, birds, a glade. Anywhere is beautiful in the morning, with fresh eyes.

Words whirled in my mind last night like streamers snagged in the trees. I got up and wrote till my eyelids sank but still sentences swung. "Sleep!" I told myself, "you can't write now, you'll be incoherent, you can't even think!" But the words kept fluttering, teasing, out of reach.

If only I could memorize my time! I stare and stare: what do I see? I scribble frantically, like the last student in the exam room, the proctor impatient.

A friend, reading one of my dispatches, wonders if I'm depressed.

"Depressed?" I blink, incredulous. "I couldn't be less."

"But you wrote, 'Does your existence matter much? Does mine?'"

"Well, does it?"

"That's a depressing thought."

"If it depresses you."

"But if your existence doesn't matter much—"

"Don't think about it. Just work. Get busy and you won't be bothered. I'm too busy thinking to think."

Yesterday I visited James Polk's only surviving home, in Columbia, Tennessee. As often happens at less frequented Presidential sites, I was alone on the tour. When this occurs, a slightly embarrassed intimacy develops. The script, composed for groups, sounds stilted delivered to one. My guide was a stout roseate lady with a curious habit of speech and a delighted smile. She knew the Polks—not as a text, but as familiars, a big brother and sister maybe, who had just stepped out. She felt free to kid them, to sigh at some of their choices, because she loved them, and they her—they had lived together so long.

Polk is generally ranked among our ablest Presidents, though of that bright crew he's the least known. For most Americans, our history from the departure of Andrew Jackson in 1837 to the roistering arrival of Teddy Roosevelt in 1901 is a blur, with the dazzling exception of 1861 to 1865. This is not because the events during those other 65 years and 15 Presidencies are inherently less interesting or important—America burgeoned then from a fascinating experiment, far from civilization's center, into the world's great power. It's because history is drama—and a single enthralling actor or episode casts others in the shade. Lincoln, above all, is the marquee name in the drama of America—the greatest of the great—our Zeus, our Jesus, our Gandhi. He looms greater even than Washington—because he saved us, and because his story is nearer ours, in its hard beginnings and endless struggle, and because he died for us, and because his eloquence pierces our armor of indifference. I cannot hear the Gettysburg Address or the peroration of the Second Inaugural without tears welling. It's embarrassing, but so it is.

James Polk had about him nothing of the theatrical. When he was nominated in 1844—he is credited with being the first "dark horse" candidate—the opposition Whigs ridiculed his lack of what we'd now call name recognition. "Who is James K. Polk?" they whooped, exulting in the renown of their standard-bearer, "the Great Pacificator," former Secretary of State, Senator Henry Clay. Polk won because he represented the mood of the moment. America wanted to expand. We believed in ourselves back then with a prophetic zeal—it was our "manifest destiny" to occupy the continent, from sea to sea—and Polk promised to achieve that. "Fifty-four forty or fight!" his alliterative campaign slogan, referred to the longitude of our northern boundary. He almost delivered. By adding to the American domain most of the territory from Texas west, Polk more than doubled the size of the United States, establishing a geographical advantage that has helped make us (for the present) insuperable. He also lowered the tariff and restored an Independent Treasury—his two other pledges. And he did this all in four years, which were all he'd sought.

Polk entered the Presidency at 49, the youngest man ever to have been elected, and he left looking like the oldest. The contrast between his portraits in 1845 and 1849 make one gasp. His hair has turned from abundant dark to limp white (they didn't have Grecian Formula then); his cheeks are gaunt; his gaze hollow as a skull's. One suspects illness undiagnosed—he'd always been slight and sickly. But there's a readier explanation, amply documented. No man ever worked harder at the job. Polk never took a vacation; he didn't believe in them. He rose at dawn, met every caller, answered every letter, read every piece of legislation, gave (liquor-less) receptions at the White House twice a week, and returned to his desk afterward, to leave it clean. He never traveled more than a few miles from the White House. His no less assiduous wife served as his secretary 10 or more hours daily. He knew what he wanted and he spent himself like a candle in that cause. "They have been four years of incessant labour and anxiety," he wrote. "I am heartily rejoiced that my term is so near its close."

Three months after leaving office he was dead of cholera.

xi.

Paducah's Alben Barkley is the last of our log-cabin leaders. He was big and strong, one of eight children of a tobacco farmer, who kept changing farms when he went bust.

Barkley had a big smile and big hands and joined any club or civic group that would have him. Like another big strong log-cabin kid, born seventy miles and seven decades distant, Barkley told stories. One (borrowed from an earlier Vice President, Thomas Marshall) was about that farmer who had two sons who vanished, one at sea and the other into the Vice Presidency.

Another, from Lincoln's inexhaustible trove, concerned the man being ridden out of town on a rail. Asked how he liked it, the man replied, "Well, if it weren't for the honor of the thing, I'd sooner walk."

Barkley would have been President but for one decision. As Senate Majority Leader and FDR's close ally, he was odds-on favorite to replace the left-leaning Henry Wallace on the 1944 Democratic ticket. But then Barkley and Roosevelt differed over a tax bill, and Barkley organized an override of the President's veto.

Effective Presidents, while democrats in theory, prove autocrats in practice. Roosevelt wanted a Vice President who would be seen but not heard. He passed over Barkley for the less prominent—but more pliant—Senator Truman of Missouri.

Truman tapped Barkley as his running mate in 1948. Truman's reelection looked doomed; he needed all the help he could get. Barkley became the first Vice President to work the office. He ranked ahead of Truman as the most requested speaker of the Democratic Speakers' Bureau. *Look* magazine named him and General Eisenhower the two "most fascinating" Americans. He's the only Vice President honored by the public with an affectionate nickname: "Veep."

Barkley hoped to succeed Truman in 1952, but at age 74 he was deemed too old. Not done with public life, he ran for the Senate again, age 76, unseating a Republican incumbent.

Two years later, after one last rip-snorting speech, he collapsed and died, the applause still ringing in his ears.

xii.

"Country" is one of those words you've got to watch for, especially in Tennessee and Kentucky.

It does not mean place; it does not mean nation; it does not mean rural, though it incorporates a sense of all three. This Country is an adjective: defiant, self-gratulatory, polemical. It juts its jaw and is ready to draw to defend itself. It expects to be saluted, and if not, friend, well mebbe you've just taken you a wrong turn and should head back where you belong.

Country carries a chip on its shoulder, which it braids into epaulettes. Country means "folks"—of less wealth, privilege, education, or sophistication than the gentry or the urban elite. Country was born in the Appalachians, where farms were small and stony and it was all a body could do to keep alive. Country dislikes banks because it always owes them and never owns them. It dislikes big words and abstractions and intellectuals, who think they're so much better than anyone jes because they've got them some learning. Subtle distinctions, to Country, are the devil's snares. Country, through the bitter end of the Civil Rights movement, resented Negroes as much as they'd resented the slave-owners before the Civil War. Country favors its own kind: white, evangelical Christian, skin roughened by weather and pinked by elevated blood pressure. Jews spell trouble to them, the way they keep ending up with the money: Shylock and Fagin they'd deem fair portraits.

Insecurity brags. Country glorifies what it is out of embarrassment at what it's not. It appropriates the flag and defines patriotism as adherence to its values. It respects guns and the military and distrusts disarmament and diplomacy. It doesn't think twice about singing a Christian hymn in a political assembly. (In the Tennessee legislature the other day, they joined hands for a teary rendition of "Amazing Grace." Try that in the New York State capitol and you'd be slapped with a dozen lawsuits.) Its creed commends common people, the working poor, so-called plain talk, simple melodies, bland inexpensive cuisine. They brand those aspects of their lives they most admire ("country music," "country cookin'," etc.).

All creeds are splendid and ridiculous. None is superior, per se. The Country critique of the citified elite can be dead-on. Big-worders like yours truly may get lost in our own discriminations. Fashion-fixated cosmopolitans can produce art that repels. Manhattanites who rhapsodize over some sea urchin marinated in lime (for thirty dollars a nibble) or an '83 Chateau Whoseewhat make my gorge rise. Sometimes diplomacy *is* a trap, when dealing with punks whom only force persuades.

It is good to belong to a religion. The conviction of the congregation helps us walk aright. Bereft of any communion, we tend to lurch, arrive at peculiar conclusions. Loners are dangerous.

It is good to belong to a religion but bad to be blinded by it. Rejoice, yes, in your God, but do not denigrate mine. If God had meant us all to worship a single version of Him, wouldn't He have seen to it? No sect's got a lock on sanctity.

Yesterday, emerging from the wondrous depths of Mammoth Cave—earth's longest, more than 350 miles and still mapping—I felt in the mood for humanity, so dined at a restaurant called Cracker Barrel. I enjoy eating in chain restaurants to observe the tactics. Cracker Barrel caught my eye when passing one on Father's Day. I noticed its parking lot was jammed, while adjacent restaurants' lots were sparse. Cracker Barrel was doing something right, to win hearts and wallets hereabout.

Beware anyone who comes on real simple like. Cracker Barrel styles itself an "Old Country Store" (at least it's "old," I thought, not "ole"). Cracker Barrel refers to the barrel of hardtack on which farmers would sit, in the era before TV and Interstates, talking about weather, politics, neighbors. But cracker also conjures a pejorative for country rubes—"cracker," "hillbilly," "redneck," all synonymous—just as "barrel" brings to mind not only a hooped wooden container but the metal shaft of a gun. As with that squirrelly word "country," behind a modest, aw-shucks exterior we feel a shudder of defiance ("Yeh, I'm a cracker, I'm country—want to make something of it?").

Cracker Barrel's formula is "down home," home being early-twentieth-century rural America. Patent medicines, rifles, snowshoes, antlers, washboards, tattered top hats, boaters, pitchforks, and a lot of sepia uncle and auntie so-and-so's with their frozen frowns, adorn the rough walls. Interspersed are quaint ole (I mean, old) ads for businesses like International Tailoring Company, Orange Crush, and (my favorite):

SPECIAL

Electric Scalp Massage
with the SENSATIONAL Q.E.D. DANDRUFF TREATMENT
All for 75¢

The menu is as calculatedly homey as the décor. "Comfort food" they call it, by which they mean everything's stewed or fried or casseroled. I weigh the selections under "Fancy Fixin's":

Meatloaf Dinner
Chicken Fried Chicken
Grilled Chicken Tenderloin
Cracker Barrel Sampler (ideal for our investigator)
Roast Beef Dinner ("roasted in the pot roast tradition")
Country Fried Steak (the beef again disguised)
Deep Dish Chicken Pot Pie
Fried Chicken Tenderloin Dinner

Where, you might ask, are yesteryear's orchard fruits or fresh garden vegetables or the peculiar pickles and relishes you won't find in the supermarket? Well, fruit and vegetables, which vary, might disappoint (also, they cost more) and a pickled egg or pig's knuckle might cause discussion so, no—in deep-fryer and stewpot and mixin' bowl we trust! *E pluribus unum.*

The portions are ample and punctual; the textures, leathery to mucilaginous. Flavors—what flavors? Prices: pleasin'—I see seniors here and when it comes to food prices, seniors know.

And what's Cracker Barrel's unique "hook"? Cracker Barrel, as they proudly proclaim, is "more than" a restaurant. Adjacent to the dining area is a *store*, where you can purchase old-fashioned kids' toys and T-shirts and wind chimes and flag-decorated button-boxes and picture frames and "hand-crafted" elves and greeting cards and quaint kitchen implements and perfumed candles and potpourri and country hams and videos and fudge and candy galore. Thus Cracker Barrel combines contemporary Americans' two ruling passions: eating and shopping.

At the end of his long life, Benjamin Franklin wrote a pamphlet promoting our nation as a place to settle. He said it was a happy destination for those who wanted to get rich, but happiest for the "laboring poor," "for nowhere else are [they] so well fed, well lodged, well clothed and well paid as in the United States of America." Here, he concluded, "a general happy mediocrity prevails."

Mediocrity is the byproduct of democracy. One size fits all: comfort food, comfort clothes, comfort travel, comfort candidates. A "Do Not Disturb" sign dangles over the doorknob to America.

Cracker Barrel beguiles with a past that never was. It's comfort history, a Disneyfication, a pastel vision as tasteless as their dumplin's.

I prefer the real, the unscripted, the original, even if it stings. I do not want comfort food to put me to sleep, or comfort government to rock in like a cradle, or a comfort past. Truth can be hard, bitter, disturbing: you can break your teeth on it. But you will learn. And discovery, for my money, is the blessing of life.

5
Land of Lincoln

i.

It's interesting how we learn.

When I was a small boy my grandmother, in summer, lived up the hill. She was a recent widow, so often during the day found herself alone. I too found myself alone, not because I'd been abandoned but because we had money so nobody needed to do anything they didn't like. My older sisters did not want to play with their younger brother and my younger brother, more than five years my junior, was too young to be amusing. My schoolmates lived in houses near each other but my house was on a farm too far to walk to. I could talk to the help, as we called them, and did, and learned from them, but they, unlike me, had work to do, and what kind of kid, I wondered, spends his time with the help? That left my grandmother. I'd climb the hill to visit her while she was eating lunch—alone, in the library, on a tray.

Many people in my family were scared of my father's mother. That was because she was smart and decisive and didn't suffer fools. She said what she saw and what she saw was often not flattering. I was never scared of my grandmother. She recognized in me, I suppose, across a gap of 68 years, another person who liked to see and say.

She was always glad when I came. She'd be reading a book. Reading a book, as I've learned since, does not prevent loneliness. Not that she complained. She complained so little that when my father died at 47, her youngest child and the fourth of five to die, she had a chair placed in the middle of her bedroom, shut the door, and sat for 36 hours without taking "nourishment," as she called it. At the end of that time she rose without a hint of loss. She did not cry—not because she did not feel like it but because her emotions were her business and nobody else's.

Looking back I can see how good a grandmother she was because conversing with even a precocious eight-year-old is not necessarily fascinating.

She made me think what I had to say was worth hearing. It may be what got me started in this line.

Our conversations ranged as conversations will and I felt giddy after. One evening, lying in bed in the slow dusk—we children went to bed at bedtime, dark or no—I began piecing together my grandmother's and my conversation of that afternoon. I could remember the beginning and the end and some moments in between but I couldn't figure out how topic A led to topic B and so on all the way to Q. It seemed stupid that a conversation of only a few hours ago had disappeared in my mind like water in sand and I was frustrated with myself, almost to the point of tears. Painstakingly, I lay there reassembling our topics like scraps of a paper you've torn up and wish you hadn't. It was agonizing, I thought I would never manage it, then suddenly, just like that, it was done. I had reconstructed the sequence and could tell it over—and over—dazzled how one thing leads to another. I felt proud of myself and slept to wild applause.

As a small boy, before anyone taught me history, I studied the entries on the Presidents in my World Book Encyclopedia and practiced their signatures. I spent a lot of time on my signature in those days. Fancy signatures, I now know, are an ominous indicator, but then they struck me as fine. William McKinley had the best signature—it zigzagged all over the place. John Adams's, with its perfect tall slanting letters, was handsome too, and James Buchanan's with its J coiled like a cobra. (Jefferson's, by contrast, was an indecipherable heap: I thought less of him because of it.)

I knew the Presidents by their faces and their signatures and gradually over the years I knew something of who they were and what they'd done, but I was never able to make them link up, arm to arm, from A to Q. There were always gaps, especially between Jackson and Lincoln, and Johnson (Andrew, but we'd only had one President Johnson then) and Teddy, whose script rushed like a race car.

When my daughter Becca, who's now 25, was in eleventh grade, I helped her remember all the Presidents for an exam but that was by rote, where memory balances precariously on the sounds of syllables and easily topples off.

Tonight I woke up and for the first time all the Presidents had linked in my mind. Jackson handed off to Van Buren who conceded to Tippecanoe—and Tyler too—who bowed (stiffly, with no good grace) to Polk and so on to an uncomfortable Clinton (I think of him as ham somehow) in his Bush sandwich. I knew the story—not all of it: no one knows that—but where it began and where it ended and in general what happened in between. And the more I studied it the simpler it got. First there was the founding of our nation, steadying ourselves, learning to walk. Then there was the period of relentless, often ruthless ambition as we acquired most of our continent—and at the same time an enormous tussle with the problem that made John Quincy Adams characterize our Constitution as "a compact with hell." It took 600,000 American lives to settle the slavery question, but once we managed it, there was no looking back. America just got mightier and mightier, inventing, discovering, amassing wealth, winning wars, wriggling out of economic jams that unraveled other nations, gradually repairing the inequities in our system, and in general having a grand old time. Clouds might gather—the cloud of Vietnam and Watergate, the cloud of militant Islam—our assurance might be shaken—but sooner or later, with our strength, decency, and luck, we would find our way.

Others will find in our 226 years a different story—that's the fun of history—but I had mine, I knew it, and knowing it I could see how the Presidents fit. Once again I had found my way to Q. There is nothing like it.

ii.

Red Hills Lake State Park, Lawrence, Illinois. Nearly dark (just past the solstice, as late as dark gets). A place I'd never heard of until a few hours ago when, realizing I'd miscalculated, I pulled over. Passing big-rigs rattled Migrant as I studied the map.

Mariah, my electronic navigatrix, has many virtues: among them, acuity, availability, attention, courtesy. Her polite and slightly coquettish electronic voice surprises hearers if I am on the phone. I explain Mariah, and they believe me, but suspicion lingers.

Mariah, like any helper, is imperfect. She knows her job but not my mind. Efficiency is her programmed objective, the quickest route, which usually means the dreaded Interstate. Her second defect is obstinacy. She knows she is right and repeats her instructions tirelessly if she thinks I've erred: "Make a U-turn if possible." Silencing her with a button feels ungallant.

That Red Lakes State Park isn't where I'd planned makes it sweeter. It is a splendid wood, more splendid because of its emergence from interminable fields. The leafy hills of Kentucky are behind me. I have returned to that boundless alluvial patch-quilt we call the Midwest. As one who covets variety and vistas, it surprises me anyone could live here.

80

I like this park. It is large and quiet. The services aren't much, but neither is the cost. In a KOA Kampground, we're paying customers; we feel entitled to hole up, as in a motel. Here, in a public park, having paid only a nominal fee, we are fellow citizens, and aggressive privacy feels like rudeness. My neighbors, with hand signals, help back me in. (Backing in a 23-foot RV reminds me of those 3-D video games I'm no good at.) Having thanked them I do not immediately curtain my cubicle as I would at a KOA. I eat—and return their glance. (They are wondering, I suppose, why this middle-aged man is camping alone.)

A public park is more real, more personable than a commercial chain, yet in a month on the road I've found myself opting for KOA's. Why? I'd set out to see, hadn't I? Why camp where I'd learn less?

All of us are more or less fearful. We crave only as much unfamiliarity as we can cope with. That is why we eat at McDonald's and shop at Wal-Mart and vacation at Disney World and check into Motel 6. We know what we're getting. We know the routine, the layout, what to order from the menu, which button to press for a wake-up call. We present our card that rewards frequent usage and feel as if we're doing something by amassing points.

Man's kingdom is his Comfort Zone. We recoil into our Comfort Zones like turtles into their shells. Variety, we say, is the spice of life—but that's all it is, the spice. Sameness, routine, safety, predictability are our bread and butter.

The bear went over the mountain to see what he could see. But the bear got scared sometimes, and lonely, and dubious about his enterprise. He sought the familiar to reassure himself, to make himself feel competent and knowledgeable. It feels good knowing where the laundry is and the dump station. There were times after a long strange day when I wanted simply to draw my blinds and gaze at the things I'd brought. "Human kind," observed Missouri's T. S. Eliot, "cannot bear very much reality."

Solitude strengthens a man if it does not sour him. I thought of this yesterday visiting Lincoln's boyhood home on Knob Creek. Knob Creek is located on the outskirts of Hodgenville, Kentucky, itself on the outskirts of nowhere. For 70 years Knob Creek was run as a tourist trap. The cabin was an imaginary replica, but the location itself was certifiable. Recently, the site was acquired by the state, and as a result, the gift shop has been shut and entry into the replicated cabin prohibited. Attendants at the other Lincoln sites tried to warn me of my likely disappointment: "You know you can't go in," said one. "All you can do is look at it."

Which was what I did. Look. At a small rough cabin surrounded by fertile flatland, hedged by woods, and at the sun slanting through the leaves and a squirrel hesitating on a split rail. Here Thomas Lincoln planted beans and pumpkins, and young Abe spent hours alone. A childhood chum named Austin Gollaher is remembered in the literature, but with miles between farms, and locomotion pedestrian, it is evident that young Abe's most intimate companions were the grass and birds and trees.

The simplicity of that scene, the absence of things "to do," moved me more than the heaped-up Lincoln Birthplace Memorial, 12 miles distant, a monumental homage to our secular saint. The Lincoln Birthplace Memorial is impressive in its way, as a grandiose expression of our nation's grief. Lincoln, one suspects, would have hated its pomposity, while understanding the yearning those pediments represent. We need to believe in something, cling to something, and we Americans believe in Lincoln above all.

At Knob Creek I experienced not Lincoln the legend, but Abe the boy, pausing in the sun, listening to the leaves, puzzling out the questions we encounter in time.

iii.

I hadn't been expecting George Rogers Clark. Truth was, I'd never heard of him. Maybe mounted on a sentence in some long-ago textbook he galloped through my brain, but he never paused. The Clark I knew was the explorer William, whom sad brave Meriwether Lewis had recruited and hyphenated into history. William, it turns out, was George's much-younger brother. (Some family, those Clarks.)

I might never have met George if, driving across the Wabash into Vincennes, there wasn't this monument, in scale and shape reminiscent of Jefferson's on the Potomac. Vincennes is on Indiana's Illinois border. I'd come to visit Grouseland, William Henry Harrison's home when he was Governor of the Indiana Territory (1800–1812). Mercifully and magnificently restored by the Daughters of the American Revolution (it had been slated for demolition in 1909), Grouseland is as politically incorrect an erection as you can think of. Vincennes, in 1800, was a scruffy, perilous frontier post (it is scruffy still). Until 1806, when Lewis and Clark returned from their expedition, west of Indiana was pretty much a blank. No one imagined the Rockies. The job of the territorial governor was to keep peace among the arriving settlers and make peace with the Indians (the peace of the grave).

Grouseland, alien as a spaceship amidst the rough cabins of frontiersmen, is a handsome reminder of the Virginia manor where Harrison grew
up. A soaring two-storied white portico supported by Doric and Ionic pillars projects from its thick red brick walls. Shawnee chief Tecumseh, who
sought in vain to negotiate with Harrison for his people, would not enter
Grouseland, sensing evil spirits. Grouseland was meant to intimidate: "I'm
boss and you're not!" its opulence sniffs.

In Grouseland we feel both the magnificence and ruthlessness of America's westward drive. Poor Tecumseh. Honorable by all accounts, he was ill-
equipped to oppose the white man's aggressive greed. These lands, he held,
had been given by the Great Spirit to all the tribes and could not be ceded
or sold. When negotiation failed, Tecumseh organized to fight. Tecumseh's
defeat vaulted Richard Mentor Johnson to the Vice Presidency in 1836 and
Harrison to the Presidency in 1840.[12]

Grouseland made Vincennes worth visiting. But who was George
Rogers Clark?

Born in Virginia in 1752, Clark is another from that astonishing generation of patriots. Washington, Jefferson, Adams, Madison, Hamilton, Patrick
Henry—where do we find their like?

Clark had been a surveyor for Great Britain's Ohio Company. When war
came, he was commissioned lieutenant colonel in the Virginia militia and
with 175 men undertook a campaign against his former employer.

In 1778 he captured Kaskaskia (in today's Illinois) and Vincennes (in Indiana) from the British. It was the patriots' one military success that year.
Irked, the local British commander, Henry Hamilton, retook Vincennes in
December 1778, leaving Clark and his followers in Kaskaskia to finish off
later. The weather in those days mandated a winter respite from combat.
The flatlands of the Midwest swamped as rivers rose. Settlements became
islands in an endless pond.

Clark didn't stand a chance against Hamilton and he knew it. Prudence
dictated that he abandon Kaskaskia and hightail it back to safety. Only
Clark wasn't prudent. He dreamed of liberty. He was young and strong.

To attempt a march across 180 miles of "drowned country," as it was
called, with bone-chilling waters often chest-high, was crazy. Think: 20
days of soaked, cold, half-starved stumbling across invisible submerged
ground, holding rifle and provisions over your head, losing your footing,

---

[12]See pages 54–56.

falling in. Imagine the weary band huddling against the night, teeth chattering, toes clenched in their boots. And this was not to save their lives, but risk them! Clark was some persuader.

His secret arrival flummoxed Hamilton. By keeping his troops hidden, Clark convinced Hamilton his force was numerous. Hamilton, spooked, must have thought he was grappling with Satan. It couldn't be done—marching all that way through a swamp—they must have flown! History does not record Hamilton's reaction to the size and condition of the ragtag crew he eventually surrendered to. He had two years to brood about it in a Virginia cell, his thoughts recurring—how often?—to that—that—that *man*, if that's what he was, Colonel Clark.

I shivered that night, dreaming of their long slog. I despised my luxury. How pampered I was, how squeamish, how modern, fretting whether my mattress was springy or my pork chop pink!

I dreamed of George Rogers Clark, his audacity, how characteristic he was of an earlier America. I doubt he thought himself a hero. Duty was clear: you did what you could, without figuring the odds. The impossible became possible if you ventured forth.

How American is his story: its boldness, strangeness, shock, the improbable prize. Wasn't that the story of our founding? It couldn't be done! It was crazy even to try! Those madmen in Philadelphia would draw down the king's wrath and get us all killed!

The essential American story is of one man or a few, against all odds—and prudence, perhaps—on a lonely journey. Ishmael, Huck Finn, Thoreau, Whitman, Emily Dickinson, Lewis-and-Clark (a zygote, really), George Rogers Clark . . . Lieutenant Governor Hamilton was a company man, a European, well schooled, no doubt, in procedures. He knew what could be done and what shouldn't be. He could tell you the odds. His plans made sense.

And he lost.

iv.

There are crosses and there are crosses.

Round the Effingham bend on Interstate 57, a 198-foot steel cross rises like a shriek. I was drowsy, peering for my exit after a long sit. I almost swerved into the rumbling semi beside me.

The cross rises from a cornfield. No hills or buildings or signs compete for attention. It is alone against the sky. The design is ingenious and quite beautiful. Everything is angular—points and edges—as if one giant obelisk, the Washington Monument, say, had intersected another. The striated stainless steel glows without gleaming.

That night it woke me. And the next. This morning I am 400 miles away and it is still glowing. The intent of art is to infiltrate consciousness. In its scale, its passion, its stark elegance, the Cross at Effingham is comparable to Stonehenge.

It is also politics, the expression not of an individual but a collective. "This is who we are in Effingham," it proclaims. "Bow or beware."

Effingham hardly existed until, in the Sixties, two Interstates met here. To be sliced by a single Interstate is a windfall, especially for the farmer whose fields flank the exit. To be chosen as an intersection of two such commercial corridors is like striking oil. (Senator Stephen Douglas, of Illinois, understood this. His passionate advocacy of the northern route for the first transcontinental railroad arose—who can doubt?—from his devotion to his constituents. The fact that he owned much of Chicago's South Side, where the trains would stop, was happenstance.)

Will Murphy remembers Effingham from the old days. He was born here, as were his father and his father's father. He can trace his ancestry back through his mother's line to one Bricker, born Broecher, who'd emigrated from Germany to the Illinois frontier in the late 1700s with his children—24 in all, by a single wife. Broecher, now Bricker, had either bought or been given 2,000 acres. It was a terrible chance: the land, the Indians, the language, the pitiless winters. That first winter the family huddled in their covered wagon: there hadn't been time to build cabins. (And I think Migrant is tight!)

Genealogy is Will's passion. After a career in the Army, Will enrolled in barber school and set up shop here. That was more than 20 years ago. Will is a barber, he notes, not one of these hair-cutters. His customers are men; he'll shave them, too, some of the older fellows, for whom a foamy barbershop shave still defines luxury. Will's greatest frustration is the passenger manifests kept by ship captains in the 1790s. They lacked almost all information: only, "Bricker, A., wife, and fourteen children." (Others of the children came after.) No names, no indication of origins. He'd never have known the name was Broecher but for family lore. It frustrates Will that he can't follow his family to its source. His father's line came from Ireland—no

85

name change there!—but the same problem. Go chasing a Murphy in Ireland, why don't you!

Effingham, Will told me as he clipped, was the quietest place you could think of growing up. There was hunting down in the Creek, near where the Wal-Mart and Days Inn are now. You could shoot deer. Aside from that, not much excitement. Hardly 2,000 in population, if that. After the Interstate came through, things really took off. "It's good and bad," he opined, the razor buzzing pleasantly. "It's always that way, isn't it, good and bad?"

"What's bad about it?"

"Oh, you get the business, the hotels and such. But with the truck drivers, you get the drugs. At the truck stops. Not so much the drivers maybe, but the girls who, you know, take care of them. Then the young people from town find their way there. It's a problem."

I asked him about the Cross. "Oh that," he quieted suddenly, intent on my neck. "Isn't that something?"

There are 848 yards of concrete in the Cross's footing, 33.92 tons of reinforced steel. There are 180.8 tons of steel in the structure. Its span is 113 feet. 35,000 vehicles pass it daily, 18,000,000 travelers a year.

The ubiquitous flier invites me not only to visit the Cross, but to contribute to its mission. "No symbol more clearly speaks of God's love, forgiveness, and salvation. Used by civic, religious and commercial organizations, the Cross represents the human qualities of honesty and decency and forever stands as an emblem of hope . . . to passersby from every faith, background and circumstance reminding them of the positive values shared and cherished by all."

The Cross is not mentioned in the colorful 36-page booklet published by the Convention and Visitors Bureau: "Effingham! In the heart of it all!" The Annual Corvette Funfest, the Schuetzenfest ("shooting festival"), Bliss Park, Drave's Archery, My Garage Corvette Museum, 24 houses of worship (all churches), even a Monastery Museum are celebrated, but not the Cross. I wonder if that's on advice of counsel. I can imagine the interchange between town attorney and councilman (in executive session):

Councilman (agitated): "What do you mean, we can't mention the Cross? The Cross is the biggest thing in Effingham. Everyone loves it. Eighteen million people a year—"

Town attorney (with determined calm): "I understand your feeling, Councilman. But the Constitution—"

Councilman: "Damn the Constitution. This isn't some kind of slave state. This is America! Aren't we free to be who we want to be?"

Attorney: "Yes, unless—"

Councilman: "Unless nothing. Either we are or we aren't."

Mayor (intervening): "I think we all share your feelings, Jack, but the law—"

Councilman (conclusively): "Fucking police state, that's what it is."

v.

Adlai Ewing Stevenson, Grover Cleveland's second Vice President, is buried pleasantly beside his grandson, Adlai Stevenson, twice the Democratic nominee for President, in Evergreen Cemetery in Bloomington.

The younger Stevenson is remembered as an idealist. His granddad was anything but.

In 1895, the senior Stevenson traveled to the state of Washington, where a debate was raging whether to name their big landmark Mount Rainier or Mount Tacoma. Partisans were hot, as Americans tend to get over matters of no importance.

The Vice President's endorsement was sought. Never one for taking sides (he supported both "free silver" and "sound currency" in the era's most divisive controversy), Stevenson arranged to give a speech from the rear platform of his train. He extolled the beauty of the mountain and pledged not to rest until the mountain was named. The name he supported was—At that moment, per instructions, the train's whistle blew, drowning out Stevenson's recommendation (if any), and the train pulled out from the station.

vi.

Lincoln is buried in Springfield. I mean, really buried. Beneath a soaring 117-foot-high white granite mountain, massive bronze sculptural groups, inscriptions, eulogies, wreaths. His crypt is the deepest and dimmest of all the Presidents: you enter through cavernous marble corridors, flanked by the great man's words. Unlike most of our Presidents, who rest amiably beside their brides, Lincoln lies alone. Mary Todd and their three sons who died early are entombed in the wall opposite.

We bury deepest those we fear will rise. We love Lincoln where he is, as we love Jesus where he is. Imagine if they returned.

The beatification of Lincoln is curious. No other President approaches him in volume or variety of veneration. We tell over the details of Lincoln's life as we do Christ's, struggling to understand. Lincoln is an industry: you can "do" his life, trace his zigzagging footsteps from birth to boyhood to early manhood to his lawyering days. You can track his train ride from Springfield to Washington to be inaugurated and his return trip, which featured 10 massive memorial services in a dozen days. Lincoln literature proliferates. His name is everywhere. There are enough collectors of Lincolniana to form a mid-sized city.

Why? And why not other Presidents? Why not Washington? Or Jefferson? Or Jackson? Or either Roosevelt?

That Lincoln was killed—martyred—is part of it. Violent deaths stick with us. There is no slow fadeout to accustom us to the idea of absence.

Lincoln was not just killed, he was killed by a famous actor, who gave himself lines (in Latin, no less).[13] The other Presidential assassins were seedy sickos. Booth was a matinee idol. He meant to star, and did, in his greatest role. He was not insane. This was vengeance, an act of war, the murder of the murderer of his hopes.

Lincoln also died on cue. Five days after our all-damaging war was done, when perhaps for the first time since 1861 he could wake without dread, crack, and he's gone. Garfield and McKinley lingered exhaustingly: only Lincoln—and later Kennedy—went out like lights.

Lincoln was our first President to be gunned down. Coming at the close of our murderous family feud, here was the final extinction of our innocence. On Good Friday, to boot.

His Presidency was as dramatic as his death. No President, with the possible exception of Washington, was more necessary to our survival. Lincoln, we feel again and again, by his sound sense and stubborn courage, really *did* save the Union. Sooner or later someone would have freed the slaves, but it was Lincoln who did it. And he died at his apogee, before he could be ensnared in the messy consequences of his accomplishments. Our chapter on Reconstruction would probably have made unhappy reading no matter who was in charge.

---

[13]Or maybe not. Like nearly every other detail of Lincoln's death, there's doubt about Booth's exit line. *Did* he roar *"Sic semper tyrannis"* or, in view of his temper and profession, *should* he have? No national calamity disorders our collective memory like a Presidential assassination.

The drama of Lincoln's life and death and its historical significance go a long way toward explaining his canonization. But still we are puzzled. Nine months before dying, Lincoln was convinced he would not be re-elected. He was not beloved. Many in his own party treated him with scorn. Is all this worship the result of a bullet?

We bury more than a body in a casket. We bury history, guilt, our insufferable past. In the Christian contention that Jesus by His death carries away our sin, there is a psychological truth. A coffin can be a convenient container for old distress.

We needed a fresh start after the Civil War. We needed to put away our shame and remorse. No one won the Civil War. Winner is loser and loser winner where both are one.

Our Civil War still astonishes us. We tell the tale over and over, repeat the causes, and still we cannot believe it. Are we the kind of family that butchers one another?

We make saints to help us bear the burden of being. Lincoln bears the burden of America. We scrutinize every aspect of his history to fathom how one man could be so "great." But of course, Lincoln, good and wise as he was, was not that "great." Sure, he was our tallest President, but not a hundred times taller than the rest. We made him great because we needed him to be great, so he could carry off our shame. If one among us, an ordinary Abe, could be so good, perhaps we are not so bad.

The difference between the Lincoln and Washington monuments in our capital is telling. Washington's is an abstraction, an idea. The focus of Lincoln's is his face. We need to see him—again and again—to know he is really a man.

At the front of Lincoln's tomb, at ground level, is an oversized bronze bust by Gutzon Borglum (the sculptor of Mount Rushmore). A tradition has developed of rubbing this Lincoln's nose. As a result, the nose gleams while the rest of the head is dark, as if Lincoln were a drunk.

I watched a seemingly intelligent couple photograph each other engaging in this ritual.

I asked them why.

"For luck," the man smiled uneasily.

"Do you really believe that?"

Husband and wife exchanged a glance. "Can't hurt," he shrugged, hurrying off.

23 days and not a word.

Not that I blame you. You were angry when I left. I was angry.

Anger is so strange. We mean not to be and then, before we know it, one of us has said something, and the other's said something back, and we're holding onto a runaway horse for dear life. A quarter century we've been married—more than half our time. We know each other well—better than anybody—yet sometimes it seems not at all.

I'd surprise you, I think, on the road. I surprise myself. I was scared heading out. I'd wake up before I left, worrying. What if I got sick? What if I got lonely? What if I had a crash? What if lust got the better of me? What if!

Turns out, like most things, it's easier than one fears. For starters, there are some 16,000 places to camp in North America. That means hundreds in every state. The reason we don't know this is there are almost none near Manhattan. It's too crowded, too expensive, and our parkways don't accommodate these big machines. Ever noticed those little parkway signs— "Passenger Cars Only"? They're not kidding. Twice, early on, I almost headed onto roads where I wouldn't have fit.

You and I don't know anybody who owns an RV. But that makes us odd, not them. One out of ten Americans spends time in an RV every year. There are more than 12 million of these rigs on the road or waiting in backyards. RV-ing is the affordable vacation. A family of four can visit almost anywhere—in comfort—for little more than 10 bucks per person per day— travel, food, lodging, recreation, the works.

There are three types of RVers: young families vacationing; recently retired couples who still have their health and like each other (you've got to in this tight space); and the parked poor, for whom a rusting RV is one step better than a cardboard crate. Average family income for RVers is $65,000 a year, according to KOA (Kampgrounds of America). The percentage with incomes over $150,000 is negligible.

The retirees are the mainstay of the campground business, because they're on the road longer, many year round, migrating south in the winter and north in the summer ("Snowbirds" they call themselves). These contented oldsters (and they seem, in the main, quite happy) want their parks clean, courteous, quiet. The niceness startles—everyone smiling and saying good morning and asking about itineraries, weather, food (sometimes laundry).

KOA is the biggest of the commercial campground chains. It's a franchise operation, suitable for mom-and-pop proprietors, who tend to live on the grounds. You've probably seen their yellow signs with the teepees and not noticed. I never did. Now I find myself searching them out at day's end. There are nicer campgrounds than KOA's but KOA's are pleasantly boring, which may be welcome after a long day. You sign in at the office ("No wife—or pet?" the clerk double-checks). You pull into your slot, attach the electric cord and sewage hose, lower the shades, drape a curtain over your front windshield, and you're as unseen and safe as in any Motel 6, only with your own stuff.

Generally, by the time I've parked I'm ravenous, having eaten nothing since breakfast. (I don't stop for lunch. Once I'm going I try to keep going.) I'll cook—either a slab of meat and some vegetables in my big saucepan or some prepackaged "gourmet" concoction in the microwave. (It's amazing what's offered.) Not once have I used my oven, where I stow pans. I pile my plate, uncork some wine, and put on a DVD—usually about American history (thank God for PBS), but sometimes an old movie, if my brain feels spent. I gobble and glug (as you know) and soon I've got a buzz on and am yawning my head off. I force myself to clean the dishes before crumpling into bed so my dreams won't smell of olive oil. I'm asleep by 8:00 and awake at dawn, unless I've been up in the night.

My morning routine is no less fixed. Two steps to light the kettle, two steps to pee, spoon three tablespoons of coffee (Starbucks' Italian Roast) into my French press, microwave three doughnut holes for thirty seconds, pour my coffee (with two packets of sugar—loose sugar can be a hazard in a van), set coffee cup and half-liquefied doughnuts on my bed-tray, crack open my bedside window shade, turn on my laptop and I'm happy as a pup at first light, snuffling the dew-drenched lawn. After a few hours (four, tops), my brain is mush. I jog (to stay alive), knot my trash (I generate about a grocery bag's worth daily), replenish Migrant's water, unhook electric and sewer, review the map, shower, and pull out. The reason I shower last is sometimes the sewer hose slips and I get sprayed. You can't believe how the stench sticks. Two days ago the whole contents gushed, spattering chunks. It took me three minutes to rinse off the pavement. I pretended I was watering flowers.

If I were less rushed, I could be sad, but who has time? The next day's destination brings a fresh obligation to read up on . . . Lincoln, Jackson, Polk, Johnson, Johnson, Harrison, Harrison, Gettysburg, Hayes, Harding, obesity, Wal-Mart, Hobart, Taylor, Kentucky, America. I think of you a lot at times, then for a whole day not at all. Do you think of me?

6
Heartland

i.

A crow is cawing, barking rather, four, five, six staccato exclamations, a pause, then a repetition. Sometimes it is answered, and two strains twine. The crow—I'm pretty sure it's a crow—is insistent, but not upset. It has something on its mind.

The language of birds reminds me of the languages I will never know. For much of my life I vowed to learn languages, but I'm coming to see I won't. I am awed by those worldly souls who, we are assured, "speak 10 languages fluently." My goal is fluency—for an hour—in one.

The commonest question about my adventure is, "Don't you get lonely?" My quick answer is "Only when I'm tired." It's true as far as it goes. Rested I have strength to see and the world shines. The varnish of the world is applied not by the dew and sun, but by our eyes. The world is new when I am.

A more considered reply, too complicated for conversation, would be, "Yes, often. But loneliness is what I came for."

Loneliness is the longing for another. Why do we long for another? To distract us from our selves. Too long alone and we're posing questions we'd as soon not. We are standing on a ledge staring into a depthless chasm. A companion tugs us back: "Let's play." Activity rescues us from thought. We cannot be meaningless when someone we care about is waiting—impatiently—for us to lace our sneaker so we can finish the game.

My perverse desire is to stare as long as I can into that chasm, to peer as deeply as sight will allow. This takes time, time that is no time, time not "kept" by a clock. It takes waking without glancing at a watch, without dreading a phone, without wondering whether it's six or eleven, without the brambles of another's needs. Seeing and saying depend on stillness. They are lonely, as a seed waiting in the soil is lonely.

Loneliness tutors us in friendship. The soul that is always active never knows its own need. It is too busy to ask. A soul alone shapes Others who suit. He inspects the closet of his acquaintances and says, yes, this one I'll keep and this and this, because I need them—indeed, I should keep them in better repair—but this and this I am willing to discard.

Friendship is not a topic taught in schools. We're expected to pick it up naturally, like breathing, but that has not been my experience. Friendship has taken me much of my adult life to learn, and the process hasn't been pretty. My early attempts at friendship embarrass me as much as my early prose.

Friendship is something you make out of a moment. It may be born in an inkling, a glance, a grin, but it doesn't grow on its own. It must be tended—watered, weeded, sheltered from wind. Neglect it and it withers. Batter it and it breaks.

I don't have many friends—a dozen, at most. More would be fewer. A hundred "friends" can only be acquaintances. A friend is someone whose life you share imaginatively, whose presence you crave like a narcotic. I liken my friends to composers. Some are Bach, Beethoven, Handel—I return to them often. Others are Verdi or Chopin: I crave them, but less frequently. Still others are Mendelssohn or Franck: I would miss them, but find a way, without them, to get on.

I try to make the most of my friendships. I didn't use to. I'd take them as they came. Now I consider what to give my friend—what word, what enjoyment, what token—that might pulse in his remembrance. I say his, because the ways of my world make friendships with women problematic. Be "seen" with "another woman" and gossip is astride quicker than Paul Revere. Men friends are not "seen" with each other in the same way. It would not be murmured, with arched eyebrow and roll of eyes, Carll "was seen" with Seth.

I think of my friends as I drive, wonder where they are, how their stories are unfolding, and smile at the prospect of our reunion. I would not know how I treasure them were I never alone.

ii.

Hannibal, Missouri, is a back-broken burg on the western bank of the Mississippi. Its claim to fame, now that the river is no longer the aorta of mid-American commerce, is the boy who sprouted there for a decade, till he was 17. Poor Hannibal. Poor Sam Clemens. Both ended unhappily. Clemens died, broke if not broken, deprived of wife and all but one of four children, his greed for riches thwarted—still (only) a humorist and pundit, who had dreamed, from his modest beginnings, in the long tense quiet hours of steering his steamboat up and down the Mississippi, of being a Great Man.

(Mark Twain, of course, *was* a great man, greater, certainly, than the plutocrats he envied. Only Clemens didn't see it that way.)

Bankrupt, bereft, alone, Clemens ended his life as his epoch's class clown. He clung to the role, for even if he claimed to hate it, he needed an audience, a live audience, and would throw over everything—family, so-called respectability—to win one. If he wasn't being funny—and laughed at—he'd feel funny—adrift, which was no fun at all. So, long past his pleasure, he kept the quips coming, lest the silence sear.

The demise of Hannibal was more predictable. Hannibal used to be something, a river port. Now it is a former something, only, unlike an embarrassed gentleman, it can't emigrate. It must make the most of what it's got. And what it's got is Mark Twain.

Mark Twain was a writer of occasional genius, who once, at least, drove that genius into Beauty and Truth. *Huckleberry Finn* is gift enough. But Twain was not content with the product of his own hand, he wanted, needed, innumerable strangers' hands, clapping. He needed, too, to be rich. So he speculated. And went bankrupt.

Hannibal's ambition was less fervent. It longed to be what it was: essential, prosperous, growing. But then . . . the steamboats stopped docking, the customers stopped coming. Railroad killed river, then highway killed railroad.

Deprived of its original purpose, Hannibal adopted a substitute—Mark Twain—which it hyped into cheesy acclaim. With Mark Twain this and Mark Twain that and Becky Thatcher this and Tom and Huck and Pudd'nhead and whoever else, the once-proud town has managed to scrape up a maintenance. Only, say, a fifth of the crumbling downtown buildings are boarded up, all offered on "reasonable terms."

Their determination to fleece me made me flee. Maybe (I'm skeptical) the so-called Mark Twain boyhood home was once graced by Clemens. But don't, please, assure me that this is where Becky Thatcher lived, or where Huck hallooed in the night and pinged pebbles. Becky and Huck and Twain's whole cast of characters are just that—characters. They cannot be memorialized because they have no past (or future, for that matter), except what their maker provides.

Pulling into the Mark Twain Cave Campgrounds, I asked about these ballyhooed caverns. "Oh that's where Tom Sawyer and Becky went," I was assured.

Fiction is not history. Our growing tendency to conflate them cheapens both. Extrapolate a story any which way for your own amusement but do not force your shoddy vision on me. Mark Twain has told me all I need to know about Huck and Tom and Jim. Tell me more—about what they ate, where they played, their neighbors—and you'll only confuse and rile me. Neither Becky Thatcher nor Tom nor Huck ever slept anywhere, except where their maker tucked them in.

iii.

Truman and Eisenhower. Opposites, we think. Democrat-Republican, civilian-soldier, liberal-conservative, "give 'em hell, Harry" and "I like Ike." The map sees differently. If I-70 were a railroad, Kansas City, Lawrence, Topeka, and Junction City would be the only stops between Independence, Missouri, and Abilene, Kansas. These are boys next door.

They might have played football against one another, if Eisenhower were six years older and Truman weren't sidelined by bad eyes. Missouri and Kansas aren't likely homes for Presidents. There aren't many people here. They aren't near much. You can't even ride the train across them anymore, unless you're a freight container. Air-travelers from New York to LA sleep over Missouri and Kansas.

Growing up in Independence or Abilene, before the car, there was nowhere else. You lived on an island in a sea of fields. Your world was complete. You knew your neighbors and lived with them. You couldn't rebel—where would you go? No one was really poor or really rich. Some were abler or luckier, but all were family. You did what your dad said, pretty much. You got along.

What a gift to a child—the time and peace to evolve a certain soul. Choices breed bewilderment. The rich plague their children with opportunities. The disease of modern man, noted the poet Auden, is "paralysis in the void of infinite opportunities." Parents who encourage their children to "find themselves" are abusers. How can you "find yourself" if you don't know where to look?

Truman and Eisenhower knew who they were. They had no doubt. They knew where they belonged. Those of us bred on city excitement might see these small towns as stifling. Both Truman and Eisenhower returned to their small towns gladly. His greatest boast in life, said Ike, was he came from Abilene.

Strolling leafy North Delaware Street or Buckeye Avenue on a sunny Sunday, you can sense why both these men had contagious, natural smiles. In minutes the serenity seeps in, the certainty that all will be all right. Everything is orderly, genial. Streets are straight. Porches greet. Church, post office, bank, filling station, stores, school—all stand where they belong. The harsh wrangle of urban life, the cruelty of racism, the rapacity of ambition, seem a dream here. There are sorrows, of course, the usual ones, but life is not sorrowful. Life is good. America is good. Just use your head, do your duty, and everything will turn out.

After hard wars we seek security; sometimes we get it. We choose either successful generals (Washington, Grant, Eisenhower) or hometown boys (Harding, Truman). We hanker for an essential goodness and quietude we consider, somehow, American.

I envy the clarity of men like Truman and Eisenhower. I wish my father and town had told me who I was, with a force that settled the matter. Wondering is wandering—lonely, bewildering, inefficient. You discover things, perhaps, but at a price.

iv.

Herbert Hoover, the evidence suggests, was a man who kept things tidy. This is no mean feat.

Take my cabin. Twenty by ten. It shouldn't be so difficult to maintain.

And I want to. I hate tacky surfaces, dishevelment.

Yet order eludes me. Dishes pile. Laundry piles. A hinge snaps. My generator won't start and its lid, beneath which, I'm convinced, a reset button nestles, refuses to unlatch. Things taunt. Only the occasional spasm of organizing saves me from being swallowed by my sloth.

Herbert Hoover, it seems, was a man who insisted on order. There is hardly a picture of him, as an adult, without a necktie. He fished in a suit and waders. An engineer, he worked unswervingly. Penniless, orphaned, he amassed a fortune, not by craft or theft or luck, but by finding gold. He managed mines around the world. He founded a company that employed 175,000 workers from Siberia to Peru. When the World War came, he gave up his business, which was boring him, and fed war victims. The Belgians, hemmed in by the German army on one side and the British blockade on the other, were starving. Hoover's Commission for Relief in Belgium rescued them. He became the world's most celebrated humanitarian, but praise meant little to him. He called medals toys. He did things because they needed to be done. When children are starving you feed them. Appointed Secretary of Commerce by Harding, Hoover kept doing things. He was the busiest man in the quiescent Harding-Coolidge Administration. Coolidge, who believed in doing little, didn't like Hoover. He called him "the Wonder Boy." It's tempting to speculate how history might have differed if Hoover, not Harding, had been nominated by the Republicans in 1920. But the Republican bosses didn't want Hoover. People who do things make trouble.

Hoover's first try for public office came in 1928. The bosses could no longer stop him. He is our only President who was neither soldier nor politician nor protégé prior to running. Hoover was famous for civilian accomplishments. Honored for his industry, integrity, decency, intelligence, and achievement, he was as good a man as we've ever elected.

And history made him a donkey.

It's hard not to feel bad for the guy, though Hoover would have recoiled from pity. "I have had every honor to which man could aspire," he said, in his retirement. "There is no place on the whole earth except here in America where all sons of man have this chance in life." It must have hurt, though, being vilified for a Depression he had not caused and had cautioned against. As a humanitarian, he had walked on water. In the White House, he and his wife, Lou, carried guns for their protection.

His passion surprises me.

"Dear Addie," he writes to his classmate, Addie Colip, age eight,

Let your days be days of peas,
Slip along as slick as greese.

At 14 he is pining again. "Friend Daisy," he pleads in boyish script, "(and I hope you are more than my friend, allthough I do not dare to head it that way yet) You do not know the extent to which I am enthralled, and I am sure that no girl should be allowed such mastery over any person's heart, unless there are such feelings in her own heart. I could not have helped paying my attentions to you, if I had tried and I am sure I did not try very hard. I do not think you care. Do you? Answer this please. Bert"

History has painted Hoover as the starchy friend of industry. "Hoovervilles" (shanty towns of homeless) and "Hoover handkerchiefs" (empty out-turned pockets) conjure an ogre. Franklin Roosevelt, born rich, and Hoover, born poor, are each seen as the enemy of his origins.

But wait: "We shall never remedy justifiable discontent until we eradicate the misery which the ruthlessness of individualism has imposed upon a minority." *Justifiable discontent—eradicate—misery—ruthlessness?* This is the molten vocabulary of a reformer, not the cool complacency of a Coolidge.

I wander the gentle grounds of the Herbert Hoover Presidential Library-Museum in West Branch, Iowa, in a sort of daze. History is never what you think. I remember a grade school classmate whom everybody abused. He was our butt until one day he was gone. Thirty years later I learned the cause of his oddity. A disability we would call it now. I flushed with shame.

Herbert Hoover was a great man. But great men need great occasions to become great leaders. It is no accident that most of the Presidents we acclaim led us in war.

Americans recognized Hoover's greatness—before fury at the Depression redepicted him. "He certainly is a wonder," wrote Franklin Roosevelt in 1920. "I wish we could make him President of the United States. There could not be a better one." John Nance Garner, Roosevelt's first Vice President, said of Hoover, "I never reflected on (his) personal character or integrity. I never doubted his probity or his patriotism. In many ways he was superbly equipped for the Presidency. If he had been President in 1921 or 1937, he might have ranked with the great Presidents."

Herb and Lou Hoover rest beneath two white marble slabs, unadorned except by their names and dates. The graves, which Hoover designed, are on a little hill that looks across a greensward toward the two-room cabin where he was born.

Hoover's father, a blacksmith, died when Bert was six; his mother four years later.

In his 20 years as a widower, Hoover could never dine alone.

v.

"Are those New York plates I'm seeing?"

I didn't want to talk. It was dusk, hot. My brain ached from too much seeing, my legs from too much driving. I'd meant to push to Des Moines tonight, but couldn't. Yawning, my attention had drifted from the road—a jolt of horror made my fingers tingle. Now I wanted to draw my blinds, eat, swig, watch a movie. Migrant has a DVD player and a TV. I've not yet watched the TV—I'm not certain it works—but half a dozen times these 40 days I've soothed myself with a movie. Most movies make me sorry I watched them. The printed word never disappoints, because I can stop reading, let my mind drift. A movie enslaves. My attention is stuck for the duration. Some people can turn movies off. I can't. I'm too curious.

I didn't want to talk, but this jolly woman had a smile that was hard to refuse. A true smile, not those rictuses they teach in hospitality school, is a gift that obligates. You can't turn your back on it without making yourself feel low. There are villains—I know some—whom smiles cannot soften. Often this type of person is good at getting rich. I lack such assurance. A smile is like an invitation to dance. Who am I to say no?

The woman's smile made me look at her, which I hadn't wanted to. I'd been looking all day and my brain was crammed, like a suitcase that won't latch. One problem with this enterprise is my relentless itinerary. I have to process impressions as fast as I receive them, otherwise they'll be buried. Poor Thomas Hendricks, for example, or Zachary Taylor, or Grover Cleveland—gone, with barely a nod. I need an itinerary, otherwise I'll dawdle. Still, needing something—like an itinerary—does not make you love it.

This jolly woman was oddly shaped, sixtyish, I guessed. She dressed without a mirror. Where I come from, women dress with mirrors and are seldom jolly. Maybe that's an axiom: mirrors conduce to unhappiness.

Yes, I worked up a small smile, they were New York plates.

"Where in New York?"

"Westchester. Just north of New York City."

In the endless flatness of the Great Plains, amidst cornfields, you do not expect people to know Westchester.

"My husband's folks come from Westchester—Fishkill, Peekskill—I remember the kill part. And my grandmother used to live in Tarrytown. We lived in Yorktown when we were first married."

"Remember a newspaper called *The Patent Trader*?"

"Sure. Used to get it—every week, I think—for the local stuff."

"That was my newspaper."

"I'll be."

Now a silence, not long, measurable in seconds, but crowded with deliberation. Having discovered a basis for conversation, we could pursue it, one thing leading to another, but to what end? Her cordiality was real, but so was her supper. An older man I took to be her husband was sitting with

100

another couple at a picnic table under the trees. They were waiting. I ached for the solitude of my cabin, for my chicken breast and zucchini, for mindlessness. Still, there was this coincidence. Two refugees from one corner of the globe encountering each other more than a thousand miles away, in a cornfield. You can't help asking: How? Why?

"Why did you leave Westchester?"

"Oh," her gaze clouded. It is not a look the young can replicate.

My question was unkind. Clearly, this was a pair who'd moved often in their years and their reasons for moving weren't happy. Want had harried them, as it had the early settlers, deeper and deeper into the heartland, where living was cheaper and they might finally fit. Running a small RV camp, far from the traveled road, is the economic equivalent of hardscrabble farming. They'd landed here and they were glad—it was pleasant with the sun angling in and supper waiting and the breeze—but their way had not been glad. It was unpleasant to look back on.

"Well, here you're a long way from nowhere," she announced cheerily. It was a line she used often. Then: "I guess we're just not city folk."

vi.

Heartland: A (usually extensive) central region of homogeneous (geographical, political, industrial, etc.) character. Scholars trace the word to the start of the twentieth century. Before then, no region needed a consolatory label to buttress its pride. Places made their natives and natives their places. Cars changed that. Talent drained from the heartland to bustling coasts, winter warmth, long views, opportunity. De Tocqueville, as usual, anticipated the exodus:

Agriculture is perhaps, of all the useful arts, the one which improves most slowly in democratic nations. . . . Suppose a man to be active, educated, free, comfortably off, and full of desire. He is too poor to live in idleness; he is rich enough not to be in fear of immediate want and is anxious to improve his lot. One man has formed a taste for physical pleasures; he sees thousands around him enjoying them; he himself has tasted some too, and he is very keen to acquire the means to enjoy them more. But life goes by, and time presses. What is he to do?

To cultivate the ground promises an almost certain reward for his efforts, but a slow one. In that way you only grow rich little by little, and with toil. Agriculture only suits the wealthy, who already have a great superfluity, or the poor, who only want to live. His choice is made; he sells his field, moves from his house, and takes up some risky but lucrative profession.

The endless fields of Iowa, Kansas, Nebraska, Missouri, South Dakota wave like a thoroughbred's mane. Seed manufacturers' signs at rows' ends testify to ceaseless tinkering to improve yield, durance, sweetness. Farms are laboratories. But men have shrunk. No longer owners, farm workers are employees of distant corporations, paid in money but not in pride. As the risks of agriculture were reduced, so was its excitement.

Our heartland leaders were born before the heartland got labeled. Hoover, Curtis, Wallace, Truman, Eisenhower feel pre-hybridized. All were true to their nature: straightforward, confident, indomitable optimists, not the artful dodgers bred by caroming crowds. Liberal or conservative, they steered dead ahead. Urban traffic makes drivers devious. In the heartland, roads are straight and empty. You can see horizons.

What these men also possessed, which the decades have diluted, was pride of place. Each was an inevitable son of his soil. They could not have been from Virginia or California or New York. Farming made them clear and firm. Monotony—of terrain and employment—made them constant. Coastlessness made them modest. Unlike their pioneer forbears in Kentucky, Tennessee, Ohio, Illinois, and Indiana, the peoples between the Mississippi and the Rockies never enjoyed their hour of national glory. Once gold was discovered in California in 1849, the West leapt to the Pacific. Kentuckians were once Westerners; Iowans, though further west, never more than *Mid*westerners.

Charles Curtis and Henry Wallace, our 31st and 33rd Vice Presidents, make an interesting comparison. It's the map's idea, after visiting their graves—in Topeka and Des Moines—within a day.

Charles Curtis was an American Indian: eighth-blood Kaw, with a touch of Osage, but as with American blacks, the least tincture was enough to earn the designation. Curtis, in his Library of Congress photograph, looks Indian. His skin is swarthy and his eyes have that sad, far-away look that makes Anglo consciences squirm.

Curtis was raised in Kansas by his two grandmothers, on and off the Kaw reservation. He rose as persons of color must in a white society, by ingratiating. Minorities, to get ahead, can either confront or coquette. Indians who confronted the United States ended up dead.

102

Curtis, according to his celebrated fellow Kansan, journalist William Allen White, wasn't interested in issues. Kansans were regular Republicans, and Curtis represented their views. His talent was political. He seemed glad to see you. He remembered your name and a fact about you (which he noted in a small pocketbook). He had endless patience for small talk. In the House of Representatives and the Senate, he cozied up the ladder, seldom orating, tirelessly schmoozing. His eloquence was a backslap, a wink, easing the legislative path for Coolidge and a smug Republican majority.

He became Senate majority leader. If the insiders had had their way, he'd have been nominated President in 1928. Charley Curtis, ever agreeable, was their kind of guy. But Herbert Hoover was too accomplished and admired to be denied. Curtis sadly accepted the second slot—and vanished into the Vice Presidency. He was renominated in 1932, but with the Depression raging, not even Houdini could have rescued Hoover.

The paths in Topeka Cemetery are cratered; purple thistles swallow stones. Curtis's ugly gray marker, on an awkward cobbled plot, has the grace of an IRS form. It lists his name and jobs, adding "Son of the Kanza Nation."

Henry Wallace, Franklin Roosevelt's second Vice President, was as liberal as Curtis was conservative. Curtis, born poor, wanted to protect the prosperous; Wallace, born prosperous, wanted to protect the poor. Curtis supported the status quo. Wallace was a changer, tinkerer, corn-hybridizer, rearranger of bureaucracies, would-be reorganizer of our nation. Curtis had few ideas; Wallace too many for his own good. Curtis was a pol; Wallace abhorred political maneuvering. Curtis puffed cigars; Wallace exhorted Senators to get physically fit.

Curtis was a realist: he read people right and knew the challenge of change. Wallace was an idealist, easily duped, a believer in human perfectibility.

When Wallace visited the Soviet Union in 1944, he reported favorably on their agricultural experiments, never suspecting Stalin of gulling him. He was popular with the public but his radicalism alarmed Roosevelt and the party regulars who arranged for his removal from the ticket. In 1948, Wallace ran for President as a Progressive. His campaign was infiltrated by Communists. Trounced and repudiated, he returned to his first passion, agricultural genetics. Plants are easier to perfect than humans.

What connects Curtis and Wallace is their consistency. Each followed his track unswervingly—Curtis, the amenable pol; Wallace, the dauntless man

103

of ideas—and expected to be rewarded with the Presidency. In the heartland, roads are straight and empty.

Consistency in purpose inspires. We like to believe our leaders stand for something. Too often they seem to stand for staying in office.

Our ablest leaders, while consistent in purpose, have been flexible in tactics. They swerved, doubled back, contradicted themselves. This is because the desires and expectations of a democracy fluctuate. Sometimes we are angry, sometimes equable; sometimes eager, sometimes torpid. A gifted leader rides the waves of public sentiment as a skipper steers across the sea, jibbing and tacking toward his end, as winds allow.

Our heartland Presidents reached office via other careers or by accident: Hoover was a humanitarian, Ike a general, Truman a fluke. Curtis and Wallace, both politicians, expected politics to carry them to the heights. They plotted straight. But America is trickier than Kansas or Iowa.

Wallace's grave reflects his ideology. In the vast Glendale Cemetery, headstones are waist-high and plain. No one's better, no one's worse. The Wallace family marker looks like everyone else's. "WALLACE" it announces in unornamented capitals.

A few yards from the Vice President there's a splotch of brightness. The headstone, while not large, is irregular and maudlin—a weeping angel on a cloud, a girl's face etched from a photograph. Red and pink flowers, real and fake, yellow plastic smiley faces, a gift wrapped in cellophane, a handmade memento, compose a garish mound. I lean closer: "Cara K. Carpenter, June 22, 1989–Oct. 29, 2000." In two days, I'll be dining with my daughter, Becca, in Pierre, South Dakota. Suddenly I miss her very much.

vii.

I am seated outdoors in my collapsible chair, sipping wine, dandled by a stiff breeze. I am in Heartland RV Park in Harlan, Iowa, not because I want to be but because the Omaha KOA had no room. There is nothing near Harlan but balletic corn, shimmering in the gusts, and round hay bales scattered like tires from a titan's cart. So much green! And tan! And punctuating the landscape half a dozen trim silos and barns, and, peeping from their stockades of trees, the modest but ample homes of farmers.

Before me dart two prairie dogs, skittish humorous rodents who rise on their hind legs, like captains on a foredeck. They eye me in my chair, with that black rectangle in my lap. Danger! But that red bottle in the grass is promising. And that blue can (of almonds) on the rear bumper.

These mammals are trash-rats. (I can say this since, happily, they cannot—yet—sue for slander.) This campsite, where vast steel boxes materialize and occasionally spill, is their grocery.

I sip—and think. Becca has made me smile all her life. She is biking this summer from New Haven to Seattle with a group of college students to benefit Habitat for Humanity. She will be fit and brown. She warned me by phone that she's wearing a small nostril ring. "Cool," I reacted dubiously.

The nostril ring returns me to a scar on Becca's temple, nearly invisible now, but once, 16 years ago, for a few hours, the locus of her parents' prayers.

We were on an island on an Adirondack lake, 15 minutes by motorboat from the dock. It was dusk. Happy voices of in-laws and friends braided. Beef hissed on the popping fire. Ice cubes tinkled in paper cups. The sinking sun was putting on a show. A brown-green goose paddled by with her goslings, patrolling for crumbs.

The world would be OK. You just knew it. Then came the shriek. Becca and her older brother had been hopping from boulder to boulder in an invented game. Peter, seven, meaning to hurry her, had given her a push, causing her to topple forehead-first into glacial granite. Blood spouted. Becca's green eyes hazed and drifted upward, lazily as feathers. She whimpered, but did not cry. Her body was limp.

The motorboat seemed not to move. This was before cell phones, so there was no way to call an ambulance. I carried her to the car. She lay on her mother's lap. She seemed asleep.

The good souls in emergency rooms are never surprised. The names they give—"laceration," "suture," "concussion"—seem less terrible somehow.

I watched the needle with dazed fascination, dipping in and out of skin bleached by lights.

The last stitch knotted (there'd been more than 20), a hand was waved before Becca's eyes. She stood, wobbly but upright. Crying, we squeezed her, careful of bandages.

"We should call camp," said my wife, "to tell them everything's OK."

We were thinking of Peter, who'd stayed behind. Peter, then as now, has a loving heart. He would be scared.

My wife dialed. Becca held the receiver as little girls do. She has always been wise, Becca, and forgiving.

"Oh, that's OK, Petuh," she lisped, in her most grown-up voice. "It was just one of those things that happen."

viii.

I blush to report how little I liked Mount Rushmore.

If you're an American, some would say, you *have* to like Mount Rushmore. As we do the flag.

I happen to like the flag. Also the *Star Spangled Banner,* however difficult to sing. They quicken my pulse. America is my story and these are its emblems, as intrinsic to the nation as its name. A name is as lovely or ugly as the person who bears it. We're unlikely to think, "He's a creep, but he has a nice name."

Our flag and our national anthem are official. They were elected. They beat out other contenders. They have histories. They tell us a lot about ourselves.

Mount Rushmore was never elected. It was born out of calculation, as a tourist draw. The Black Hills of Dakota are a long way from anywhere. In 1923 South Dakota's state historian Doane Robinson conceived the idea of carving faces in the mountain so folks would come see. Doane Robinson may be the only state historian whose name survives in our national consciousness.

I would make a bad dog. I don't come when whistled for. Tell me what I'm *supposed* to do and I stiffen, "Who says?"

Millions visit Mount Rushmore each year—coil up the steep road, park cars and RVs in the layered garage, climb the stairs, pass visitors' center and restaurant and gift shop, stride solemnly beneath flag-festooned arches, plant themselves on the viewing terrace, and gaze. Awe is mandatory. Having trekked so far, dragged the kids and relations, spent all that money and vacation, how can you admit, "I hated it, it was a hustle?"

I had the feeling, milling among the crowd this Fourth of July, that if I even murmured my true response, I'd be mugged. The ubiquitous security forces, some carrying machine guns, would have ushered me into a windowless room, grateful for this "threat" which justified their presence.

I kept quiet. I tend to—until I can retreat into my turret and aim words through slits. I want to say what I see, but carefully, into willing ears.

Mount Rushmore *is* a hustle. The religious vocabulary it's cloaked in—
"shrine," "pilgrimage," etc.—are part of the carnie act. Mount Rushmore is
a necessary component of South Dakota's economy. South Dakota is an
arid state with arid prospects. Cattle-ranching is its main industry, grazing
steer on land too barren to farm. The state keeps losing people because
there's nothing to do here. It's beautiful, all that bleak emptiness, but you
can't eat beauty.

South Dakota dubs itself, on its license plate, "The Mount Rushmore
State." Imagine, naming oneself after a tourist attraction. A chunk of the
state's retail income depends on visitors to the faces in the mountains.
These travelers, having come so far, tend to stay awhile. They patronize
motels and restaurants and low-stakes casinos and tag-along museums and
waterslides and cruddy souvenir shops. How long, after all, can you gaze
on four granite busts?

For me, six minutes was plenty. Like many inept artists before and since,
Mount Rushmore's sculptor, Gutzon Borglum, made up in razzle-dazzle
what he lacked in talent. The likenesses on Mount Rushmore are cartoon-
ish. High-schoolers could do better. Poor Teddy Roosevelt, crammed un-
comfortably behind Jefferson's ear, is a travesty. The scale and oddity of
this work are what make it fantastic. It is not, as the brochures and exhibits
reiterate as if fact, "great art."

I rushed away. A tourist trap had been sprung and we were meant not
to yelp.

So what? some might ask. If people like it, where's the harm?

I agree: to each his own. This fabrication is no worse than Becky
Thatcher's cave or Hersheypark. The technical feat *is* remarkable, blasting
and chiseling all that stone.

Still, I mourn the loss of eyes. It pains me to see us herded like sheep.
Who can say what people might notice if they freed themselves to look?
Why are we so submissive to the manipulations of our managers!

Nonconformity is the modern American adventure. Not puerile
eccentricity—wearing one's hair orange, or sprinkling one's speech with
expletives, though these may be a start—but living your own life, seeing
with your own eyes, saying out in your own stubborn tongue.

7
Everland

i.

Bobbing down the Missouri River, past the rough cliffs of the Missouri Breaks, it comes to me: "America" is not a people at all, it is a *land*. That's why "America" can't be found, because the land changes. Here in the Rockies, man is small; even today with our herds and machines, we mar the earth hardly more than dust specks. Scorching sun, cyclone, hail, flash floods, bitter winters mock man's attempts. The Westerner, as a result, thinks differently from the New Englander, the Southerner, the Plainsman or Prairie dweller. He detects a different God. God in the Rockies is a son-of-a-bitch. His mountains oppress, His sun parches, His winds shear, His dry plains stretch to the limit of sight.

Cockiness is not easy for a Montanan. Terrain here is a hard father, who whips you if you stray—or sometimes for no good reason, just to remind you who's who. Sloth is suicide. What you take from the earth you eke. The engines of man's invention make it easier but never easy. The modern diseases of dyspepsia, depression, obesity, dreariness, pettiness, self-absorption take less hold here. Who has time?

Most nations derive from an original tribe or place. They begin as one. America, from the first, was a collective: United States (plural);[14] all sorts of places and peoples.

Strife is our musculature. The inspiration of our parents was to let us mix it up. The Founders did not decree, "Pipe down! Behave!" They urged us to go at it, settle it among ourselves, but according to rules—*our* rules, which we could change if we chose, but not easily.

As the Marquess of Queensberry's code made boxing a sport, the Constitution made America a nation.

---

[14]After the Civil War, "United States" changed from a plural to a singular noun, as *pluribus* bowed to *unum*.

Government in America is bare-knuckled. It always has been—since uncouth Andy Jackson crashed the decorous debating society of our gentlemanly first six Presidents. Washington and his five successors dreaded "faction." Political parties, they feared, might doom their idealistic Republic. They envisioned the aristocracy in the agora, like Socrates' disciples, politely collaborating.

They were wrong. Contest strengthens. It makes us sinewy, wary, wise. We say we hate partisanship—maybe we do—but that's what keeps us in shape. Philosophers, history indicates, are inept at governing, because humans are never what we think. We say one thing and do another. We succumb to appetites. We go too far. Democracy is a self-correcting medium. We are our own sheepdogs, barking ourselves into line.

Gazing up at the dreamlike shapes of the sandstone and basalt cliffs, seeing in their erosions vast faces and lost cities, I am suffused with the miracle of their creation—and of our nation's. No one could have envisioned what time has made. The processes were often killing—volcanic eruptions, relentless grinding—but the result is delicate, fantastic.

And fragile. It wouldn't take much—a small army of indifferent jackhammers—to reduce this irreplaceable majesty to rubble.

Our forefathers, with dazzling forethought, preserved this and other vast tracts of primeval landscapes for our enlightenment and pleasure. It behooves us, with comparable care, to protect this unimaginable—and vulnerable—nation we have been bequeathed. The more one imbibes our American story, the more apparent it becomes how accidental we are, and how often, but for the actions of a few—in a legislature or on a battlefield or inside a voting booth—things might have turned out worse. Our past is often not pretty—yet with a fortune that feels providential even our crimes seem to work in our favor. It is horrible what we did to the natives we found here and the Africans we hauled here. It is horrible how we picked fights with our neighbors to expand our domain. It is horrible what we did to ourselves in the Civil War and on other grim occasions. Yet each calamity becomes a building block which, if removed, might diminish the result.

The Missouri's current carries me without my swimming. I gaze in awe—at these cliffs, this sky, these waters, and at the nation that secures them. How lucky we are! And how obligated! As a parent fears for a child, so should we for this bequest. So much, so quickly, can go wrong.

ii.

She will not return my call. It has been six weeks. Well, two can play that game.

I'd as soon skip this part of the story, make myself more than I am. My guide, Thoreau, was a skipper, bar none. You'd think from *Walden* he was never sad, that he chirruped through every howling night like a cricket on the hearth.

It's annoying how his account makes his successors failures. Thoreau might argue he was preaching. Does the preacher disclose doubts? The preacher's job is to convince, not confess.

These days we distrust preachers. We want to know what's eating them.

What was eating me was simple. Everybody in the Billings KOA was happy and together. Lovers, families, couples, biked, strolled, played minia- ture golf, whooped through sprinklers, splashed in the pool, grilled burgers and gabbled like there was no tomorrow. The only exceptions were a woman who looked homeless, with her mangy wolfhound—and me.

I would go to a bar.

Going to a bar alone is an American experience I'd missed. In college I went with friends. Then I was married. In 26 years of marriage I'd been faithful, not because I'm good but because I'm timid.

My marriage, like many, bumped along like a car without shocks. We love our three kids but have different notions of raising them. We'd be happy to cede our differences to some arbiter as long as he or she saw it our way. We could have selected weaklings to marry—pleasant, compliant souls, we think—but we didn't. We wanted . . . what we got—only some- times what we got didn't feel like what we wanted.

My disappearance for all these months was a slap. I didn't expect my wife to see it my way but I figured by now we'd be talking.

There are dangers I can face. Flesh isn't one of them. I'm as prim and pink as John Quincy Adams. I've never felt knuckles crack—pow—as in the movies. I do not hug easily, or seduce.

Why couldn't I be descended from the roistering Virginians instead of the prudish Puritans! What I'd give for a shot of Texas macho or the swag- gering self-assurance of the self-made! New England WASPs are God's clay baked brittle in the kiln of propriety, raised like museum porcelains: look, no touch. Sex, to my blushing father, was something one took care of. Kissing, we were meant to peck.

My comfort zone is where I can speak the language. Flesh I speak as fluently as French. I can order from the menu—that's it.

But I was alone. In Billings. My wife would not return my call. The laughter outdoors prickled like a rain of needles.

I checked on the Internet for singles bars. Billings featured two but New Orleans dozens. Something to look forward to.

I decided on long khakis. You don't go into a bar, I figured, in shorts. I hadn't felt cloth on my shins for weeks.

I trembled as I drove across the Interstate. It was dusk. At the stoplight, two children in a car were fighting. The mother was shouting, twisted in her seat. The father, in denims, gripped the steering wheel with both hands. I envied them.

The bar was The Golden Nugget or some such. In the firelight of my imagination, I foresaw a cowboy crowd in town for Saturday night, country-western music, nasal twangs, amiable curiosity. The Internet blurb had promised a rip-snorting time.

I parked Migrant around the corner and locked her. Wine and beer were chilling in the refrigerator, Vodka in the freezer. I'd made extra ice, stowed chips and peanuts, swept, just in case.

I ducked into a CVS. For a condom. All those sizes. When sex entered my life, women handled protection. Pill or IUD was up to them. No one had heard of STD or HPV or AIDS. Now who knew what diseases might lurk. My change clattered on the counter. I flushed like a rookie counterfeiter.

How does one walk into a bar? If you're Brad Pitt or Robert Redford, it's easy. Your appearance is a fanfare.

But if you're a nondescript 50-year-old stranger, OK-looking but nothing to write home about?

The storefront was jazzy with beer signs, pulsing lights, tinsel. I inhaled, straightened my shoulders, pushed open the door.

Dim. Stale smoke. Eight patrons slouched at a bar that could accommodate three times that number.

I debated. Rip-snorting looked more like gut-wrenching. Wherever everyone was in Billings this Saturday it wasn't here.

But hey. *I* was here, wasn't I, equipped, my small courage summoned? I could turn tail but then? It would be hours before the laughter at the KOA quieted.

The bar-woman was a weathered, husky-voiced survivor of countless affairs. Two trim, nice-enough-looking ladies in their thirties sat beside

111

one another and, two stools apart, a respectable looking older man—no, not older, my age. They were in shorts. I sat beside the ladies, ordered a Bud.

"Where you two from?"

"Omaha."

"Massachusetts. Worcester."

"What brings you to Billings?"

"An airplane." Small laugh.

The other: "We work for United."

"Flight attendants."

"Just here for the night?"

"That's right."

It surprises me how few people respond to questions with answers instead of questions. If a stranger in a singles bar asked me a question I'd ask one back. Any story's interesting—for a while.

The legs nearest mine were tan, tapered.

"I was just through Omaha a week ago," I pressed. "I went to school not far from Worcester."

"That so."

The bar-woman, wearily: "You gals need another?"

The ladies exchanged a glance. "One more can't hurt."

Two brimming glasses of draught. Nonalcoholic. But I was making headway.

"You two had dinner?" It was past seven.

"Yes." "We're expected—" their answers tripped over each other.

I let it go. "You like being flight attendants?"

Another glance. They were good legs, really.

"It's OK."

"Better than home."

"You can say that again."

The voice belonged to the man on my right. A pilot. One of those chummy baritones that wake you with midflight travelogues.

A conversation ensued—across me—about hubs, schedules, work rules, medical benefits, unruly passengers, weather. I smiled hard. Within 15 minutes the three had exited to dinner—together. A minute later I checked my watch, as if I had somewhere to go.

iii.

This morning I am in Salt Lake City. My schedule is relaxed this week, so I am catching up on the news. A news junkie at home, I've been far from the news on the road and find I don't miss it. A news addiction isn't all that different from absorption in daytime soaps. Tuning in daily makes us feel that we belong. Skip a week or five and we find, to our surprise, not much has happened.

The big story this summer has been a series of revelations about corporate shenanigans that caused the stock market to shudder. Everybody is poorer; and since almost everybody in America spends more than he has, almost everybody is anxious. I'd be anxious too, if I were home. The gallows humor of friends in the money business would snake into my sleep. I'd find myself tallying losses and extrapolating the trend. Here on the road, far from the hubbub of buying and selling, I am relaxed. So what if I own less? The happiest lesson of my journey is how little it takes to be content. Possessions possess us, not the other way around.

To catch up on the news, I purchase three magazines—*Time* and *Newsweek,* produced by Americans for Americans; and *The Economist,* a British weekly, increasingly circulated in the United States.

The editors of *Time* and *Newsweek* think alike. Last week's "news," in their view, was condensable to 10 topics, plus tidbits, celebrity gossip, and commentary. Pictures are large, and serious articles tend to be illustrated by cartoons. Of this week's topics, three overlap—the markets' jitters; the skull of a seven-million-year-old hominid, discovered in Chad; and (on both covers) the risks of hormone replacement therapy. Two articles in each concern events beyond our borders.

The Economist sees the world differently. It offers articles on more than 60 topics, a dozen or so about the United States, the rest about everywhere else. Where *Time* and *Newsweek* make the globe feel small, *The Economist* makes it feel huge.

The editors at *Time* and *Newsweek* are not stupider than those at *The Economist;* they see a different reader. The *Time* and *Newsweek* reader wants to be tranquilized, not challenged; beguiled, not disturbed. Offer him too much information and he'll discard the magazine discouraged. *The Economist* is edited for a reader who will be excited, not dismayed, by the immensity of his ignorance.

The stupefaction of America, our almost bovine lack of curiosity about the rest of the world or even our own nation, astonishes foreign visitors.

How with so much freedom and education and information—and with so much opportunity to affect civilization—are we so dull?

In four dozen days on the road, I have not overheard a single discussion about current events. Conversations concern food, weather, vehicles, vistas, sports, laundry. Try to induce even the mildest interchange about the headlines and people recoil into their shells.

It wasn't always this way. Dickens—and many others—noted the passionate, even brawling interest of ordinary Americans in their nation. Tens of thousands of Illinoisans would attend a Lincoln-Douglas debate, straining to hear hours of intricate (and unamplified) argument (and this before Lincoln was "Lincoln"). There are plenty of accounts of scarcely lettered farmers, during the Depression and World War II, hunched over their radios for fireside chats.

America bores Americans, except when hell breaks loose. Today's news is not less interesting, but we are less interested. The fate of the world is someone else's business.

It's a shame. Also a danger. The less aware we are, the more apt to be stampeded. Liars and manipulators prey on ignorance. That monster just *may* be under the bed, if you haven't looked.

Twenty years ago, I'd have found many more topics covered in *Time* and *Newsweek,* maybe even 60. Pictures would have been smaller, cartoons and gossip infrequent. Editors would have strained less to amuse.

Will only horror wake us from our torpor? Is Osama our only alarm clock? I long to shake my neighbors: "Quick, quick, get up!"

But I have only words.

iv.

By the time this movie is over it will be almost nine and somehow I've forgotten to eat. Shopping for groceries alone at night makes me uneasy. Finding a restaurant in this early-to-bed city might be a problem.

Did Sister Jackie know where might be open at nine?

Sister Jackie wore pearls and a fashionable grandmotherly dress. She was one of an army of attractively attired retirees who volunteer as "hosts" at Temple Square in Salt Lake City. These hosts have been successful in their careers. Their smiles feel unrehearsed, far from the practiced pleasantries of hospitality "professionals." I was a tourist, an unbeliever, underdressed, yet they treated me as if they were glad I'd come. The only strangers glad to see me in my seven weeks from home have been people expecting to be paid. The exception was Bob Bolyard, in Indianapolis, the retired coal miner who, with his wife Brenda and 84-year-old mother-in-law, traveled the country in their RV, singing Gospel music in churches that would have them.

Sister Jackie said she was almost sure the rooftop restaurant on the tenth floor would still be serving. Then she went off shift, another pleasant grandmother, equally well-dressed, taking her place. Sister Jackie's whisper in my ear, 10 minutes later, startled me (the theater was dark). Yes, she said (she was wearing a sweet perfume), she'd gone upstairs to be sure, and if I hurried after the movie I could make it.

It is easy to sneer at the Mormons: their implausible revelations and indefatigable niceness. I was raised Episcopalian. In the elegant Episcopalian church, belief is frowned on as evidence of instability. Many of our Presidents have been Episcopalians: Washington, Madison, Monroe, the elder Harrison, Tyler, Taylor, Pierce, Arthur, FDR, Ford, Bush senior. Episcopalians don't worry others with their religion because they don't seem to have one.

No President yet has been a Mormon. That tells you something. Then again, there are more than five million Mormons in America, and less than two million Episcopalians, who had a two-century head start. That also tells you something.

I was prepared to sneer. Joseph Smith, the founder of the Mormons—or the Church of the Latter-Day Saints, as they're properly called—remains, to the uninfatuated eye, one of America's great con men. What spectacular audacity—to declare that God, through his oddly named angel Moroni, had dispatched a second gospel—inscribed on gold plates in hieroglyphics, no less—for Smith to "translate" and promulgate! The gold plates, needless to say, vanished into heaven afterward, though their existence is attested by 11 of Smith's disciples, so it must be true.

He had to have been some operator, this Smith. In the approved cult tradition, he convinced his followers to give him their all, including wealth and women. Smith's "discovery" of the doctrine of plural marriages— "spiritual marriages," he called them—freed the goat to help himself to an estimated 48 of his followers' wives and daughters—though Smith's original wife, Emma, remained dubious. Smith was one of a crowd of crackpot Messiahs spawned by the fervor of the Second Great Awakening, just as Jesus was one of many new-religionists in his day. Both Smith and Jesus solidified their sects by getting martyred: sanctity is easier to stoke when you're dead.

If my hosts recounted their stories with a wink, I'd have felt less uncomfortable. Any religion, after all, is built on myth. The Mormons insist on the literal truth of their malarkey. One after another intelligent, tranquil, smiling face will describe Amnihu and Amnor and Antiparah and Cumorah and Irreantum and Onidah and Zerahemnah as if they were real.

Two feature films—about their founders' travails crossing the continent; and about Jesus's appearance in America during some vague, quasi-Mayan prehistory—were especially ludicrous, rife with handsome hunks and moony virgins and suffering sages and swelling violins. My hosts' reverential awe before this bad art could not be sincere, could it?

Most of the art in Temple Square is bad: lurid, idolatrous, mawkish. The smooth music of the Mormon Tabernacle Choir swaddles to suffocation. The sentiments expressed by the young missionaries and hosts and by elders on ubiquitous video screens cloy with relentless sweetness.

Younger I'd have inveighed against such surrender of self to this screwy consensus. It is ghastly being assured by a grown man in his right mind that those golden plates really were—no, I mean, really—sucked back into heaven.

And yet, sitting at my solitary tenth-floor table, gazing out over that famous gingerbread temple, sipping my soft drink, I could not mock. Here, for all its silliness, was something large and good: a big rich organization that brought comfort and clarity and gladness to its adherents, that encouraged charity, sobriety, industry, probity, family, comeliness, and respect. The measure of a religion is not its origins or doctrine, which are almost always weird, but what it does. Is it, on balance, a force for good? Does it help lives or hurt them? Independence of mind is hardly a boon if it leads to despair.

The newest addition to the Temple Square complex is a six-acre conference center, which includes a 21,000-seat auditorium, without a single sight-obscuring pillar—the largest such cantilevered structure in the world. It is really something, the contemporary equivalent of a St. Peter's or the mosque at Mecca, a dazzling demonstration of means. Our guide was a pleasant-looking gentleman in his early seventies, I'd guess, who also served Sunday mornings as an usher at the Tabernacle. Again and again he repeated what fulfillment his church work provided, how lucky he was to hear the choir each week, how amazing it was—miraculous, really—this auditorium could have been made. His talk was a little boring: once you've seen a new auditorium, you've seen it; yet I found myself reluctant to break away. There was nothing of the proselyte about this grandfather, nothing scheming or bamboozled or strange. He was just happy, really happy.

I basked in his glow.

v.

If you have the chance, treat yourself to a drive from Provo to Price on a hot, dry, summer afternoon. Make it, if you can, on a summer during which hardly a flick of wet has fallen, when the bridged bed of the Price River is a cracked gully; when the rough burning wind off Book Cliffs shakes your steel flanks and the gates of cattle pens swing emptily. The terrible beauty of the scene may make you seize your steering wheel, lest, dazed, you are puffed off the concrete into the sage. There are other cars and trucks on this exitless 50-mile straightaway; a railroad track, too, and a long parade of leaning wooden crosses bearing power lines. If your mount buckles beneath you with a rasping cough, you will not die here, as pioneers did, straining desperately westward. Today a trucker with a CB will stop and summon a helicopter to lift you to cool white coats and sneakers squeaking on clean tiles and the beeps and clicks of unaccountable machines. It takes work these days in America to find where you cannot be rescued. This long, dry trail across the Wasatch Plateau, under the gaze of those towering red-gray cloud-mottled cliffs, is now only the sensation of an hour, traveling at 60, air-conditioned, but still you can imagine how hot it must have been—and long—and how small they must have felt—and prayerful. I sip my nippled water bottle nervously.

Beauty, of course, is a transaction, not a fact. There are plenty who could pass this splendid emptiness with only impatience for a bright red Dairy Queen sign, sprouting from the desert like a flower. There are others who might find the gaze of the mountains too belittling to enjoy.

God—or Evolution, His surrogate—has given man so much. Not the least of our gifts is to imagine our own importance. He gave us, alone among the species, the foresight of our death, but also a passel of strategies to face that erasure. Yes, we are dust, but divine dust, we say, possessed of some spirit unattached to time. Or we immerse ourselves in enterprise, doing this and that, reaching that goal and the next, as if these actions signified. We join clubs and congregations, recite pledges, bellow fight songs, and convince ourselves the answer is Yes, Yes, when we know, sure as sunshine, it is No.

117

Each of us responds differently to evidence of our nonentity. Some redecorate their homes or buy pets. Others hit the road, like so many of my neighbors in these RV camps. Others find in their insignificance the sweetest dispensation, release from the burden of expectations.

I like to think I am not old yet, that I will attain at least my actuarial allotment, or if not, my Biblical portion of three-score and ten. I have no reason to believe this but then, my doctors assure me, I have no grounds to think otherwise. The ancient admonishment to live every day as if it were your last is silly, taken literally. If today were my last, I'd devote it, I suspect, not to adding a page to an incomplete manuscript, but to saying good-bye.

For most of my life I fretted about time. On every anniversary—of my birth, my marriage, my children's births, holidays, religious and calendar years—I'd berate myself for slowness, laziness. I'd wake sweating in the night at how little I'd made.

Then one day, as if by a wand, my fear vanished. I was certain never to succeed—or fail—for these notions were fictions, endlessly malleable. I was free—not to do nothing: nothing could interest me less—but to do as I pleased. I enjoyed seeing—so I would see. I enjoyed saying—so I would say. Whether my words found hearers, that would be as it might. But I am certain, as I have been certain of little else in 50 years, that I am not wasting myself on someone else's dream. No dream makes sense: therefore live your own. It at least you know is something true.

vi.

Yesterday was cleaning day. It began with my laundry bag bulging out of its cabinet. A full laundry bag is as importunate as a full sewage tank: ignore it at your peril.

The camp, in Green River, had a nice big Laundromat, with windows overlooking the mesa. This Laundromat was for the public as well as campers, so it had to be nice. Laundromats exclusively for campers tend to be cramped. No one cares if you use them.

My Laundromat system is to jog during the 40 minutes of washing, transfer the damp load to the dryer, shave, shower, straighten the cabin, then return to fold the toasty heap. Some people watch their clothes revolving in the round glass window. They thumb old magazines without interest.

There's one street in Green River, so that's where I ran. It is straight and wide and flat, like most streets in the desert. There are gas stations, convenience stores, motels, a restaurant or two, sometimes a water slide or gift shop. In Green River, I ran by a trim little museum devoted to John Wesley Powell, the nineteenth-century geologist and ethnologist who introduced the Rockies to white America. Powell and Lewis and Clark are the patron saints of the mountain states: their names are everywhere. I made a note to visit the museum, but by the time I remembered, I was 60 miles down the road.

Next to my camp there was a car wash that could accommodate an RV. The car wash in my hometown is a fancy automatic affair, with whirring sprays and caressing brushes. You can watch through a window as a swarm of Guatemalans towels, calling to each other in Spanish. An RV wouldn't fit in my hometown car wash. That makes sense, since I'm the only person I know there who owns one.

The Green River car wash is a do-it-yourself affair—a steel shed, fitted out with two long hoses, one attached to a power spray, the other to a brush that spouts fluffy pink suds. You get wet. It was fun.

Having folded and stowed my laundry—and swept and swabbed the inside of my van, including toilet and sinks—I felt unaccountably joyous on the highway, singing along to a piano concerto by Saint-Saens. Migrant had been so dirty and now she was, well, not spotless, but at least bright and bugless in the sun. Bugs out west are a problem when you drive fast. They splatter against your leading surfaces and bake until they're hard to scrape off.

I smiled—I am still smiling—at the prospect of my friends' reaction to this account. Most of my friends don't clean their cars, or fold their laundry, or cook their suppers. None drain their sewage. My friends have others do these things; so until two months ago did I. My friends, in the main, are busy and successful, and when they have free time, play golf.

Joy is wiser than thought. I was happy at my cleanness because I had made it. I had not needed a laundress or cleaning person or industrious immigrant. I was happy too in the realization that no task need be a chore if undertaken in a spirit of adventure.

George Herbert wrote about this. Herbert was a younger contemporary of Shakespeare's, who described his antsy inner life with a tenderness that wrings the heart. "Teach me, my God and King," he prayed,

In all things thee to see,
And what I do in anything,
To do it as for thee.

A servant with this clause
Makes drudgery divine:
Who sweeps a room as for thy laws,
Makes that and th'action fine.

Beauty and ugliness are not facts: they are ways of seeing. Label a flower a weed, a task a chore, an obstacle a doom, and that's what they become. Sadness is not our fate; it is our fault.

vii.

Sometimes we notice before we notice.

Along Route 160, heading west, a gleam of glass in the sage. Beer bottles. Well, litter is common enough. But a mile of it? Five miles? *Twenty* miles? Who owns this parched property? Not the state: the citizenry would never tolerate such filth. There would be a special assessment, a new sheriff.

I consult the map and wince. These are Indian lands, one of those strange half-sovereign nations within our borders, so much poorer, so much sadder, it is hard to look. And these bottles, millions of them, the accumulation, it would seem, of decades, what are they? A tradition? A proclamation of penury? An affront to the oppressors, whooshing by on a perfectly paved federal road? A glittering gesture of indifference?

I am yawning at the Towaoc Texaco. Fifty gallons is a lot with no nozzle-latch.

A jolly burly Ute is filling his dented pickup. He smiles broadly. He has half his front teeth, the left half.

"You from New York I see."

"Yep," I attempt a vernacular. "You?"

"Just over there." He points across an indefinite expanse of sage, dust, khaki grass, sagging barbed wire, broken cars, and rusting mobile homes.

"Where you going?"

"West. I'm a writer."

"Ohhh," he considers this. "I catch wild horses. You know wild horses?"

"A little. Catch them to tame them?"

"Oh no," he laughs, delighted. His cheeks are broad, cherubic. He could pass for an Indian Santa Claus. "Too long to tame. Horse meat."

I grew up riding horses. We loved them. Even when they were too old to ride, we'd never kill them unless we had to. Then we'd bury them. We wore polished leather boots and crisp white stocks and soft tight gloves. Grooms helped us into the saddle. For horse shows, manes and tails were braided. I got good at braiding. It was part of our training.

"Palominos?" I search for a thread.

"All kinds. Government horses. Ponies." He points to the high mesa. "They up there. Big problem. Eat all the grass. Specially now. It's so dry."

"What do you get for the—meat?" It's a writer's job to ask questions.

"Between 35 and a thousand each. Once I got 27 of them all at once."

"With a lasso?"

He beams. He seems to like me for my ignorance.

"No, no. That's no way."

"You shoot them?"

"No! Water trap. They come to the water and then—" He splays his brown fingers, then joins them. I can almost hear the snap. "Last spring—" this is his funniest story, the one he longs to share, "two white guys come to the tribe say they'll clear away the horses—three months—for a hundred and forty thousand dollars. Then they ask, 'Where are the horses?' So we show them." He points again. "And they say, 'Oh no, we can't do that. We only work in *pastures*.'" Now his shoulders are heaving with glee. "I don't charge nothing. The tribe knows that."

"Is that your work?" Migrant was full, but I wasn't.

"Hobby. I'm a heavy machinery operator."

"But if those white guys thought it was worth a hundred and forty thousand . . ."

"I know, I know," he shakes his head: it's an old argument; "but then it wouldn't be fun."

The ranger at Mesa Verde, the ancient Indian cliff dwellings, speaks of Anglos with a note of disparagement. He's an Anglo himself.

"Our native Americans were wandering peoples. Real estate meant nothing to them. They'd use up the land and move on. Or there'd be a drought—or cold spell—or both. The seed wouldn't germinate. Their prayers wouldn't be working. They'd blame the witch, the evil spirit.

"We know when they left here but not why. Maybe it was war, maybe water, maybe weather, we just don't know. We do know when—some time in the 1200s. They made their way south to the Rio Grande. Then they wanted to come back. It was not good there, either, not the right place. That's the heart of their religion, looking for the right place. Only now they weren't free any more. First the Spaniards, then the Anglos, told them where they could go and where they couldn't. The Indians did not understand about private property. It was never part of their thinking."

Out west I've grown lax about where to spend the night. Every county, it seems, has an RV park or several. (There are 27 KOA's, for example, in Colorado, compared to none in Connecticut.) I drive in the afternoon until stopped by weariness, hunger, or dusk. (What use driving in the dark? I came to see.)

Leaving Mesa Verde, I figure I'll drive as much of the way to the Petrified Forest, in Arizona, as I can manage. There are not many towns on the map but there are some. I'll be fine.

On the way I pass "Four Corners," the only spot where you can touch four states simultaneously (Utah, Colorado, Arizona, New Mexico). The Navajos, who own the land, have put a "monument" here, a photo-op you can visit for three bucks a head. Only in America do we erect monuments to a surveyor's anomaly and make money by it. Even past seven there's a line to the platform from which you snap relatives squatting with a limb in four different states. (Not having a relative, I borrowed a little blonde, already posing for her dad. Her mother, wary, was about to object.)

Now I am off into the desert. The beauty of this landscape is aggressive. You can no more ignore it than you can play Beethoven's Ninth as background music. The limitless arid flatness, punctuated by strangely carved mesas and buttes and fins of red rock, the vast variousness of the sky, the sparse clinging vegetation, the occasional dust-scoured hovel or fence, leave scant hope for man. Ruin is the theme; the ceaseless glorious ruin of geologic time, the heaving up of mountains, their grinding down, the evaporation of oceans, the endless recollection of dust. Here, we sense, is the underlying truth beneath man's pretensions, the bedrock beneath our cocky metropolises and crops.

I drink the pastel dusk: nothing could be more grand! But now it is turning into night, no sign of a town, only dimming ribbons to nowhere. It is nearing nine, I am hungry, but these clutches of hovels I pass can't be the names on my map!

I pull over to study. Oh: the Navaho Nation, those hundreds of thousands of acres granted by America to our vanquished predecessors. Such a gift! Nothing can be grown here, nothing. There is no water. It is all red dust. (Perhaps that's why the "red man" was called red, for his skin is brown.)

My uneasiness grows. How far to civilization, the Interstate, a glowing bouquet of neon—Wendy's, Texaco, Best Western, Kentucky Fried, KOA? In theory, I can pull over anywhere and pass the night: Migrant is as self-sufficient as a sloop, at least for a day or two. My worry is, it is not ocean around me, but an alien people who have reasons to be angry.

The Indian question tongue-ties even the most articulate Americans. That's because it has no answer. The consequence of separatism is this—an embittered, impoverished ghetto in the midst of plenty. The consequence of assimilation is loss of identity. Losers in history face an unpalatable choice: embrace the conqueror or endure subjection. The white man won. Only we white people don't like to think of ourselves in that light. We are idealists. We declare "all men are created equal"—and mean it—while conveniently excluding populations from our definition.

The white man won—with tactics frequently abhorrent. We almost cheer for Custer's butchers at Little Big Horn. We had it coming.

But now? Can we endure the shame of such squalor in our midst? Can we say it's not our fault? Should we, then, compensate these benighted people by making them our drug lords, licensing them (by whatever bizarre theory of law) to feed our gambling addiction?

There are no RV camps in the Navajo Nation, none that I can find. White people, I suppose, who form the majority of RVers, wouldn't want to stop here, so it wouldn't pay. Three hours' driving brings me to the Interstate and a welcome invitation to a "full hookup." I'm sorry to have passed so much of the Navajo Nation in the dark. But I sleep relieved.

8
Neverland

I'm bad at rocks. Grand Canyon, Arches, Painted Desert, Petrified Forest, Mojave Desert—I look and say, well, what everyone says—"Amazing! Fantastic! Amazing!"—feeling small.

Down the road from Petrified Forest, in Holbrook, Arizona, Jim Gray's beckons, world's largest purveyor of petrified wood. I'm not one for souvenirs—Migrant hasn't room—but for these dreamy agates, so strangely striated, I make an exception. I purchase a box full of bookends at prices a fraction of Manhattan's. I will enjoy seeing them, eternity propping the hour's effusions, on my friends' shelves.

ii.

"Schundler," replies the creamy voice beside me.

At the Flagstaff KOA, at five on a summer afternoon, there are two check-in lines.

I look. Could it be the recently defeated candidate for Governor of New Jersey? He'd have time. But in Arizona? At a KOA?

"You wouldn't be *Brett* Schundler?"

The Face. Yanked down like a window-shade. The abler the politician the more impenetrable the Face.

Local politics are more fun to report on than national. Local candidates, less schooled, tend to be frank.

Candidates dreaming of the heights make themselves puppets of their purpose. Brett Schundler becomes "Brett Schundler, rising star in the GOP."

I invite him over for a beer. It is cruel, I know: the last person he wants to be now is "Brett Schundler." That's why he's in Flagstaff—in a rented RV—with his pretty wife and kids—to shuck that striped suit.

124

He accepts, of course. Politicians treat journalists like stray dogs—politely, lest one's rabid. We sit beneath the pines, in the smoke of a hundred grills, sipping, nibbling peanuts.

I wish I could remember what he said. It wasn't that I was awed, Lord knows, or put off: it was just . . . predictable. Consultants standardize candidates, make them dress alike, talk alike, evade alike. Consultified candidates know to call blacks African-Americans and Indians Native Americans and problems challenges. They never admit to ambition. It is the "opportunity to serve" that entices them.

Americans are bored by government because politicians have made government boring. Seeking the majority's favor, candidates espouse the majority's opinions, so that even important campaigns seem as empty as "Queen for a Day" with its applause-o-meter. We read the text of the Lincoln-Douglas debates with wonderment. Imagine in backwoods Illinois, all those thousands of voters straining to follow closely reasoned arguments, fanning themselves, hushed, no PA system or AC. Serious candidates make serious voters. If elections are TV shows, why not change the channel?

Rising in office today requires candidates to accept the captivity of quotation marks. The higher a politician rises, the more his every word and gesture is sifted for that single inadvertence, that blurted frustration, that might embarrass. Lens and recorder never forget. Thus mini-cams make cowards of us all.

Once we elected men, not mannequins, neighbors we knew, whom we allowed to err. Now candor is suicide. Candidates are drilled to stay "on message" lest they veer off course.

Brett Schundler is the very model of a modern major candidate: smooth, polished, practiced, impossible to find. I know he is lying when he grips my hand and says he is glad we talked.

iii.

Simon Rodia and J. Paul Getty never met, I'm guessing, though they shared a passion for collecting and lived in the same city.

Rodia was born in Campania, Italy, in 1879. A poor man, he was sent to the United States in his early teens. He worked as a laborer. In the early 1920s he bought a pie-shaped plot in Watts, a working-class neighborhood of Los Angeles, and began building a series of eccentric, whimsical towers. The tallest is almost a hundred feet high. Rodia had no money, no written plans, no bolts, no scaffolding, no engineering degree, no co-workers, no welding tools. Short and agile, he clambered over the high, open, hand-made girders, pressing bright bottle and tile fragments into the concrete casings. In 1954, he decided his life work was finished. He gave his home to his neighbor and moved away, never to return. When he died in 1965, Rodia and his creation were beginning to be talked of. Plans to demolish the towers were opposed. Today, Rodia's towers rise, protected, from a shabby barrio, their jolly tips teasing the sky. They and their maker are famous.

Getty was born in Minnesota in 1892. He followed his father into the oil business. He became the richest man in the world. He divorced five wives and buried two of five sons. He spent lavishly on himself and his art collection but as little as possible on others. On his 700-acre estate in England, he installed a pay telephone. At his estate in Malibu, he built a museum for his collection. After his death in 1976, a new Getty Museum was erected atop a small mountain in Brentwood. It is made of stone and steel and glass. It is vast, spectacular, and sumptuous, as ambitious in its way as Rodia's towers.

Both Rodia and Getty were reclusive souls. Both tried marriage and gave up on it. Both had estranged sons. Both were murmured about by their neighbors. Both channeled their loneliness into collecting and sorting treasures. Rodia's treasures were scraps; they cost him nothing. Getty's were old and cost a lot. Both built fantastic storehouses for their finds.

To visit the Getty, you park far off (when the main lot is full) and are bused up. The Getty is a standard Los Angeles tourist attraction, like Sunset Boulevard or Disneyland.

Not many people visit Rodia's towers. The Chamber of Commerce, I suspect, would prefer you didn't. Watts is famous for violence as well as towers. In 1965, rioters ravaged the commercial strip, in an outbreak still cited in histories. In 1991, Los Angeles police mauled a black man called Rodney King, again lofting Watts into the world's headlines. My brother and sister-in-law, who have lived in Los Angeles for 20 years, had trouble finding Rodia's towers. My brother's car is shiny and expensive. The glances we attracted were disquieting.

I'd expected to be wowed by the Getty, and I was. Architect Richard Meier has created a fantastic and original hill-town. From the base of the hill, it resembles a fortress—neighbors, wary of its proposed height, kept it squat—but inside, one is transported. Big modern buildings often make us feel small. The Getty welcomes and beckons. Around every corner is a nook and chair. Low walls and fountain rims invite perching. Each corridor leads to a deck from which one can gaze at the shimmering city stretching east to the mountains and west to the sea.

Rodia's towers I'd expected only to smile at. How great could it be, this oddball's sport? Sweet—spirited—folk art maybe—but not Art with a capital A.

My first glance confirmed my expectation. The street is cramped and ugly. The base of the towers is fenced off, so you have to peer at the ground floor through wires. Shovels and buckets indicate a restoration effort, but the site reeks of neglect.

I was almost sorry I'd dragged my brother and sister-in-law here. But then, look: how the green of bottle shards glistens in the fretwork like emeralds. And how each of the eight towers comments on and cajoles the others. And how those dreamy stairs spiral to nowhere. And how those elegant patterns in the concrete remind you of—what?—antique heating grates? And how, as dusk deepens, these improbable spires choir into the blue. Then I imagine that spry little man, solitary and strange, clambering, for thirty-three years, nimble as a chimp, no cranes, no structural engineering, no reinforced concrete to withstand earthquakes, no nothing except his dream: "I had in my mind," he explained, in broken English, "to do something big and I did."

J. Paul Getty left a monument to himself, for us to admire. We are grateful to him for his generosity and daunted by his wealth. He deserves the fame he purchased.

Simon Rodia gave no thought to fame or fortune. When he felt his work was done, he gave it to a neighbor and went away. He created for joy, as you'd sing a song.

J. Paul Getty was among the famous figures of his age. No one ever heard of Simon Rodia. Now history is redressing that balance. A century hence, Getty will be a name on a building, a bronze bust in the foyer. And Simon Rodia will have blossomed, like Paul Bunyan and Johnny Appleseed and Davy Crockett, into American myth. His towers will be visited by multitudes. They will rise from the field of flowers they deserve.

iv.

It's no accident that the Magic Kingdom sprouted from Southern California. Or the movie business. Or Rodia's towers. Or the Getty Museum.

Or Hearst's castle. Or Richard Nixon. Or Ronald Reagan. These are all fantasies—and fantasy is the native flora of this fairest of American climates.

Americans have trouble with the idea of fantasy. We think of ourselves as a sincere, plain-speaking folk. George Washington 'fessing up to his cherry tree, suffering Lincoln, the taciturn cowboy, give-'em-hell-Harry are our kind of guys.

Actor suggests liar. Lying is un-American, right? Yet we worship actors and their works. We gorge on TV and movies. Show-biz is our lingua franca. Performers are our royalty, whose every dalliance and overdose we dissect. We never allow our actors to retire. An ex-Senator can fade into obscurity, but not a movie star.

Southern California is a made-up place. Enter it from the east, by highway, and you feel that powerfully. After endless miles of empty desert, presto!—palm trees and skyscrapers and cosmetics. Fords and Chevys become Lexuses and Jaguars. Mozart's on the radio again. Starbucks bloom, where before there were only Dairy Queens.

Made-up does not mean false. It means put on, selected, like a hat. In much of the country, only one sort of hat fits. Anything different seems odd. In LA, there is no indigenous hat—or architectural style—or dogma. You *have* to choose one: there's no norm to default to. With so many choices, reality feels like a play.

(Ambling in Pasadena, I worry how I look for the first time in months. My Brazilian chicken with couscous splattered my shirt. I need a haircut. My sandals are scuffed.)

Richard Nixon and Ronald Reagan were both actors. Every President's an actor, of course—that is, he performs on a vast stage. Yet most Presidents we feel play the only role they could have. FDR, JFK, Bush the First were typecast as patricians; Truman, Ike, and Ford as no-nonsense mid-Westerners. LBJ could only have come from Texas; Jimmy Carter from Georgia; Bill Clinton from Arkansas. All of these men had accents and gestures and patterns that betrayed them. Nixon and Reagan feel, by comparison, rootless. They don't talk Southern Californian. They don't look Southern Californian. They didn't govern Southern Californian. Because Southern Californians don't talk or look or govern any one way.

Nixon was an awkward actor, whose forced smile never convinced anyone. From the Alger Hiss hearings to his excruciating Checkers speech to his haggard appearance in the 1960 Presidential debates to his farewell remarks to the White House staff in 1974 to his worldly-wise narration at his library in Yorba Linda, we feel Nixon flogging himself onto center stage, because that's where he had to prove himself. Bad actors can be more interesting than good actors: through the imperfection in his imposture, we glimpse the man.

Nixon was my nemesis because he made me his. I was one of the despised unsilent minority on college campuses who clamored against a misguided war. Nixon's Vice President Spiro Agnew pelted us with alliterations like spitballs—Agnew, who vies with Aaron Burr and Schuyler Colfax for our worst Vice President. (Maybe it's animus, but I give Agnew the nod. Burr was a scoundrel and Colfax a thief, but Agnew was both—and a brute, to boot.) Nixon's Vietnam might have collared me or sent me packing. (I can't say what I would have done if drafted.) I hated Nixon. His Watergate comeuppance delighted me. Today I feel sadness toward him, even sympathy.

Nixon was a hero—in his battle with Richard Nixon. Beneath that stickish performer and indefatigable politician we sense a determined public servant, bent on doing right. Some people fit easily into their skins: what they want and who they are melodiously chime. Nixon was a misfit; never suave or glib or privileged like the resented Jack Kennedy, but a jut-jawed plugger, always embattled, always persecuted, but never quashed. With a paranoid's invention, Nixon revised his world with himself in the role of victim. (His library's account of Watergate ludicrously portrays the President as a defender of Presidential rights, while his critics are partisan and unscrupulous.) Nixon was not a nice or pleasant or attractive or comfortable human being; but he was a patriot who, whatever his limitations, would serve his country till his last breath.

Reagan was Nixon's opposite—a born actor. He became his part so thoroughly that one scours the record for a single utterance "out of character," like Nixon's rant to the press in 1962. Even when he was shot, Reagan's quips seem scripted—"Honey, I forgot to duck" and, to his surgeons, "I hope you guys are Republicans." Only an able actor could have admitted lying to the American public—"In my heart, I knew it was not true, but the facts show differently"—and had his ratings rise.

Where Nixon writhed in crisis, Reagan floated in sunny ease. Reagan seemed to feel the pain of others—at least he acted it—but none of his own. Reagan, like McKinley, Taft, and Eisenhower, was always cheerful. He refused to have enemies. Nothing fazed him.

This is admirable but off-putting. Our hearts enter only where invited, where doubt and dismay beseech. Ronald Reagan never seemed to need us, except as an audience, to applaud. Even when he retired from public view with his moving handwritten letter about his Alzheimer's, he had

everything under control. Such consistent geniality, beyond our experience, is beyond our ken. We can't quite believe it. It does not seem real.

The Nixon and Reagan libraries resemble each other: low, pleasant, un-
obtrusive buildings with characteristic Californian vistas (Nixon's is flowers;
Reagan's rugged hills). Both tell their stories chronologically, with lively in-
teractive exhibits. But where Reagan's progress is from triumph to triumph
(even his failure to win the Republican nomination in 1976 is portrayed as
a necessary—and therefore happy—prelude to his victory in 1980), Nixon's
is from siege to siege. Nixon is ugly, scowling, awkward, defying his enemies, beating odds, coming back. Having vowed we "wouldn't have Nixon
to kick around anymore," he gave us just that, and kicked we did, and hard,
and we're going to keep kicking, because Nixon is complicated, and needy,
and feisty, and won't lie still. Reagan is handsome and idolized and serene.
His quiet grave[15] faces the setting sun, like an old Western. The epitaph
reads, "I know in my heart that man is good, that what is right will always
eventually triumph, and there is purpose and worth to each and every life."
He will rest in peace.

v.

Having zigzagged up the five-mile driveway in the tour bus and climbed
a hundred steps, one expects to be awed by the view from Hearst Castle.
West stretch the craggy undisturbed coast and the Pacific; north, south, and
east, the smoothed tan cliffs of the Santa Lucia range; and before you, en-
circled by concrete Roman-ish columns and salacious French-ish statuary,
a swimming pool half the size of a football field. And all was the property
of its proprietor, all but the ocean. (San Simeon, comedian W. C. Fields
quipped, was a great place to raise kids; you send them out to play and
when they get home they're grown-ups.)

It was so busy this summer Sunday I had to wedge in on standby on the
day's last bus. Fifty passengers times six times eight hours, I find myself
calculating, times fourteen dollars—or maybe more, since five different
tours are offered, each showing different rooms—times fifty-two . . . no, I
felt no urge, despite prompting, to become a "friend" of Hearst Castle.

---

[15]When I visited Reagan's Presidential library, he was technically alive but practically dead.
His handsome grave had to wait another two years for its handsome occupant.

Reactions among our group varied. The gigglers found our guide humorous forbidding chewing gum. (When was I last part of a group ordered to "spit out"?) A pair of grimly overweight females knew the name of every bygone movie idol and sighed to envision them lolling beneath the palms. The unfazed attention of various head-nodders declared their refusal to quail before so much splendor. Home-improvers pointed to this or that brocade as just the thing for their den. A trio of nose-ringed teenagers scoffed. And the moralists muttered—that so much wealth should be squandered on an old man's games.

I count myself among the mutterers, I suppose, but that's only after sleeping on it. At the time I wasn't sure what to think. Part of me squirmed with envy. I too want to be salaamed: any maker does. Part of me admired the theatricality of architect Julia Morgan's designs, as "authentic" as the corny costume dramas Hearst made into movies. Part of me was saddened by so much piling up, room upon room, thing upon thing, as if you could buy your way to ease.

I woke up angry. A philippic bubbled, hot as nausea.

Our guide, an older lady, smitten with the glamour, had urged us not to take any of it "too seriously." Lillian Davies, Hearst's mistress, was a kid in her twenties when this all began, as were her Hollywood playmates—Clark Gable, Greta Garbo, Johnny Weissmuller, among others. San Simeon was a goof to them, a doting uncle's indulgence. They did not think themselves superior, lounging on this Olympian summit. They didn't really think much at all. It was party time among the beautiful people and the music seldom paused. There was lunch, languorous relaxing, a dip, tennis, a horse ride, drinks, dinner, a film, and on and on. That's how the beautiful people manage it in all generations, doing nothing exquisitely.

And yet, this colossal stage set was not folded away with the rest of their airy lives. The castle remains as evidence. The flip side of freedom is folly. Only in America can we amass such fortunes and deploy them unconscionably. William Randolph Hearst proclaimed himself a liberal, preoccupied with the welfare of the poor. Yet what could dishearten the poor more than such massive portions of privilege heaped on the plates of a few? When church or state erect fantastic monuments, they embody a community and enforce its pride. I'm all in favor of grand public buildings: they inspirit, being owned by all. But where's the public purpose for San Simeon, unless it was to keep the public far off? This is self-aggrandizement, braggadocio at a scale unimaginable, grotesque profligacy now presented as admirable artifact.

The tactful application of wealth is a tricky topic. We do not expect the rich to live in shacks. Flaunting is OK—up to a point.

The greater one's wealth, however, the greater one's responsibility to exemplify. Honor is measured not by what one has, but by what one has made of it. Penniless Simon Rodia, who created his towers in Watts for the delight of his neighbors and posterity, was a great man. So was Andrew Carnegie, who said it is not a shame to acquire great wealth, only to die with it.

William Randolph Hearst, by comparison, is a sorry footnote.

vi.

I am in Ukiah, California. I had never heard of Ukiah, but my encyclopedia had. From 1899 to 1903, its International Latitude Observatory was home to Frank Schlesinger (1871–1943), an astronomer who developed "a photographic method of determining parallaxes." Parallax, per my Oxford English Dictionary, is an "apparent displacement, or difference in the apparent position, of an object, caused by actual change (or difference) of position of the point of observation." In other words, reality shifts as we shift our stance.

Ukiah is also remembered as the headquarters, in the late 1960s, for The People's Temple, the cult of the notorious Jim Jones. On November 18, 1978, in Guyana, 913 of Jones's followers were killed or committed suicide by drinking cyanide-laced Kool-Aid. Two hundred seventy-six of the dead were children. Jones, who began his career as an Indiana evangelist, died of a bullet to the brain, probably self-inflicted.

I drove here yesterday from San Simeon. My first 80 miles were on US 1, Earth's most famous road. At the edge of an ocean we expect lowlands, gradually rising. Here America feels cleaved. The coiling two-lane highway clings to the cliffs. It is better not to look down onto the rocks and foam. The beauty is terrifying. Three times I had to pull over—to gaze and settle my pulse.

Until this journey I disliked driving. How one got anywhere was mechanical. Airports were my paradigm for travel: grin and bear it.

I settle into the cab of Migrant as into a theater seat. Every vista interests. Even the dingiest neighborhoods strain to tell their stories. (More and more, in urban areas, walls are rising around highways, blocking views. The same is happening in my hometown as newcomers erect fences to preserve "privacy." This impulse to evade neighbors is a bad sign.)

Last night, a dark figure entered my dreams, a sort of all-purpose apparition embodying death, guilt, dread. It began quizzing me, as it often does, about my life's value and direction.

Younger, I'd cower before this recurrent visitor. I'd accept its accusations as just.

Last night, I surprised myself by my defiance. "No, I *don't* know what my book is about—or my life, for that matter. But guess what? I don't care. My brain brims with 'finds.' I'm not looking for 'America' or any marketable conclusion. Who concludes, excludes. America is inexhaustible: its largeness is its largesse. It will exhaust a thousand portraitists.

"I write as a painter paints—what I see. If a few folks choose to hang my words over their mantels, bless them. If not, I'm still the luckiest guy I know. How many souls can say, 'I am living the life I dreamed. I am giving my all'?

"I wake every morning excited as a kid at Christmas. So many moments to unwrap! Sure, I've had my share of losses, sadnesses, but I wouldn't alter one, because they all—together—have brought me to this hour.

"Understand, can't you? Joy is the arbiter of worth. Only the heart's yes is irrefutable. So beat it, you gloomy creep."

vii.

Northern California is burning this summer. So are Oregon, Arizona, Colorado, New Mexico, Nevada. Drought and arrogance have made the forests tinder. The forests are beautiful; men wanted to live there. They said to themselves, We can prevent fires. And they have, more or less—for a century—while the underbrush piled like kindling. But forests seek to burn now and then (Smokey the Bear notwithstanding). It's nature's way of cleansing, rejuvenating, reopening the sky to the shaded soil. Dead wood is hard to get rid of, literally as well as figuratively.

Route 199, which slices conveniently from the northern California coast to Interstate-5 in Oregon, was closed due to fire. Road closures in the trafficked East mean detours of a few miles. My detour today—onto Route 299-West, then north on I-5—added, I see now, in horrified hindsight—130 miles! And not just any 130 miles. These snaked through the Salmon Mountains, along the precipitous banks of the Trinity River. Thirty-five miles per hour, through this primeval landscape, is a respectable average.

I'd chosen for my daily briefing a tape I knew I would dislike: *A People's History of the United States* by Howard Zinn. This is history from the vantage of its victims: the trip as seen by the roadbed. Zinn never met a loser who hadn't been screwed. From Columbus to Washington to Jefferson to Jackson to Lincoln to TR to FDR to Kennedy to LBJ, the victors in the American saga were all venal and cruel, while Indians, slaves, immigrants, factory workers, grape-pickers, feminists, gays, and inmates were noble and oppressed. Ideals never moved America's leaders. If we made any progress softening our civilization, it was only because the aggrieved arose and forced us.

Some people prefer to hear only agreeable opinions. I like being riled. It makes me think.

I settle on two objections to Zinn's version. First: if history had gone his way, if all his victims had prevailed, would we be a better nation today? Second: how is progress possible without pain? Can there be a new forest without burning the old?

America's history is rife with lamentable chapters. So is the history of any conscious adult. As the cadences of the Book of Common Prayer remind us: "We have left undone those things which we ought to have done; and we have done those things which we ought not to have done; and there is no health in us." We would repair our treatment of the Indians, if we could. We would storm into the Constitutional convention in Philadelphia in 1787 and insist that slavery be abolished. We would reconstruct Reconstruction, so it didn't grind down those it was meant to raise. We would unbolt the Triangle Shirtwaist Company so 146 young seamstresses didn't incinerate. We would, but we can't. Time is padlocked: it contains all we've done and will not let us revise.

Decrying ancient wrongs is presumptuous. Who are we to chide our forbears? Whatever our grandparents did, for good or ill, is entombed with them. Our focus should be our own conduct: "What next? What now?"

Winding between the crags and evergreens of the Salmon Mountains, glancing uneasily into the shining river below, my speculations drift. If America had not become America, if we had not grown big and strong, where would our world be today? Mightn't the barbarians—the Nazis and the Communists—have prevailed without America to oppose them? Mightn't that barbarism have plunged mankind into a new dark age?

I cannot wish away even the grimmest chapters of our past. They, no less than our proudest moments, made us who we are. I also cannot forget the fragility of this accomplishment called America. Zinn may pummel America as if it were as lasting as the pyramids—that is his right—but any acquaintance with our past shows how easily all might have been different. The miracle of America is not that we damaged so many in our ascent, but that we learned from our mistakes and tried to stop making them. It pains me, judging from its availability in bookstores, that Zinn's history is among the better sellers.

You'd have been proud of our daughter in Seattle, tan and fit and happy after her cross-country bike trip, surrounded by fast new friends. Their joy together was contagious, their laughter, their nicknames, their ache at parting. And the nose-ring—don't freak—looks just fine. The message of a nose-ring is "I won't be led by the nose"—that's what we want, isn't it? Besides, the cartilage, I'm told, heals with barely a trace.

My week with Becca and her new boyfriend—heading south through Oregon, then west to Idaho—was wonderful for my heart and terrible for my book. One cannot look outward and inward at the same time. With Becca aboard, the talk was about family, memories. Time flew—but so did the scenes, few of which I can recall.

In Portland, we smoked pot. I haven't smoked pot since college. Remember those acrid dorm rooms with the shades drawn, passing around joints and talking drivel? I never experienced the high that was promised—booze is more my thing—and the heat seared my gullet. I smoked to belong. Since my earliest school days I never felt "in." It stung. Now I no longer care.

The pot in Portland was no more effective but I loved being included. The affection of grown children is a grace like no other. As parents, we've botched plenty, I fear, but not that.

Your continuing silence is becoming something of a quandary. In eight weeks I will be home—to what? Silence changes colors. At first I figured you were too furious to speak. Then I thought you were punishing me. Now I'm guessing you've called it quits. Truth is, any of these readings may be wrong. I just don't know.

I'm pretty sure you think this venture nonsense, my talk about a book a lot of guff. I'm not exploring, I'm running away, in your view, shirking. Writers don't need to abandon their families to write.

You're not wrong, not entirely. I did need to escape. I was scared and angry and frightened of what I might do. I needed air.

But I also was traveling toward—not toward any particular book that the world required, but toward a chance to see. See what? For whom? These are questions that ridicule askers. What use is a song? Why clip roses and arrange them in a vase? Why spend hours readying an elaborate supper

Presidents and Vice Presidents

(In Order of Service)

Served	President	Served	Vice President
1789–1797	George Washington	1789–1797	John Adams
1797–1801	John Adams	1797–1801	Thomas Jefferson
1801–1809	Thomas Jefferson	1801–1805	Aaron Burr, Jr.
		1805–1812	George Clinton
1809–1817	James Madison		
		1813–1814	Elbridge Gerry
1817–1825	James Monroe	1817–1825	Daniel D. Tompkins
1825–1829	John Quincy Adams	1825–1832	John C. Calhoun
1829–1837	Andrew Jackson		
		1833–1837	Martin Van Buren
1837–1841	Martin Van Buren	1837–1841	Richard Mentor Johnson
1841	William Henry Harrison	1841	John Tyler
1841–1845	John Tyler		
1845–1849	James K. Polk	1845–1849	George Mifflin Dallas
1849-1850	Zachary Taylor	1849–1850	Millard Fillmore
1850–1853	Millard Fillmore		
1853–1857	Franklin Pierce	1853	William Rufus deVane King
1857–1861	James Buchanan	1857–1861	John C. Breckinridge
1861–1865	Abraham Lincoln	1861–1865	Hannibal Hamlin
		1865	Andrew Johnson
1865–1869	Andrew Johnson		
1869–1877	Ulysses S. Grant	1869–1873	Schuyler Colfax
		1873–1875	Henry Wilson
1877–1881	Rutherford B. Hayes	1877–1881	William A. Wheeler
1881	James A. Garfield	1881	Chester A. Arthur
1881–1885	Chester A. Arthur		
1885–1889	Grover Cleveland	1885	Thomas A. Hendricks
1889–1893	Benjamin Harrison	1889–1893	Levi P. Morton
1893–1897	Grover Cleveland	1893–1897	Adlai E. Stevenson
1897–1901	William McKinley	1897–1899	Garret A. Hobart
		1901	Theodore Roosevelt
1901–1909	Theodore Roosevelt		
		1905–1909	Charles W. Fairbank
1909–1913	William H. Taft	1909–1913	James S. Sherman

Presidents and Vice Presidents

(In Order of Service — *continued*)

Served	President	Served	Vice President
1913–1921	Woodrow Wilson	1913–1921	Thomas R. Marshall
1921–1923	Warren G. Harding	1921–1923	Calvin Coolidge
1923–1929	Calvin Coolidge		
		1925–1929	Charles Gates Dawes
1929–1933	Herbert Hoover	1929–1933	Charles Curtis
1933–1945	Franklin D. Roosevelt	1933–1941	John Nance Garner
		1941–1945	Henry A. Wallace
		1945	Harry S Truman
1945–1953	Harry S Truman		
		1949–1953	Alben W. Barkley
1953–1961	Dwight D. Eisenhower	1953–1961	Richard M. Nixon
1961–1963	John F. Kennedy	1961–1963	Lyndon B. Johnson
1963–1969	Lyndon B. Johnson		
		1965–1969	Hubert H. Humphrey
1969–1974	Richard M. Nixon	1969–1973	Spiro T. Agnew
		1973–1974	Gerald R. Ford
1974–1977	Gerald R. Ford	1974–1977	Nelson A. Rockefeller
1977–1981	Jimmy Carter	1977–1981	Walter F. Mondale
1981–1989	Ronald Reagan	1981–1989	George H.W. Bush
1989–1993	George H.W. Bush	1989–1993	J. Danforth Quayle
1993–2001	William J. Clinton	1993–2001	Albert A. Gore, Jr.
2001–	George W. Bush	2001–	Richard B. Cheney

Presidents and Vice Presidents

(In Order of Appearance)

Garret A. Hobart
Paterson, NJ

Grover Cleveland
Princeton, NJ

Aaron Burr, Jr.
Princeton, NJ

George Mifflin Dallas
Philadelphia, PA

James Buchanan
Lancaster, PA

William McKinley
Canton, OH

James A. Garfield
Clevland, OH

Rutherford B. Hayes
Fremont, OH

Warren G. Harding
Marion, OH

William Henry Harrison
North Bend, OH

Benjamin Harrison
Indianapolis, IN

Thomas A. Hendricks
Indianapolis, IN

Charles W. Fairbanks
Indianapolis, IN

Thomas R. Marshall
Indianapolis, IN

Zachary Taylor
Louisville, KY

Richard Mentor Johnson
Frankfort, KY

John C. Breckinridge
Lexington, KY

Andrew Johnson
Greeneville, TN

Andrew Jackson
Nashville, TN

James K. Polk
Nashville, TN

Alben W. Barkley
Paducah, KY

Adlai E. Stevenson
Bloomington, IL

Dwight D. Eisenhower
Abilene, KS

Herbert Hoover
West Branch, IA

Abraham Lincoln
Springfield, IL

Harry S Truman
Independence, MO

Charles Curtis
Topeka, KS

Henry A. Wallace
Des Moines, IA

Richard M. Nixon
Yorba Linda, CA

Ronald Reagan
Simi Valley, CA

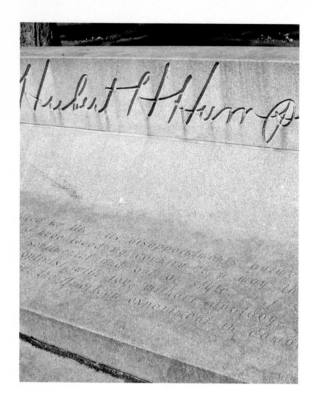

Hubert H. Humphrey
Minneapolis
MN

Charles Gates Dawes
Chicago, IL

Millard Fillmore
Buffalo, NY

Schuyler Colfax
South Bend, IN

James S. Sherman
Utica, NY

Levi P. Morton
Rhinebeck, NY

George Clinton
Kingston, NY

Franklin D. Roosevelt
Hype Park, NY

Nelson A. Rockefeller
Sleepy Hollow, NY

Ulysses S. Grant
New York, NY

Daniel D. Tompkins
New York, NY

Theodore Roosevelt
Oyster Bay, NY

Chester A. Arthur
Albany, NY

Martin Van Buren
Kinderhook, NY

William A. Wheeler
Malone, NY

Calvin Coolidge
Plymouth Notch, VT

Hannibal Hamlin
Bangor, ME

Franklin Pierce
Concord, NH

Henry Wilson
Natick MA

John Adams
Quincy, MA

John Quincy Adams
Quincy, MA

William H. Taft
Arlington, VA

John F. Kennedy
Arlington, VA

Woodrow Wilson
Washington, DC

Elbridge Gerry
Washington, DC

Spiro T. Agnew
Timomium, MD

George Washington
Mount Vernon, VA

John Tyler
Richmond, VA

James Monroe
Richmond, VA

Thomas Jefferson
Charlottesville, VA

James Madison
Monpelier Station, VA

John C. Calhoun
Charleston, SC

William R.D. King
Selma, AL

Lyndon B. Johnson
Stonewall, TX

John Nancer Garner
Uvalde, TX

JOHN NANCE
GARNER
NOV. 22, 1868
NOV. 7, 1967

when a 10-minute microwave zap would feed us fine? Why play tennis? "Beauty is its own excuse for being," wrote Emerson, our first intellectual. Discovery is a blast. And sometimes—not often, but sometimes—a melody will linger after its maker's still.

I do not assume I am such a maker. Any maker who does is an ass. The brag on John O'Hara's tomb in Princeton—"Better than anyone else, he told the truth of his time"—sneers at his yellowing tomes. There is no telling who will go the distance in the posterity sweepstakes. Bestsellers sprint, then falter. Slow starters, ignored at the gate, pick up pace. (Walden and Moby Dick *sold a few dozen copies. Emily Dickinson directed that her trunk of poems—only one of which had been printed—be dumped.) Lasting writing doesn't pay and paying writing doesn't last.*

And yet—the old "and yet"—people do it—invisible legions of poets, painters, sculptors, tune-makers, knitters, weavers, whittlers—now and always, not for the glory but the glow. Writing their world they right it somehow. Singing they make it sing.

I spent a lifetime avoiding my vocation because it made no sense, doing boastable jobs, scribbling poems in embarrassed secret. Poets were contemptible and doomed to starve. Real men didn't write poems.

Then I passed the age my dad was when he died and figured what the hell, why not do the only work that has ever made me feel meant?

So, yes, I am running away—from our pain—but from futility, too. Here, on the road, among Americans living and gone, I am heart-whole as never before. Inconsequential, I have never felt of more consequence. Anonymous, I have never felt more named. It sounds nutty, I know, but it's the way I feel.

I hope one day you will understand.

9
Fast East

i.

I wake from my week off with eager eyes. It was good to be away, better than I would have thought. It is good to be back.

Yesterday, I drove from Ketchum, Idaho, where Hemingway shot himself, to Bozeman, Montana. My schedule puts me in a hurry now and the West is wide. My route crossed the Craters of the Moon National Monument, where the earth is black and crusted as charred toast. There is nothing to do with charred toast: even the birds won't eat it. There is nothing to do with this grim landscape but gaze, then look away. This feels more like Judgment than Geology. The God who scalded these acres, making them infertile for eternity, was in a bad mood.

I tried not to stare at a couple in the check-out line in the Albertson's in Idaho Falls (Albertson's is a food store chain in these parts)—sub-subsistence farmers, it seemed, from their tattered denims and haunted eyes. I couldn't tell whether they were 30 or 70. They recalled the faces Walker Evans photographed during the Depression. They looked dazed in the shiny supermarket. They were buying a 12-pack of Coke and the transaction seemed complicated.

I had passed through West Yellowstone a month earlier, heading west, but it felt like an age. These months on the road have wakened me to the largeness of life. While I never lacked for interest—there's always something to discover—I never felt so helpless before a profligacy of views, so incompetent to capture even a particle of this immense trove. Who has time to moan with all this morning! I do my damnedest to rescue memories, but they rush away, and I will never catch up.

When I began my adventure, I would plot my daily course and reserve at campsites. To arrive at a definite destination is its own kind of fulfillment. Now I drive till I feel like stopping, hoping for a park before dark. Dusk becomes ominous. Yesterday, winding north on Route 20, beneath the towering Rockies, crisscrossing the Gallatin River, I grew pleasantly worried as crags flattened to silhouettes. Those little roadside crosses that have sprung up in recent years to memorialize traffic fatalities added to my alarm, like spooky movie music.

In Bozeman, the familiar yellow, red, and black KOA sign glowed like home. There are times when the familiar is all one craves. Yes, they had a spot—one of two remaining, in a campground that accommodates more than a hundred—and the computer recognized my name (yes, Carll with two l's). I cooked my T-bone and sliced and dressed my tomatoes as fast as I was able, and sat to my steaming plate and tumbler of Merlot. A pleasant baritone read *Huckleberry Finn* as I ate. *Huckleberry Finn* is a story I never tire of, the most genial of companions.

ii.

Hurtling still—past Idaho, Montana, North Dakota, Minnesota, Wisconsin. Tonight I wake, anxious, in Galena—Illinois' northwest corner—on the Mississippi. Grateful citizens gave General Grant a house here after the war. The Mississippi was majestic then, the continent's sole superhighway, key to its possession. Grant, one can argue, won the Civil War on the Mississippi, when he captured Vicksburg and bisected the Confederacy. That was before railroads and highways and airplanes made the Mississippi a mere puddle to jump. There's a sadness about river towns. Their founders dreamed of glory: a landing on the Mississippi! Think what a City might rise here! They failed to foresee trains and airplanes and big rigs bearing goods independent of tides.

I am traveling faster than I can say. How will I do justice? We never do— justice, but we may feel we have. Memory, groping, seizes an impression, like a ship's rail, to steady itself. In my last two dozen hours I have witnessed 1,200 miles but what have I observed? We'd like to think we can pack perceptions to unpack later but moments fade faster than flowers. Already some towns on my itinerary call nothing to mind: I pull open the drawer and it is—empty!—as if a thief had come.

I had meant particularly to say a word for North Dakota. North Dakota is less populous than even South Dakota. Its only boast—on its license plate—is "Gateway to the West." A gateway is not a place, it is between places, neither here nor there. North Dakota exists to be passed through, which is what I did, its whole drab width in a single day. From the badlands in the west, where young Theodore Roosevelt carried his grief after losing his young wife and beloved mother in a single day, to the rocky grazing lands in the east, I searched for some place to pause if I had the time, but found none. I mused—as bugs splattered my windshield and a pebble from a truck cut a crystal spider in the glass—what I'd do if North Dakota were a company I'd been hired to "turn around." My only ideas were lurid—sex and gambling will entice folks anywhere—but the fix would be worse than the fault. North Dakota's only option, it seems, is to embrace its status as least—least populous, least temperate, least tempting of the states.

Passing through Fargo to Minnesota is like entering a garden. As harsh as North Dakota is, Minnesota is gracious. Suddenly there is water and green rolling hills and trees and fat cows and trim farms and steeples and crop-thick fields. There are people who smile and a pervasive promise of pleasantness. I had come to Minnesota to visit Hubert Humphrey—one of the pleasantest politicians in memory—and within hours was house-hunting in my imagination. Each of us has his dream place, that landscape where his soul might find ease. For some it is the jostling city; for others the craggy West; for others the teeming sands of Florida or the chill hush of a mountain lake. Mine is Minnesota in the summer, modest, serene, equable, fruitful, quiet; where the view is long but contained by a neighboring hill; where unburied rocks do not threaten like fists, or the weather with winds or droughts.

I saw little of Minnesota beyond the highway and Lakeview Cemetery in Minneapolis, one of the nation's prettiest. The little I saw was persuasive. Minnesota *feels* light-hearted—sensible, grateful, scrubbed in body and mind. Could any other state have produced Garrison Keillor with his infallible sentimental charm; or that intrepid innocent, "clean Gene" McCarthy, undaunted by the towering LBJ; or Jimmy Carter's Vice President, modest Walter ("Fritz") Mondale; or happy Hubert Humphrey, who seems to keep smiling from his tomb? Would any other state have the self-confidence—or optimism—or whimsy—to elect a flamboyant wrestler Governor?

As usual, having mistaken my driving time, I had to forsake inviting stops on my way to Galena. The Sinclair Lewis Interpretation Center, Frank Lloyd Wright's Taliesin, a preserved Mississippi village, a Swiss cheese factory, the World Lumberjack Championships, each would have bettered me. But I had "promises to keep"—my Presidents and Vice Presidents; appointments that reeled me like a hooked fish.

Toward sundown, the urge to rescue my moment became too much. I was south of Prairie du Chien, on Route 133, a two-lane road that weaves along the Mississippi's eastern bank. Route 133 is a designated scenic byway, but few travel it, because it's slow. In America we like to get where we are going, even if it's nowhere.

I crested a hill, the sun at my back, and saw a straight road between fields of soybeans and corn, all scrupulously tended. I had been eating fried chicken and chugging red wine as I drove, too hungry to wait, and the liquor loosened my heart. The abundance, the precision, the goldenness, the happy farmhouse with its glad wooden sign decorated with two winking cows—

THE OSTERHAUS'S

LARRY CINDY

HOLLY

LINDSEY

the parade of power poles, the neat silos dotting the distance like fingers skyward . . . suddenly wetness spangled my cheek. I pulled Migrant over and clicked pictures, hoping not to worry anyone with my attention.

You can visit the spot yourself, just south of the junction of County VV and Squirrel Hollow Road in some town—I'm not sure which—in Wisconsin. Depending on the time of day and the time of your life, you may find it as exalting as the Sistine Chapel—or nothing special. For me the beauty of the place depended on its usualness. Here was America—its order, its industry, its decency and confidence and kindness. How dare we respond with less than praise.

iii.

The road rushes but Hubert lingers.

Hubert Humphrey practiced the politics of joy. His face was round and happy. His alliterative name was happy. (Parents who christen their kid Hubert Horatio Humphrey must be feeling fine.) He began his career as a pharmacist and most pharmacists I've known were happy. Happy Hubert came from a happy state. His eyes twinkled. Finally, in 1968, he got the nomination for President he'd wanted for years. He was happy. And the nation had never been more glum.

The collision between Hubert's buoyancy and the nation's despondency was bad for both. How could anybody smile after our losses in Vietnam and the assassinations of Martin Luther King, Jr., and Bobby Kennedy? Hubert, with his shining eyes and Humpty Dumpty bravado, seemed a little loopy.

Hubert did not see it that way. That terrible things had happened didn't make America terrible. Think of all we'd accomplished. Remember how the Minneapolis Police Department was purged of anti-Semitism and racism when he was Mayor? And how the national Democratic party was transformed, at the convention of 1948, from a party for Southern whites into a party for all? (Hubert's incendiary speech still soars: "To those who say, my friends, to those who say, that we are rushing this issue of civil rights, I say to them we are 172 years too late! To those who say, this civil rights program is an infringement on states' rights, I say this: the time has arrived in America for the Democratic Party to get out of the shadow of states' rights and walk forthrightly into the bright sunshine of human rights!") And what about all our new laws protecting blacks, women, sick folks, old folks, poor folks, workers on the job, our natural resources? America could do miracles, my friends, we had and we would, you only had to believe.

Hubert was happy but I and my schoolmates weren't buying. Objecting to America had become our identity. Despising Lyndon Johnson—and nightstick-brandishing pigs—and the suits who made us cut our hair and put on our pants—and who drafted us and locked us up for a puff of weed—and who offed anybody they didn't like (this was the heyday of conspiracy theories)—made us feel important. How often do kids change the world! Clean Gene McCarthy was our man, then Bobby, but after Bobby was rubbed out (and who *was* Sirhan Sirhan working for, anyway?), we got . . . Hubert? Hubert was LBJ's lapdog. For his decades of making America a more decent nation we gave him no credit. The issue we cared about was Vietnam. And on Vietnam Hubert was stuck. Oppose LBJ's policies and LBJ would block his nomination. Support the war, no matter how tepidly, and his lifelong allies would abandon him in disgust.

Rage over a single issue blinded voters to the deep differences between the candidates. Instead of Happy Hubert we elected Tricky Dick (by a whisker). Nixon brought us anger and Agnew and Watergate. The recovery of America's optimism was deferred 12 years.

I'd like to tell Hubert "sorry." He'd brush off my apology with a laugh—why, my friend, America is *about* making mistakes—but unfairness is not so easy to forget. I had no doubts in 1968. I knew who wore black hats and who wore white. I was sure—and wrong. Happy, sensible, equable Hubert was the leader we needed to set us right.

His happiness lifts from his epitaph. "I enjoyed my life. Its disappointments are outweighed by its pleasures. I have loved my country in a way that some people consider sentimental and out of style. I still do."

iv.

The voice on the telephone: "Where are you now?"
"That's a trick question."

Last night it was Prairie Garden, Illinois—about as near to Chicago as I could camp. Big cities and RVs do not mix. RVs occupy too much real estate and RVers won't pay more than 30, at most 40 dollars a night. Also, there's the grime. RVers lounge in folding chairs beneath awnings. Big city air is not conducive to lounging. I like cities but not in my RV. Darting traffic startles me—especially those gum-chewing hotshots who gun past vans on the right. These boys are still immortal, and contemptuous of RVers. They can't imagine a day that will find *them* in one of those crates! I tend to think of myself as their age, but their glances disabuse me. I am a man with an AARP card in his wallet. I am older than my father.

You'd think Chicago would have given us a lot of Presidents and Vice Presidents, but there's only one, Charles Gates Dawes, and he was really from Ohio. Dawes is one of two banker Vice Presidents.[16] Bankers make unlikely politicians, more interested in money than men. Their profession makes them unpopular. They have funds, which we want. They are owed. Miss a mortgage or a car payment by a day or two and they're down your throat. Bank applications make us feel nakeder than a physical exam. The skeptical scrutiny of a loan officer silently rebukes: "Is that all you're worth?"

Dawes's tomb looks like a banker's. It's a mausoleum—not too lavish—in the Doric temple style. Peering through the cobwebbed metal grate I can make out three, maybe four marble caskets in the dimness, stacked like currency. Dawes was a leading man in his day. He was awarded the Nobel Peace Prize in 1924 for his work reorganizing German reparations payments after the first World War. The "Dawes plan," as it was called, put off the Second World War for a while, but that's not how they saw it in 1924.

---

[16]The other is Garret Hobart. Levi P. Morton (Vice President, 1889–1893) was an *investment* banker, a buyer and seller of companies, not a keeper of deposits or issuer of loans.

Dawes's peace was intended to last forever, not a decade. Calvin Coolidge disliked his Vice President, who embarrassed him by napping through a tie-breaking vote in the Senate.[17] For the first time in more than 60 years a Presidential nomination was rejected, by a single vote, while Dawes dozed.

Schuyler Colfax's grave is in a run-down section of South Bend, Indiana. The lettering on his headstone is worn almost to invisibility. I'd like to celebrate Colfax as a fellow newspaperman, but the evidence is, newspapermen fare poorly near the Presidency. Warren Harding was a newspaperman. Horace Greeley, who heckled Lincoln and lost to Grant in 1872, was a newspaperman. Dan Quayle and Al Gore began as reporters. Maybe it's the cockiness that comes of being a newspaperman that undoes us. Newspapermen sometimes believe we make the news we report. We are used to being petted by publicity-seekers (which includes most politicians). Our acquaintance with issues, while wide, tends to be thin. Politics is harder than reporting. Politicians have to find a way to make change happen. I wonder, was it frustration that led the self-righteous Colfax to accept kickbacks when he was Grant's Vice President? Only two of our Presidents and Vice Presidents exploited their office for material gain—a gratifyingly small percentage in light of the temptation. Colfax joins Spiro Agnew in our pantheon of Greed.

v.

More prairie.

The width of America is an exhausting miracle.

Driving, I listen. First to tapes: history lectures from The Teaching Company; audio-books. There is no end of knowing, but concentration wanes. Ten minutes the mellow voice has been telling me—what? I rewind. But my brain, like a sullen teenager, won't unlatch its door.

I try music. Satellite radio is one of those splendidly superfluous American innovations—safety pin, paperclip, VCR, zipper, etc. For a few bucks a month you get limitless music, entertainment, and news, without static. No more scratchy scanning past twanging bands, preachers, sell-a-thons, for something, anything, to listen to. Mozart, Bach, Bruckner, Menotti, Copland—I drink for hours. But still the road stretches.

---

[17] The Vice President's sole Constitutional duty, as President of the Senate, is to vote in a tie.

I think about my journey, now at its midpoint. Think is not the verb. My mind drifts, like a spoor. The man I thought I was would never have lit out across America for no reason. He was hell-bent—not ambling like this—toward what?

If I can't make myself out, maybe I can reach some conclusions about the Presidents. What makes a good President? Historians seem to have settled on a ranking system: best and worst lists are an American disease. It's silly—John Adams vying with John Kennedy for fourteenth versus fifteenth; Polk squaring off against LBJ. Better how? Is lemonade better than artichoke?

Criteria tiptoe out of the whirr, alliterating into a little poem: *Values, Vision, Efficacy, and Effect.* That's it!

→ *Values*: The President, our symbolic citizen, must embody values we respect.

→ *Vision*: He must lead where we need to go. (Bush the First, by derogating "the vision thing," demonstrated the inadequacy of his conception.)

→ *Efficacy*: He (or she) must be capable of getting things done; and

→ *Effect*: What he—or she—does, in hindsight, must prove worth the doing.

Values, Vision, Efficacy, and Effect.
Tires on interminable pavement.
Values, Vision, Efficacy, and Effect.
Easily said.

vi.

Again I find myself in one of those dead-end RV campgrounds where vacant lives are passed in corroding cartons. This is in the woods—in a bog, really—so it's not as mean or squalid as the hell-hole I happened on in Cleveland. Fat rabbits proliferate, tame on tossed scraps.

In six weeks I will be home for a three-month spell and I'm tense. Damn Thoreau for his deceptive sunniness, his refusal even to hint at grief. He reminds me of a precocious adolescent who hasn't the confidence to admit lack of confidence.

The home we return to is never the home we left. I will have been away for 92 days. I have been in communication—by telephone, e-mail—with friends and relatives. I have visited various family members along the way. Everything will be the same—only, nothing will.

I steel myself for the question, "What is your book about?" It is natural enough. We hunger for 10-second synopses.

In outline, I know what this book's about: a trip; America; our leaders; me. Part chronicle, part travel, part history, part meditation, it is a portrait of a moment. As with any picture, its sole justification is its appeal.

I feel some pressure to arrive at a Therefore, to emulate Thoreau with a stirring exhortation. But that would be a pose. The truth is that truth is hard to figure. This run-down camp may seem dismal to me, yet a paradise to that little girl out my window gaily chasing a rotund rabbit. The rabbit doesn't run far so he senses it's a game. His pink wiggling nostrils almost constitute a grin.

Therefores are delusions, redoubts from doubt. We proclaim "I believe" out of panic lest we don't. Who concludes excludes, narrows reality to a habitable hut.

My faith is in the truth. If I keep seeing and saying, maybe I'll arrive at some Yes too persuasive to resist. Or maybe not. I don't much care—as long as there's a new world out my window each morning—beckoning— with its dreamy smile.

10
New York

i.

The roar and spume of Niagara Falls are as advertised. Mini-cams shrink wonders to clichés. We have seen before we see.

The people, though, startle.

We've trekked from all corners of the world—Indians in their saris, Africans with their accents, shoulder-rubbing Asians, doe-eyed newly-weds, paddling second-honeymooners, harried Texans with towheads in tow, as polyglot a mix as a UNICEF Christmas card. Yet cameras click and jaws gape in unison.

Disembarking, pleasantly sprayed, from The Maid of the Mist (VII, I think its number was), I notice two shapely legs standing alone. They are tanned and fit and shaved from ankle to hem—high hem—of khaki shorts. Above the shorts are a modest pea-green T-shirt and backpack, then bright auburn hair braided like a sweet-roll.

The tourist at this juncture has a choice of hoofing it back up the cliff or taking the elevator. I'd been of a mind to take the elevator but this vision of an attractive young woman alone makes me think a hike might do me good.

I study the tensing and relaxing of her calves as she climbs. Arriving at the landing they proceed briskly through the leafy park.

I have no designs on these calves beyond catching up with their owner and perhaps exchanging a word. One thing can lead to another but doesn't usually.

Unexpectedly she swerves from path to grass and is crouching onto a brown blanket where a man sits cross-legged—and from which four small arms sprout. The language is middle European, not one I can name. Momma had taken a break while Poppa tended the brood. They are re-united, and glad.

I hurry on, curious, even now, as to her face.

147

ii.

We should always be driving east at sunset, the sun plating our prospect, not stabbing us in the eyes.

September weekends in western New York are a terrible wonderful time. Farm stands brim with produce—tomatoes, melons, squash, berries, potatoes, peppers, peaches, cucumbers, grapes, plums—soon to be blighted by frost. Buying my four ripe tomatoes for two dollars, the proprietress plaintively offers me a bushel for eight. There is scant time remaining for yard sales before cold, so every other house, it seems, has debouched its contents onto the lawn. The bric-a-brac and broken toys and hand-me-downs whisper powerfully.

If western New York were a separate state, it would belong to the Great Lakes cluster. Michigan, Wisconsin, Minnesota, and Ohio would welcome a fifth to the cultivation of these fertile rolling hills and the navigation of these vast inland waters. Rochester or Syracuse or Buffalo might be a capital, memorized by schoolchildren.

New York, though, is Manhattan, the capital of the world. That's where the people are, the money, the attention. Tell folks you're from New York and they think traffic, Broadway, 9/11, not lakes and silos and cows.

We are measured by comparison. Being less takes the strut out of our stride. Julius Caesar once remarked that he'd rather be the first man in a flyblown outpost of empire than the second man in Rome. A second-rateness hangs over western New York. The towns and cities feel bypassed. The soil is rich, the waters plentiful, but ambition has fled. The Erie Canal, once the aorta of a nation, now flows unruffled except by loons and the infrequent boater.

There was a time—it is hard to think this now—when western New York produced Presidents. Grover Cleveland vaulted from Mayor of Buffalo to the White House in less than two years. Two forgotten Vice Presidents—Hayes's William Almon Wheeler and Taft's "Sunny Jim" Sherman—hailed from Utica and Malone.

The difficult decades before the Civil War were colored by a quarrel between two Cayuga county boys. Millard Fillmore (1800–1874) and William Seward (1801–1872), on paper, were peas in a pod. Fillmore was born in Moravia, in the Finger Lakes district; Seward, from early adulthood, made his home in Auburn, the town next door. Both were lawyers who launched their careers in the Antimasonic party, shifting their allegiance to the newly formed Whigs in 1834. Both were protégés of legendary political boss

Thurlow Weed. While Seward served in the state Senate, Fillmore sat across the hall in the Assembly. While Seward was Governor, Fillmore was Congressman. When Fillmore was nominated as Zachary Taylor's Vice President in 1848, you'd think Seward would have been pleased for his long-time ally. Not one bit. With Weed's mysterious acquiescence, Seward set out to eviscerate Fillmore. When Taylor died and Fillmore became President, Seward hissed: "Providence has at last led the man of hesitations and double opinions to where decision and singleness are indispensable."

Seward's hatred hardly makes sense until one visits Auburn and Moravia. Fillmore was born in a cramped cabin, far from town. (His birth site, if you can find it, is marked by an empty field, a flagpole, a broken picnic table, and a road plaque.) A tall strapping handsome farmer, Fillmore was 17 before he saw a dictionary. He rose, as poor boys must, by industry, grace, and accommodation.

Where Fillmore was big and strong and dashing, Seward was tiny and ugly. He stood five-four and weighed little more than a hundred pounds. He had a huge nose. But he was rich. Both father and father-in-law were prominent judges and Seward swaggered. His home in Auburn stands as testament to his pride. You can feel the rage in its ostentation, his resentment at being denied the Presidency. And to think that that ignorant good-looking lout from Moravia should have made it to the top!

Fillmore might have made a good President. He was smart, conscientious, industrious, modest. But his strategy to prevent the Union from splitting over slavery, what history calls the Compromise of 1850, didn't work. No strategy, it appears now, was likely to. This probably was "an irrepressible conflict," as Seward intemperately observed. One doubts even Lincoln, had he reached the White House a decade earlier, could have saved the Union without war.

Seward made certain his loathsome rival was not nominated in 1852. The Whigs' eventual candidate, Mexican war hero General Winfield Scott, was drubbed and with him the Whig party. Seward later became a distinguished Secretary of State, under Lincoln and Andrew Johnson, forestalling Great Britain's embrace of the Confederacy and purchasing Alaska from the Russians (for a nickel an acre). Fillmore, misreading the temper of the times, joined the racist Know-Nothing party, and as their Presidential candidate in 1856 got the licking he deserved.

How might history have been different if these two Cayuga boys, this Mutt and Jeff, had hit it off? With Seward's brains and assurance and Fillmore's looks and charm, what mightn't they have achieved? Why, we wonder, didn't Boss Weed insist on their getting along, instead of siding with one against the other? How much of the tide of history, seemingly inexorable, can be traced to petty spite?

iii.

Oneida. I wake with a poem.

> so much depends
> upon
>
> a red wheel
> barrow
>
> glazed with rain
> water
>
> beside the white
> chickens.

A famous poem, I'd say, only today that's an oxymoron. Poetry is slow and hard; Americans are fast and easy. A poem that won't explain itself irks like an evasive witness.

This poem is by William Carlos Williams, a New Jersey physician. It hangs—or depends—from that first line like a raindrop from a bough. The twin senses of "depend"—of consequence and suspense—entwine: what happens after, what happens because. The least thing—a rain-slicked wheelbarrow beside chickens—alters the history of earth.

I think of our Presidents and Vice Presidents. For them, too, so much depends—on circumstance, geography, chance. In hindsight their careers seem inevitable: we speak of destiny, the mating of man and moment. Before they occurred, their ascents seemed improbable. Only four Presidents—out of 43[18]—strike us as foregone conclusions: Washington, Jackson, Grant, and Ike. But then we recall how these four became great generals, and no outcome seems farther-fetched. If General Howe had pursued Washington from Long Island in 1776; if a duelist's bullet had veered

---

[18]Really 42—stout Cleveland fills two slots.

half an inch closer to Jackson's heart; if Lincoln had been put off by Grant's drinking; if Colonel Eisenhower had not caught General MacArthur's eye . . . if, if, if.

For those who rise by politics, residence counts for more than capability or character. As of this writing, 13 Presidents and Vice Presidents have hailed from New York, 8 from Ohio, 6 from Indiana, and 5 each from Virginia and Massachusetts, 4 each from Tennessee and Texas. Had these men made their careers in less populous states—the Dakotas, say, or Delaware—they're less likely to have elbowed into history. Not even the two Roosevelts could have overcome geography with their large personalities.

Where we're from is who we are. Presidents and Vice Presidents raised in New York, while of various parties, share this coloration: they're politicians. New York breeds politicians because it's big, rich, and variegated. The money men of Manhattan have interests different from the farmers up north. Control of the state, since the beginning, has swung between parties. Campaigning has been rough-and-tumble. The country's first "political machine"—a murky but useful term—is credited to New York: Martin van Buren's "Albany Regency." Here, too, rose Tammany Hall, the most influential and rotten of the genre. New York bosses like Thurlow Weed and "Boss" Tweed and Tom Platt and Roscoe Conkling and Jim Farley manipulated national outcomes for eighty years. A New York candidate had to learn to cope with these complications. Candidates from more homogenous states could sail "above politics," espousing large principles. New Yorkers are trained to ceaselessly sniff for self-interest.

New York's crop of Presidents and Vice Presidents ranges from the inspired (the Roosevelts, and some would say Cleveland) to the impressive (George Clinton, Daniel Tompkins, Levi Morton, Nelson Rockefeller) to the wily (Aaron Burr, Martin van Buren) to the middling (Millard Fillmore, Chester Arthur) to the better-forgotten (Hayes's sour number two, William Almon Wheeler, and "Sunny Jim" Sherman of Utica). Whatever their parties or politics, all were pols. Political skills are useful in politics—knowing how to get things done—but they aren't enough. You need luck.

So much depends.

iv.

I dreamed I was at Levi Morton's funeral. It wasn't crowded. He was old—96. It was 27 years since he'd been Vice President. Many Americans

151

no longer knew his name. Rhinebeck, a village on the Hudson River, wasn't easy to get to (this was 1920). Neighbors followed the casket, and a few local worthies. Others sent notes.

How different an occasion, I thought, if this had been *President* Morton. And it would have been. In 1880, Republican nominee James Garfield had invited Morton to be his Vice President. Morton accepted, but then the New York boss, Senator Roscoe Conkling, told Morton not to. Conkling wanted more out of Garfield than a worthless Vice Presidency. He wanted assurances that the spoils of victory, New York's patronage jobs, would be his to dispense. Morton was no pushover—self-made, he'd amassed one of the country's largest fortunes[19]—but he bowed to Conkling's wish.

If Morton had held to his acceptance—and the deranged assassin, Charles Guiteau, had gotten off his shot—Morton, not Chester Arthur, would have become President a year later. And unlike his fellow New Yorker, who had no trouble defying Conkling and accepting this windfall, Morton might have found a way to keep the job.

Morton was supposed to be Secretary of the Treasury—that, at least, was Conkling's plan. The Secretary of the Treasury, unlike the Vice President, had jobs at his disposal. President Garfield had a different idea. He wanted to get rid of the spoils system. So, to everybody's surprise, did President Arthur. Conkling stormed—but it was too late. The high tide of the bosses' power had passed. The Pendleton Act, providing for open competitive exams for government jobs and shielding civil servants from political pressure, became law in 1883. In 1884, Americans chose a grumpy newcomer as President, New York's Grover Cleveland, whose sole credential was his honesty. Americans were sick of being ignored. They wanted their leaders answering to them, not to unseen puppeteers.

Morton, a prodigious fund-raiser, was awarded various consolation prizes, including, in 1888, his party's nomination as Vice President. Benjamin Harrison did not die in office (though he might have felt like it). Morton was not renominated as Vice President in 1892, not that it would have mattered. In 1896, Morton, now Governor of New York, sought the Republican nomination for President and placed fourth.

---

[19]Morton is our first instance of a conspicuously successful plutocrat seeking political office. The rich, from Andrew Jackson's presidency onward, did not dirty their hands by pressing the flesh. Politicians were servants. Morton, like Teddy Roosevelt, FDR, Averell Harriman, the Rockefellers, the Kennedys, John Heinz, John Corzine, and Mike Bloomberg after him, recognized that refusal to do battle in the arena disqualified them from condemning the result.

Morton was not one to complain. Life had been good to him. He'd started with nothing. He'd grown rich beyond imagining. He'd risen higher in government than any Wall Street graduate, before or since. He'd been Congressman, Ambassador, Vice President, Governor, partner of J. P. Morgan—not bad for a poor parson's kid from Vermont. He'd lived longer, by half a dozen years, than any previous President or Vice President.[20]

Yet how often, before sleep, must his thoughts have returned to that hot smoky hotel room in Chicago, June 1880. His heart was high with the prospect of becoming Vice President. He was ready; he'd said yes. But then Senator Conkling was shaking his head gloomily.

Morton did not much like "Lord" Roscoe. But he believed in his power and was reluctant to oppose it. Chester Arthur had no such compunction. He was used to accepting what was offered. Conkling, sulking at the rejection of his Presidential candidate, ex-President Grant, wanted *no* New Yorker on this filthy Garfield ticket. He'd told Chet Arthur that—Chet, who owed him *everything*! But Arthur, out of—what? disloyalty? greed? a surge of patriotism? a sense of destiny?—had disobeyed! Why, Morton must have asked himself over and over, till sleep spared him, hadn't *he* had the nerve?

v.

Maybe the oddest marital arrangement of our Presidents was FDR's. We have had philanderers aplenty and May-December weddings and a bachelor who favored men and a married man who may have[21] and wives who were emotionally incapacitated and myrmidons who ruled their husbands and love-matches so firm they seemed a turret against the world. But only FDR was so obviously married to his mother.

The facts one knows from books: how, a beloved only child, young Franklin's papa died when Franklin was 18 and the boy lived the rest of his life, until four years before his own death, in his mother's house. One knows from his mother's desperate reaction to the news of Franklin's engagement at 21 and Franklin's slavering attempts to mollify her, the strength of this emotional umbilicus. Eleanor herself testifies, with chilling matter-of-factness,

---

[20]Morton, our longest surviving President or Vice President, lived three years longer than Reagan.

[21]Did Lincoln and his soldierly bedmates get it on? Don't we have better questions to explore?

how her mother-in-law made all the decisions about the grandchildren as they arrived, relegating Eleanor to the role of companion, stage wife, and baby-machine. One can hardly doubt, from early photographs and Franklin's protestations, that he loved Eleanor. But it seems, in light of his various extramarital liaisons, that he loved as a pasha loves: wife two, three, and twenty may be delectable, but there's no question who's wife number one.

The facts are unusual. But only by visiting Springwood, Sarah Delano Roosevelt's home in Hyde Park where Franklin was born, buried, and lived all his life, can one feel the enveloping weirdness of this ménage. Sarah is ubiquitous. Her portraits are everywhere, at all ages, busty as a ship's figurehead. We see the little office where she made the arrangements for the estate. We see noble sculptures and portraits of the adored Franklin. And where's Eleanor? Cramped in a narrow room between her husband's and her mother-in-law's bedrooms, as if to keep them apart. One feels Eleanor's suffocation and frustration, her need finally to flee to her own cottage on a far corner of the estate, leaving her husband and his mother in their nest. When in 1939, King George VI and his wife Elisabeth visited the Roosevelts, the official photograph, taken on the porch, includes five: Eleanor and the king on the right, Franklin and the queen on the left, and in the middle, forward as a prow, Sarah, queen of all.

Our characters leave clues to their nature, little windows, like those peepholes onto construction sites. Some characters are transparent, unafraid to show themselves; others huddle in the dimness. One clue to James Buchanan, for example, is his bizarre signature: the tail of his florid J coils half the length of all the letters, like a snake. Here was a soul preoccupied with appearances, with an exact and prissy perfection. A clue to Calvin Coolidge is the two-seat privy in his Vermont homestead, a tacit rebuke to all luxury or show. The oversized white marble bust over Martin van Buren's desk in Kinderhook—of the man himself—proclaims the occupant's insecurity, his insatiable need to boast.

FDR's domestic arrangements give away the man. We understand better his infectious, imperturbable smile, the engaging smugness of a boy who knows he is safe and adored. The two principal challenges of maturity Roosevelt didn't have to tackle: getting a living and getting loved. They were already, for all time, taken care of, freeing him to focus on wooing and winning the multitude.

That Eleanor endured her demotion and went on to establish a confident public identity and productive career is a moving saga of self-reclamation. How painful it must have been to be always second—or third—or umpteenth in line for her splendid husband's regard. FDR's famous terrier Fala is buried almost as close to the great man as Eleanor herself. Were there nights when she envied even a Scottie its hug?

vi.

Wrestling sheets like Laocoon, weird notions ricocheting like trapped bats. It feels like Halloween in my mind—not the sweet Kodak Halloween of parading tots, but the dark Halloween of smashed pumpkins and whooping teens.

Seeking the cause of sleeplessness is a futile exercise, but hey, what else are you going to do, lying rigid, praying for release? Was it something I ate? Something I saw? Something I fear? Do great souls suffer such nights? I sometimes fantasize encountering, say, a President or Pope at the refrigerator door, fumbling for a glass of juice.

Perhaps it is what I saw yesterday. Mansions. Along the Hudson. Relics of that age we call gilded.

I admire America. But there are passages of our nation's past, as there are of my own, I cringe at. The decades between the end of the Civil War and the arrival of Teddy Roosevelt make me want to look away. Maybe the poet Hardy had them in mind when he described his sea-worm: "grotesque, blind, dumb, indifferent."

We have always been, at our best, a proving-ground of ideals. The "shining city on the hill," the founders' republic, Jacksonian democracy, Manifest Destiny, the abolition of slavery—these vast and stirring goals drew us out of ourselves. That dreaming intensity returned in the twentieth century, as we battled behemoths—the inadvertent cruelty of capitalism, the Huns, Hitler, Stalin, racism, sexism, pollution—and strove crazily to reach the moon. In the late nineteenth century, however, the gleam in our eye was replaced by the feverish flicker of cupidity. To hell with ideals, which had left 600,000 young Americans dead in the Civil War! We were going to enjoy life, grab all we could, and ignore the whimpers of the impotent. Survival of the fittest—hurrah!

Immersion in the art and architecture and politics of this period leaves me feeling bloated, as after a debauch. My stomach is sour and I can smell the cigar smoke in my clothes. What got into us? We knew better. Yet somehow we forgot.

The proliferent mansions of the Vanderbilt scions assail me especially. The one in Hyde Park, New York, a few doors down from Sarah Roosevelt's, is typical. It is gorgeous, of course: one of those faux-palaces favored by the plutocracy and extravagantly realized by the likes of Richard Morris Hunt and Stanford White. A tall pillared palazzo poised high on the eastern bank of the Hudson, it gleams in the sunset like Wotan's Valhalla. The high-ceilinged rooms knock your eyes out—movie sets before there were movies.

In public buildings such grandeur may be grand, for it honors all. In a private residence, designed to be occupied for perhaps a month a year, it appalls. Though no revolutionary, I can imagine myself gleefully toppling these pomposities. And it's not as if this particular Vanderbilt or his siblings ever did much but be born. Their grandfather amassed the pile, and their father increased it, to where it seemed impossible to stay its inexorable rise. This generation did little more than live exquisitely and labor manfully to spend.

Interesting homes, for me, are the homes of interesting people. Who can abide the vapid exhibitionism of the oblivious rich? It enrages, suffocates, ignores and insults our republican premise. It also ruins the lives of its proprietors. Whatever these pretty puppets had in them they couldn't express. They had a "duty"—to live suitably and keep their noses aloft.

The politics of the period reflects this perversion. "Gentlemen," needless to say, did not stand for elective office. A public servant was like a household servant, someone you hired. Messrs. Johnson (Andrew), Grant, Hayes, Garfield, Arthur, Cleveland, Harrison, and McKinley were not bad guys: they tried to do right, as they saw it. But they were powerless to swim against the tide of wealth. Elections were bought and sold and the people knew it, but what could they do? The great capitalist captains and their party bosses were too mighty to oppose.

We grow by oscillation. We strive, we rest. We dare, we are cautious. We despise the face in the mirror, we blow it kisses.

Impossible adolescents give way to imposing adults. In the twentieth century, beginning with Teddy Roosevelt, the people wrested power from the plutocrats. We became less obnoxious as a nation, more mindful of our variety. We humbled ourselves by our mistakes, even as we grew mightier.

Our idealism did not die in the Gilded Age; it was only dormant. It can still be heard rumbling in the rebukes of Mark Twain and Henry James; in the courage of labor organizers; in reform of the civil service; in muckraking and a willingness to question our magnificence. Gradually we opened our eyes to what asses we'd been. The gaudy mansions were put up for sale when their owners died—and found no buyers.

Across the Hudson from the Vanderbilt Mansion, on the western bank, is Holy Cross Monastery. The brethren there forsake all possessions, all worldly ambition, and live simple lives of prayer, poverty, chastity, and service. The founding prior of Holy Cross Monastery was a refugee from the ruling class. He too was a product of the Gilded Age.

vii.

I knew Nelson Rockefeller slightly. He lived down the road and was always running. As a fledgling reporter I'd be invited to press receptions at the Rockefeller estate in Pocantico Hills. You went when invited, to say you had. The receptions would be held in a high-ceilinged complex called "the Playhouse." Before the Governor's arrival, we would mill and gawk, pretending to be comfortable. Like the Vanderbilts, the Rockefellers practiced brutal ostentation. They lived behind guarded gates in a vastness that made you feel small. They moved in a swarm of toadies and retainers.

In America anybody can become rich, which is why the rich are resented. The trudging majority assume the rich are either lucky or crooks (unless they're inventors or celebrities, for whom we make an exception). We wince with envy—why them and not me! We exult in the mishaps of the rich. In an aristocracy, where ranks are fixed, the lower orders can respect, even love their masters, but not in America. In America, we itch to deflate those whose success demotes us.

The American rich barricade themselves in citadels. They huddle in enclaves and clubs. Those who earn their fortunes are unlikely to be frightened by the mob. Their heirs, less capable, turn timid and exclusive. Snobbery is panic. Only small souls treat others as small.

For Nelson Rockefeller, politics was penance. He would demonstrate that despite the gates and walls and bowling allies and golf course and liveried servants, he was no hothouse plant, too tender to endure the common air. He would use his wealth to prove wealth hadn't ruined him. He would be average if it killed him.

There was something both gallant and pathetic in his desperation. He smiled so hard you feared his face would crack. He greeted strangers with exorbitant ebullience. "Hi ya, fella!" he gripped my hand, and every other.

He needed to be President. If he'd stayed faithful to his first wife, he might have won the Republican nomination in 1964. America, though, wasn't ready for a philandering chief. The lady who became the second

Mrs. Rockefeller, Happy Murphy, like King Edward VIII's Wallis Simpson, was reviled as Jezebel.

Findagrave.com did not indicate that Rockefeller's resting place was private. The sentry at the gate grew huffy as I pleaded. Did this pampered son of privilege, who'd striven so hard to be a man of the people, want to be the *only* President or Vice President whom the people could not call on? "That's his business, isn't it?" the man reddened. "Who do you think you are?"

I asked for someone to whom I could appeal my dismissal. "Why don't you get lost?" he waved. I'm unused to being treated as scum. The comedy engaged me. To be arrested for trying to visit the grave of Nelson Rockefeller—that would make a chapter!

The sentry's superior was smoother but equally firm. No visitors—family's orders. Was there anyone in the family I could talk to? No. What, I asked, was the family afraid of? I'd visited John D.'s obelisk in Cleveland. He was not afraid.

A friend had pointed me to the location of the Rockefeller cemetery, at the north end of Sleepy Hollow Cemetery, on Route 9. Andrew Carnegie, Washington Irving, Samuel Gompers, Mark Hellinger, and Walter Chrysler are buried in Sleepy Hollow. Visits to their graves are encouraged.

I stopped at the cemetery office. Two amiable men in parkas chuckled at my request. The Rockefellers' adamant seclusion amused them. The rich—what can you do?

I tramped around the mile or so of tall metal fence. The sky was gray. Rain was coming. Leaves were falling. Sleepy Hollow Cemetery is large and old. It would not be hard to clamber over the fence unnoticed, but I was wearing the wrong clothes. My amusement and irritation grew. This was funny—and not funny. Who'd ever heard of a private cemetery? In life, perhaps, consorting with the hoi polloi was repugnant, but in death? American cemeteries resemble America. There are better and worse neighborhoods, but the roads pass between them unhindered.

By now my shoes were wet and I was mad. Who did they think they were to keep my Vice President away from me! Our Presidents and Vice Presidents have given themselves to history. Can the gift be taken back?

I planned my invasion. I would return wearing jeans, sneakers, and work gloves, at three or so in the afternoon, as the light began to dim. I would park a way off and carry my rope ladder to a secluded spot behind the Chrysler mausoleum. I would snap my picture and clamber back, pulse racing. And if I were nabbed for trespassing? Well, that would be part of the story too. Is stealing an image, your honor, stealing?

Driving away in the rain, I thought of Nelson. Did he want to be barred from the people whom all his life he had reached for? The flushed sentry insisted that the Vice President knew about his final resting place and this was what he wanted. I wondered. The Vice President had died naked in the arms of a young female aide. He hadn't, I'm betting, been contemplating death at the time.

Among the comforts of cemeteries is their inadvertent society. Samuel Gompers and Andrew Carnegie can talk labor unions. Gompers of London, England, Chrysler of Wamego, Kansas, and Carnegie of Dumferline, Fife, all born poor, can marvel at the paths that ended here. Mark Hellinger can invite Washington Irving to a Broadway show: Irving loved the theater.

The Rockefellers enjoy the company of Rockefellers. No new faces, no variety, no visitors. When I finally found myself before Nelson's modest marker, I could almost feel his relief from the monotony. "Hi ya, fella!" he gripped me, smiling hard.

viii.

"Who is buried in Grant's tomb?" The guests on Groucho Marx's TV quiz show hesitated. Afraid of being made to look foolish, they made themselves look foolish.

The answer, of course, is America's Ulysses and his beloved Julia, in our biggest Presidential grave. Under a soaring cupola, their two elephantine sarcophagi are cramped in a dim well. (Technically, the National Park Ranger reminds me, the Grants aren't *buried* but *entombed* here—burial is *beneath* ground—though that wasn't Groucho's point.) No President sleeps less fittingly. Grant had his faults, enough to land him near the basement of most Presidential ratings, but vanity wasn't one.

No American leader is harder to figure. A genius in battle, a fool in politics. Modest in demeanor, a glutton for applause. Keen judge of soldiers, dupe of civilians. Personally incorruptible, overseer of our most corrupt Administration to date.[22] He hated hurting animals, yet was more willing than any general to spend the lives of his men. Taciturn in speech, he was eloquent in prose. A drunken knockabout before 1861, he became our most lauded hero after.

---

[22]Some might argue Harding's was more corrupt. Grant's and Harding's management styles were similar. Easy-going, chummy, they delegated and didn't look too hard.

Three vast presences hover over the Civil War. Lincoln we know: a soul whose decency and wisdom and magnanimity seem never to end. The more we learn of Lincoln, the greater he grows. He is our moral touchstone, the ideal to which we aspire.

Lee is similarly haloed. Military analysts may debate his tactics, but no one slanders his character. Wise, courageous, generous, empathetic, unflinching, he and his relative, George Washington, are our two noble Romans. Their probity and devotion seem beyond our ken.

Grant—part of him—is a national embarrassment. America in 1868 craved leadership. We were ready for it. A reunited nation elected its new President practically by acclamation. And what did Grant do with his chance? Drifted. Trusted crooks and bumblers. Let southern supremacists resume their oppression of blacks. Abandoned the Indian, to whom he had made promises. Allowed greedy scumbags to embroil the country in scandal. Charity may pardon Pierce and Buchanan their haplessness: even Lincoln might not have been able to save the union in the decade before the Civil War. Of Harding's reviled Administration, one might shrug, well, America didn't want much leadership just then, feeling snug and smug. Grant had the power and the mandate and the moment; on his vision and guidance the shape of our rescued nation would depend. And he funked it. It took almost a century—till the Civil Rights and Voting Rights acts of 1964 and 1965—to clean up the mess Grant left. (The Indians never recovered.)

A Grant dartboard would be in order. But then it was Grant, as much as anyone, who saved us. Without Grant's cool, clear understanding of war, without his courage and confidence and uncanny aptitude for selecting and inspiring generals, it's likely the Confederacy would have prevailed and our continent been doomed to an interminable debilitating feud between south and north. And without Grant's generosity and humility and sense of the tragedy of the Civil War, it's likely the aftermath, rancorous as it was, would have been worse. The surrender at Appomattox, April 9, 1865, may be our proudest American moment. That brothers fought is an old story. That brothers who slaughtered each other for four years could embrace at the close, suppressing their vindictive impulse, is a miracle. Lee was noble at Appomattox, maintaining the dignity of his cause in the ignominy of defeat; but Grant was nobler. The defeated have few options; victors may whoop, gloat, humiliate. Grant was incapable of gloating: men, to him, were men, who though they might err, deserved to be treated with respect.

Reading Grant's *Memoirs*, one of the few examples of this windy genre that could be called literature, it's as if all the faults in his character fall away, and we see him shining. What startles is Grant's innocence. He accepts himself and others as they are: without glamour or self-reproach, cynicism or sentiment, fear or favor. He is not trying to cook history's books or settle scores. He understands, as perhaps only a soldier can, who has witnessed so many random deaths, that we are all accidents, that only fools swagger. He smiles at his ascent as if from a height. Grant's clarity made him a first-rate general and writer. He could see through the fog of ego to the facts. It also made him a bad politician. On the battlefield, facts dictate; observe them clearly and you will know what must be done. In politics, direction must be generated. The course of state is a matter of opinion. A strong President must be destiny-deluded, convinced of his necessity. Small egos need not apply.

Grant failed as President, yet it's impossible not to like him, then and now. The most celebrated man of his age, cheered by kings and throngs, he exhibits not a trace of conceit. He writes of his first military victory, in the Mexican War, "My exploit was equal to that of the soldier who boasted that he had cut off the leg of one of the enemy. When asked why he did not cut off his head, he replied: 'Someone had done that before.'" Of his lauded adversary, he writes: "The natural disposition of most people is to clothe a commander of a large army whom they do not know, with almost superhuman abilities. A large part of the National army, for instance, and most of the press of the country, clothed General Lee with just such qualities, but I had known him personally, and knew that he was mortal; and it was just as well that I felt this." To Grant, one size fit all: human-size. His religion was simple: "In positions of great responsibility, everyone should do his duty to the best of his ability where assigned by competent authority." Do your duty, and you'll have done all.

Groucho's question was wiser than he knew. It is not really Grant who's buried in Grant's tomb, or dowdy, squint-eyed Julia, but a pair of auctioned stiffs. Cocky New York City, to advertise its preeminence, bid highest for the privilege of housing our most famous corpse.[23] The Grants put up with their accommodations not because they're comfortable, but because they're free—and grand—like the White House. And they've nowhere else to go.

---

[23]Destitute at the end of his life, having been duped in business, Grant needed to make money. His need resulted in his indispensable *Autobiography*, which he finished while writhing with jaw cancer. Shopping his and Julia's remains was another way to bring in a few bucks.

ix.

Manhattan is too busy for history. St. Mark's-in-the-Bowery, a treasure that any other American city would acclaim, grows gaunt as a portionless widow. Here is the spiritual home of New York's first first families; a fine sample of Colonial architecture; the burial place of fierce Governor Peter Stuyvesant (whose farm or "bouerie" gave the name to this district); Daniel Tompkins, Vice President during the Monroe Administration (1817–1825); and Colonel Nicholas Fish, a Revolutionary war hero and progenitor of the noted Fish family. What these stones might tell! Washington, the elder Adams, members of the first Congress, Alexander Hamilton, Aaron Burr, Washington Irving, the James boys (William and Henry), Martin van Buren, Millard Fillmore, must all have paused beneath this portico. Maybe young Teddy Roosevelt was brought here by his parents. (The Bowery, until the mid-1870s, was Manhattan's theatre district—until flophouses, sa-loons, cheap cafes, and pawn shops turned it sordid.)

The imagination bounds. But what we see, in this richest city in the rich-est nation, is a landmark en route to rot. Plaster dangles off the ceiling; the churchyard, where grass should grow, has been bricked over in bleak geometries; pastel flyers flap from doorposts; an overgrown "contempla-tion garden" is padlocked; in the furniture-less sanctuary a meditation ses-sion is in progress, with a score of slack middle-agers sitting cross-legged on the carpet. There are no historical brochures, no one who knows. Daniel Tompkins's tomb, fading to illegibility, is unmarked even by a flag.

x.

Andrew Carnegie and Henry Clay Frick didn't like each other. Not at the end, maybe not ever. They had, as businessmen do, a chumship, not a friendship.

A chumship is a friendship feigned for pecuniary gain. Friends care for each other, without calculating gain; chums, only if it pays.

Business people sometimes mistake chums for friends. It makes life less lonely. I tried but never got the hang of it. I envied back-slappers, who could wish me happy birthday and ask about my kids as if they cared.

Carnegie and Frick were titans of the Golden Age of business. From the Civil War to the First World War, business captains were America's idols. Money then was the thing to make, not war, not movies. Railroad, automobile, telegraph, telephone, reaper, penicillin, cameras, light bulbs, zippers, crayons, corn flakes, elevators, electric chairs, barbed wire, machine guns, grocery bags, safety razors, rubber bands, sewing machines, soft drinks, staplers, typewriters—business was transforming life, for the better, it seemed, daily.

Carnegie made steel, a new thing, Frick made the coke needed to make steel, so the two got together, to make more steel—and money—than anyone else. Their chumship fell apart, as chumships will, over money. They ended up tangling in court, to the tabloids' delight.

Fifth Avenue was where you lived back then if you could afford to (unless you lived on Madison). Wherever you made your money, you flaunted it on Fifth. Carnegie lived at 50th Street, later 90th, Frick at 70th, their mutual chum J. P. Morgan on Madison at 36th.

Carnegie, Frick, and Morgan are remembered today not for what they made but for what they gave: Carnegie his libraries and concert hall and college; Frick and Morgan, their collections.[24] We gawk at the scale of their benefactions: Carnegie Hall, the Frick Museum, the Morgan Library: that men, not kings, could amass such treasure!

I float through the Frick, a somnambulist. There are pictures on the wall so vivid I seem to have dreamed them. From castles, cathedrals, palaces, chateaux, country homes, these works have been gathered, from the apses and throne rooms and foyers and salons where they hung, it was thought, forever. Is this their final stop, I wonder, or another way station in an endless wandering?

It's spooky, what these must have cost—not in dollars, which aren't easy to feel, but in lives. Frick was a hard driver. Men were to be used and discarded. He earned a reputation as the cruelest employer in the coal industry. Carnegie wrote books praising the working man. He believed himself

---

[24]Morgan, because history has a sense of humor, is also remembered for his strawberry nose. His sensitivity to his deformity was famous—and unsettling. "[The banker J. P.] Morgan terrified people," Paul Johnson recounts. "He was righteous, and the unrighteous trembled in his presence. So did many other people. He liked to give ladies gold trinkets at his dinner parties, but they were scared of him too. He was very conscious of the effects of his skin complaint, rhinophyma, which made his nose large, red, and swollen, to the delight of caricaturists. When Mrs. Dwight Morrow, the young wife of one of his partners, had to entertain him to tea, she instructed her four-year-old daughter, Euphemia, on no account to say anything about his nose. The little girl dutifully complied, and after she had sat on the great man's knee, her mother thankfully dismissed her to the nursery. Then she started pouring and said, 'Mr. Morgan, do you take nose in your tea?'"

the working man's friend. But he hired Frick to run his steel company, because he believed in profits more.

How many lives does it take to make a painting? To build the halls and skills and education and taste and idle hours to enjoy them? How many corpses fertilize a symphony?

It is better, savoring a coq au vin, to ignore the chicken's neck. Rejoice in what's before you: you could not have prevented it. Besides, death and defeat are in the nature of things. A few are born to mastery, most to drudgery, under any flag. It's the way things are.

My eyes feast. Still there's this uneasiness—not just for the laborers spent to fill this vault, but for the man inside. It's airless here, barred from the street, gazed at by so many dead. He's stuck, Mr. Frick, imprisoned by his stuff, approached in trepidation, at risk of being murdered if he ventures out. (Only the clumsiness of a would-be assassin spared him in 1892.) He's won, big time, not only wealth but fame. But was it worth it?

Walt Whitman, contemporary of Frick, Carnegie, and Morgan, celebrated everything American, our industrial genius no less than our liberty. But he sensed the danger of stuff-worship:

> Old institutions, these arts, libraries, legends, collections, and the practice
>   handed along in manufactures, will we rate them so high?
> Will we rate our cash and business high? I have no objection,
> I rate them as high as the highest—then a child born of a woman and
>   man I rate beyond all rate.

Andrew Carnegie, near the end of his life, wanted to reconcile with his old chum Frick. Having sold his company (to Morgan), Carnegie sought to be remembered as a benefactor, not a son-of-a-bitch. He dispatched an invitation down Fifth Avenue. Frick replied: "Tell Mr. Carnegie I'll see him in hell, where we're both going."

xi.

I keep trying to like Teddy Roosevelt. He perked up the Presidency, wrested America from the plutocrats, and restored ideals.

We'd grown fat and dull since Lincoln. Teddy's zest was infectious. The first White House advocate of exercise, he booted stuffy America out of its stuffed chair. He whooped and rode and boxed and grinned like nobody's business. He dug a canal and preserved a wilderness. He personalized the

164

Presidency, inviting the press into his family's privacy (from which his successors have been shooing them ever since).

Every President reflects his times but few embody them. Teddy, like Washington, Jefferson, Jackson, Lincoln, FDR, Kennedy, and Reagan, put his name on his era. These oversized personalities transform our national character. Who they are matters as much as what they do.

Teddy made the President our leader again, not just our dorm monitor. He exhorted, execrated, preached, pointed to the stars. By transforming the Presidency into a "bully pulpit," he led us to expect inspiration from that office. Sometimes we get it.

We owe Teddy a lot. I'd like to like him. Yet I find myself gritting my teeth. Partly it's the noise. He is always shouting. Shouting is bullying. It allows no room for other voices.

Then there's the violence. Teddy loved killing. "A just war," he told Congress, "is in the long run far better for a man's soul than the most prosperous peace." In Sagamore Hill, Teddy's weird shadowy mansion in Oyster Bay, the head, pelt, claw, hoof, or tusk of some creature Teddy shot peers from every nook.

Killing when you must is one thing; killing for fun is another. Killers forget there are souls. To a killer, a hippo—or a soldier—is a target. Killers tally their bag, speak of casualties casually.

Democracy demands leaders who can hack through the underbrush of obfuscation and obstruction. It demands leaders not too tender to opponents. Those who never offend never get anywhere. Legislating is war.

Great leaders are seldom great guys. They kill if they must. But it hurts them to pull a trigger or spring a trap.

Teddy gallops into our consciousness as a man impervious to pain—his own or anyone else's. He shoots and shoots—opponents, animals—with boisterous righteousness. Without compunction, it seems, he brought down the man he'd recruited to succeed him—the loyal, amiable, gentle William Howard Taft—because he disliked not being President. He blew up the Republican Party, which had given him his political life. He hankered for his sons to face death in the World War. Better that than dishonor!

Zealots unnerve me. Knowing without doubt, they have stopped thinking.

Teddy was a zealot. His assurance gained much that was good and necessary. He was a President whose actions I can hardly fault. Yet I shudder at his cruelty. "I don't go so far to think that the only good Indians are dead Indians," he wrote to a friend, "but I believe nine out of every ten are, and I shouldn't inquire too closely into the cause of the tenth." "I like to see a mob handled by the regulars, or by good State-Guards, not over-scrupulous about bloodshed," he remarked, after the Pullman strike. "How I wish I wasn't a reformer, oh, Senator!" he wrote to an industrialist. "But I suppose I must live up to my part, like the Negro minstrel who blacked himself all over." "There is no room in this country for hyphenated Americanism," he fulminated against German-Americans, Irish-Americans, Japanese-Americans, etc., at the close of his career. "The hyphenated American always hoists the American flag undermost." Indians, strikers, blacks, immigrants, lions, buffalos, industrialists, Congressmen, his chosen successor, his own party—Teddy was ready to blast away at whatever thwarted him.

His legacy lingers. Damn the other nations of earth, here comes America! As young Theodore pummeled and pumped his sickly boyish body into indomitable brawn, so does today's America bristle with irresistible might. We negotiate by ultimatum: our way or the highway!

"O, it is excellent," sighed Shakespeare, "to have a giant's strength, but it is tyrannous to use it like a giant!" Too soon the bully pulpit becomes the bully's swagger.

xii.

North again. To Albany, Martin van Buren, Chester Arthur, ancestors.

What a city Albany must have been! Inland terminus of the Hudson's deep-water channel, hub of the western fur trade (when West meant the Appalachians and beyond), commencement of the wondrous canal that linked the fertile plains of the Great Lakes with the limitless Atlantic. Albany made Presidents then (van Buren, the improbable Arthur). Albany made plutocrats. But car and highway bypassed Albany, turning it into a dingy backwater whose only business is government.

Van Buren's "Lindenwald," in nearby Kinderhook, captures the exuberance of Albany's Golden Age. Son of a local tavern-keeper, van Buren was a poor boy made good. No soldier, like his mentor General Jackson, van Buren is remembered as America's first political operative, a wily insider, "the red fox," "the little magician," who "rowed to his object with muffled oars." He was a small natty man who smiled a lot and let everyone else do the talking.

Rich men may retire to cottages, but a poor boy who's made it needs to flaunt. "Lindenwald" preens with an endearing innocence. All is a la mode: indoor plumbing—decades before it was installed in the White House; a

166

furnace; kitchen ranges; a 51-panel wallpaper mural, imported from France; Brussels carpets; portraits; fruit orchards; ornamental ponds; picturesque porches; and a four-story Italianate tower, topped by a little loggia from which visitors might survey the expanse.

So many Presidential retirement homes, if they survive, are solemn with self-importance or drab with disappointment. Van Buren, notwithstanding his calamitous Administration, coping with the Panic of '37 (it's hard to be a good President in a bad economy), seems irrepressibly pleased with himself. In his large study, behind his desk, rises a more than life-sized marble bust of the President, above where its original would have sat.

My first stop at the Albany Rural Cemetery is Chester Arthur.

Chester Arthur made Ronald Reagan look like a workaholic. "You have no idea how depressing and fatiguing it is," he grumbled, "to live in the same house where you work."

He was a dandy and an epicure, especially by comparison with the modest Midwesterners who preceded him. He owned more than 80 pairs of pants. He served 8 varieties of wine at his 14-course White House dinners. The White House, he thought, should be elegant; he hired William Comfort Tiffany, of stained glass fame, to oversee its redecoration. His career before his improbable selection as James Garfield's running mate[25] was as a flunky. Senator Roscoe Conkling wielded the power in New York and he needed people he could rely on. The Port of New York accounted for more than a third of the national government's revenues. Those who insist on Arthur's probity as the Collector of the Port overlook the obvious. Conkling wasn't interested in probity. He wanted loyalty. That gentlemanly Chet Arthur satisfied Conkling for seven years in that lucrative post—and made a bundle doing it—is proof, at a minimum, Arthur was amenable.

Earnest industrious President Garfield couldn't stand the indolent foppish Arthur, whose sole interest seemed to be how much patronage he could dole. Garfield banned him from the White House. Arthur was prepared to live out his Vice Presidency in Manhattan, in elegant ease.

Then Charles Guiteau, a deranged frustrated office seeker, shot Garfield in the back, shouting "Arthur is President now." An embarrassed Arthur disappeared from view for the 80 days it took Garfield to die. When Arthur was sworn in, Roscoe Conkling was gleeful. His flunky was now in charge

---

[25]See page 155.

of the cookie jar. Only Arthur, like Prince Hal when he became king, rejected the fat, rascally companion of his younger days. Falstaff and Conkling both shriveled at the shock.

Arthur turned out to be a sensible if not energetic chief. With expectations so low, his responsible performance came as a pleasant surprise. (Harry Truman and Gerald Ford similarly benefited from low expectations.) He reformed the Civil Service, depriving bosses like Conkling of their clout. When Arthur died of Bright's disease, shortly after leaving the White House, the crusading Philadelphia publisher Alexander McClure wrote, "No man ever entered the Presidency so profoundly and widely distrusted, and no one ever retired . . . more generally respected." Even cynical Mark Twain gave him a thumbs up. "It would be hard indeed to better President Arthur's administration."

Having snapped Arthur's grave, I go looking for my great-great-grandfather. Yes, he's here, with his son, my great-grandfather, a stone's throw from Arthur (whom they must have known). Across the wall, in the Roman Catholic cemetery, I find my grandmother's father, Anthony Nicholas Brady.

Driven here by Ireland's potato famine, Brady found a way to wealth, by backing, among others, Thomas Edison. (Another of his great-grandsons, Nicholas Brady, served as Treasury Secretary in the first Bush Administration.)

The Brady mausoleum, surrounded by its own lawn, is half the size of the Parthenon. The long key rasps in the rusted door. I stand in the silence, a groundskeeper waiting outside. (What is the right amount of time to spend at a grave? Too short seems irreverent; too long feels like show. And what does one *do* there? Say a prayer? But to whom? About what? I want to do right by my forbears—but what does that mean? They're dust. Yet they know somehow. I sense their gratitude at being remembered, after all these years.)

The late afternoon light glows saffron through the mawkish glass. My great-grandparents eye me dubiously. Khaki shorts, scuffed sandals, digital camera . . . a *motor home?* Was it for this they muscled and elbowed and lavished their way to respectability?

Maybe it was.

11
New England

What makes a town stand tall?

Trace the Canadian boundary of New York, from Niagara Falls in the west to Rouses Point beside Vermont, and insensibly this question poses itself. Something is changing—but what? It is not the topography—gently undulant farmland, not far from significant water. It is not the climate—long biting winters and sufficient growing seasons. It is not the nation or the state or the schools or the people, which are one. And yet, as you head northward from Oswego, the amiable bounty of the roadside lapses into shabbiness. Structures seem to be flaking, rusting, leaning, warping into earth. Windows are boarded with buckled plywood. Cars and trailers gaze forlornly from front yards, pleading to be purchased for five, four, three hundred, or less. Fields have been abandoned. In one town (why shame them by naming them—they have worries enough), I see a sign for Little League. I venture up the path a way. The Little League fields in my town are sodded and edged and buffed: diamonds shine. Here I find only head-high weeds, blooming yellow and purple, and one sway-backed bench.

The people too turn grimmer as you turn north. Torn clothes and stained T-shirts suggest indifference to appearance. Attractive futures straighten our spines: that is why soldiers are made to stand stiff: their very posture constitutes a salute. Dim futures make us slouch.

The map suggests highways may be to blame: the water-highway of the Erie Canal, which the turnpikes paralleled, brought trade to Western New York, and still people pass this way, along the Interstate. No one travels through New York's northern hump unless they have to (to visit, for example, the grave of William Almon Wheeler).

These northern towns were not always stooped and shuffling. Spires and porticos and florid carpentry recall a prouder epoch, when neighbors lived where they were born and a farmer could grow, with application, into affluence and esteem.

What makes a town stand tall—or a man—is the chance to rise. We grow taller by reaching. Take from a man—or a town—or a nation—that hope and good posture no longer seems worth the effort. "Life," observed Dr. Johnson, "is a progress from want to want, not from enjoyment to enjoyment." Were we wise, we would desire nothing more than desire.

Cross the bridge into Vermont, over Lake Champlain, and the view changes. Northernmost New York, above the Adirondacks, doesn't conjure much, but Vermont is a postcard. When, we wonder, did Vermont become "Vermont," cradled in quote marks, a place of high mountains and simple values, of healthy exertion and crafts and folk art and heritage and engaging taciturnity and sensitivity to earth, a state somehow emblematically "American"? The physical variation between Vermont and northernmost New York isn't enough to explain the difference. Vermont, too, was once a place of rural communities and rugged farms. Vermont was not bolstered by great highways or large industry. Yet Vermont found hope, a hope reflected in its cleanliness and comeliness and bustle, its evident cheer. It made itself something. How?

Vermont today is so much "Vermont"—in quotes—it's easy to forget this picture is a confection, not a foregone fact. Faced with a declining agrarian economy and remoteness from urban hubs, Vermont reinvented itself. It took what it had—picturesque mountains, forests, clean air, cooler summers, covered bridges, Yankee ways, respected schools, and cows—and composed them into a "lifestyle." Calvin Coolidge, a Vermonter, helped: there was something oddly refreshing about his wry silence and curt confidence. Robert Frost helped too, who kept readers confused whether he came from New Hampshire or Vermont (his entrancing homage to New Hampshire ends with the line, "At present I am living in Vermont"). Frost conceived of an America so clear and true and vital we yearn to be swaddled in it. Grandma Moses helped with her whimsically bucolic paintings, which portrayed a paradise in the orchards and snows. Skiing helped, which became popular after the Second World War, as did cars and roads, which facilitated travel to and fro. The Sixties' counterculture helped with its anti-urban, anti-slick bias that found in Vermont a congenial setting (Ben and Jerry, of ice cream renown, cleverly packaged this bias, making "Vermont" virtually synonymous with sweet, creamy, natural, funky, and sincere; more recently, the Vermont Teddy Bear Company has been luring buyers with the same bait). Computers help, which more and more enable us to work away from cities. So does our zeal for exercise, especially hiking and biking, which the state's scenery encourages.

These were ingredients, but it took chefs, lots of them, collaborating, often unwittingly, to stir their state into a state of mind. One of these chefs was an heiress of railroad and sugar fortunes, a decorous Episcopalian one would never have taken for a pioneer. Electra Havemeyer Webb was a lady doomed to a life of pampered futility, of stupendously accomplishing nothing with exquisite taste. The deepest hurts recorded in Mrs. Webb's biography are her mother's critique of a purchase ("Well . . . if you could have seen my mother's face! She said, '*What* have you done?' And I said, 'I have bought a work of art' ") and her chagrin at her mother's being jailed for a night as a suffragette ("Of course most people think it is a joke but I felt dreadfully. . . . It was all in the papers and I was really very upset over the whole thing").

Ease is a disease: that the majority longs to be infected does not make it less crippling. Mrs. Webb survived privilege. What saved her was a mysterious avidity, her ceaseless, restless craving for the refuse and bric-a-brac we now honor as Folk Art. She saw, she wanted, and she could afford—masses of the stuff: farm tools, moccasins, dolls, toys, sleighs, carriages, decoys, bandboxes, shop signs, pill boxes, covered bridges, quilts, lighthouses, locomotives, sawmills, scrimshaw, music boxes, steamships, posters, carousels, bonnets, mittens, samplers, porringers, figureheads, spinning wheels, weathervanes, whirligigs, ladles, calipers, crockery . . . the extent of her collections dizzies. Her parents had been noted collectors of European art, whose bequests to the Metropolitan Museum in New York City include some of our most cherished images. They too deserve praise. But Electra (along with a few other early Folk Art aficionados) did more than collect: she widened and democratized our conception of art. As, through our history, we have expanded suffrage from property-owning white males to all adults, so we have expanded the parameters of preciousness, finding beauty in the quotidian and mundane. The Shelburne Museum in Shelburne, Vermont, which houses Mrs. Webb's legacy in 37 antique structures, not only draws hundreds of thousands of tourists each year to this once remote village, it contributes to the idea of "Vermont" as a land that thumbs its nose at luxury and honors the laborer and housewife and the works of their hands.

"What is man but his passion?" wrote Kentucky's Robert Penn Warren in his masterful poem, *Audubon.* Passion rescues us from the mire of meaninglessness, quickens our pulse, and gives us cause.

Mrs. Webb's passion made her life a pilgrimage. Her legacy helped salvage a small state and give it new vision and purpose. She and many

171

others provided Vermont with those cozy quote-marks that shelter it from despair.

ii.

Dark, quiet, cool. Not even the ping of acorns or the whisper of leaves soon to fall. The stillness rings.

It was two New Englanders wakened me just now, talking across a stone wall, though I don't know they ever met. By the time Robert Frost (b. 1875) embodied "New England" in the national consciousness, Calvin Coolidge (b. 1873) was long dead.

No region's name is more evocative. Granite, we think; forests; hard farms; coastal fisheries, whaling; taciturnity; Puritans; propriety; frugality; maple syrup; snow. Homage and challenge nest in the name. Not the old England this, but new, improved: in the words of its first governor, "a shining city on the hill."

Frost and Coolidge both defined themselves by this place. Coolidge is buried not two stones' throw from where he was born, in a room behind his father's general store. Across a dirt road, at 2:47 a.m. on August 3, 1923, having been wakened by news of President Harding's death, Coolidge took the oath of office from his father, a justice of the peace. Then he went back to sleep. Frost was born in California to displaced New Englanders. After his father died, Frost, age nine, and his mother brought the body home, and stayed.

Frost's two preserved farms—in Derry and Franconia, New Hampshire—aren't much; neither is the Coolidge compound in Plymouth Notch, Vermont: simple white farmhouses; wood stoves; Spartan amenities. The only toilet in the Coolidge house when Coolidge was President— and this was the 1920s—was a two-seater with no running water. Martin van Buren, who enjoyed the best things in life, installed indoor plumbing in his house in Kinderhook in 1840! But that was New York—and a social climber.

Frost and Coolidge flourished in the Roaring Twenties, but in their homes you hear no roaring. Bobbed flappers, bathtub gin, flashy spenders, the leering and the sneering, not a hint of them. The Twenties were a decade of upheaval—in politics and the arts—of socialism, cubism, Nazism, imagism, surrealism, all sorts of isms—but here all was tradition and quiet.

172

Their voices were quiet too. After Lincoln, Jefferson, and Grant, Coolidge is the ablest writer among our Presidents. Read his *Autobiography* (if you can find a copy). The prose is clean and precise—no convoluted syntax, no striving for effect, not an extra word.[26]

> During the long vacations from May until September I went home and worked on the farm. We had a number of horses so that I was able to indulge my pleasure in riding. As no one else in the neighborhood cared for this diversion, I had to ride alone. But a horse is much company, and riding over the fields and the country roads by himself, where nothing interrupts his seeing and thinking, is a good occupation for a boy. The silences of Nature have a discipline all their own.

To Frost too, being alone with a horse was memorable:

> My little horse must think it queer
> To stop without a farmhouse near
> Between the woods and frozen lake
> The darkest evening of the year.
>
> He gives his harness bells a shake
> To ask if there is some mistake.
> The only other sound's the sweep
> Of easy wind and downy flake.

"Old-fashioned" may be the adjective that comes to mind, reading these passages. Their elements—a man, a horse, nature undisturbed—recall a bygone, almost mythic past. But the style is new. Old-fashioned, in the Twenties, meant ornate periods and upholstered rhetoric. As assiduously as any of the declared innovators of the age—Pound, Joyce, Eliot, Gertrude Stein, Hemingway—Coolidge and Frost are stripping language of its encrustations, the coats of paint that had hidden its grain. But unlike the self-styled "modernists," neither Coolidge nor Frost opts for obscurity. They speak to be understood. They have something to say.

Coolidge is usually rated by historians among our lesser Presidents. This is puzzling. 1923 to 1928 was a time of economic prosperity and domestic and international calm. Coolidge was popular and respected, elected in his own right by a large margin. He was honest and clear. He made worthy

---

[26]Weighing in at 30,000 words, Coolidge's *Autobiography* is a pamphlet compared to recent Presidential tomes. Clinton's, at more than 700,000 words, requires a wheelbarrow.

appointments. He restored dignity to a Presidency sullied by scandals. He had a noble vision of America that he expressed forcefully and pursued consistently. That he failed to forestall a worldwide depression suggests that he could have.

Frost, too, fared poorly with scholars and critics, at least at first. His popularity was held against him. His clarity and simplicity and familiar forms were seen as lack of originality.

To understand judgments one must understand the judges. Historians, scholars, and critics are bystanders. They comment on the action in their fields. They favor excitement. It gives them more to talk about, which, in turn, makes them more interesting. The self-evident is anathema to the interpreter: it deprives him of vocation.

Frost and Coolidge stood for Yankee virtues: simplicity, frugality, probity, liberty, self-reliance, clarity, hard work, and turning a buck. They were not pretentious or elitist. They saw themselves as ordinary men, speaking to ordinary men. Both felt contempt, even pity, for the hoity-toity and high-brows.

They were true conservatives. That's what life in a farming community makes you. Rural neighbors have to behave to survive. Risks are avoided, strangers and innovations distrusted. Farmers are too tired to be eager for novelty.

The values espoused by a Frost or Coolidge seem right to the American majority. Greed, vanity, ambition, boredom, fear, may cause us to veer from those values but we don't feel good about it. In our hearts, we long to live a clean communal life among decent neighbors. Frost and Coolidge speak to that longing.

No vision, of course, is adequate to all occasions. Americans change things when we have to, and those moments call forth a different sort of leader. In politics as in art, the oscillation between innovators and traditionalists, agitators and comforters, is ceaseless. Americans have generally shown a sound instinct for choosing the leaders we need. Only in the decades before the Civil War did all our leaders fail and that was because, short of violence, the problem was probably insoluble.

If a President is to be measured by his values, vision, efficacy, and effect, Coolidge deserves honor. His values were sure and good; his vision—of free enterprise and less government—was constant; he implemented his plan; and his results were impressive. As Ronald Reagan noted, with his characteristic twinkle, "You hear a lot of jokes every once in a while about 'Silent Cal Coolidge.' The joke is on the people who

174

make the jokes. Look at his record. He cut the taxes four times. We probably had the greatest growth and prosperity we've ever known. I have taken heed of that because if he did that by doing nothing, maybe that's the answer."

iii.

We can smile now but Hannibal Hamlin, we feel certain, found his pigment no joke. Except for Charles Curtis, who had Indian blood, Hamlin was our darkest Vice President or President. Folks talked. The hulking, brawny comer struck back. "If the gentleman chooses to find fault with me on account of my complexion," 27-year-old Hamlin mocked a flush-faced elder in the Maine legislature, "what has he to say about himself? I take my complexion from nature; he gets his from the brandy bottle. Which is more honorable?"

Black-and-white photography bleaches. We feel Hamlin, though, behind his bushy eyebrows and jutting jaw. Here is Lyndon Johnson a century earlier: a looming, defiant, self-made politician from a scorned state (Texas in the 1930s was as remote and rugged as Maine in the 1830s), barreling toward his goal.

Hamlin's ambition descended from a grandfather who sired 17 children with two wives. Eleazar Hamlin called his children Asia, Africa, Europe, America, Cyrus, Hannibal, and the like. A man who names his children after continents and conquerors isn't one I'd mess with.

Hamlin didn't mean to be Vice President. If he'd attended the 1860 Republican convention in Chicago, he wouldn't have been. As Chair of the Senate's Committee on Commerce, he had contracts to dole out. (Lincoln's Secretary of the Navy Gideon Welles described Hamlin as "rapacious as a wolf" for patronage.) As Vice President, Hamlin could only sit and wait. ("Wheeler," he groaned to his friend and future Vice President, William Almon Wheeler, "I will take lunch with you on condition that you promise me you will never be Vice President. I am only a fifth wheel of a coach and can do little for my friends.")

Presidents nowadays select their Vice Presidents and give them assignments. Lincoln had never met Hamlin before their nomination and, the evidence suggests, didn't like him. Hamlin was too sure of himself, too critical, and too rigid on the ticklish question of abolition. Lincoln quipped that Hamlin shielded him from assassination. Do you think, he asked, that "the

175

Richmond people would like to have Hannibal Hamlin here any better than myself? In that one alternative, I have an insurance on my life worth half the prairie land in Illinois."

It is hard not to chafe with Hamlin—a man of might doomed, when might was most needed, to impotence and disregard. He had so little to do during the bloody summer of 1864 that he volunteered in the Maine Coast Guard and for two months served sailors chowder.

Lincoln booted Hamlin from his reelection ticket. He needed someone more appealing. Whispers that Hamlin was a mulatto were no advantage in a contest Lincoln feared he'd lose. Lincoln would have denied his involvement in Hamlin's dismissal; deft Presidents leave few fingerprints. But Lincoln was boss and Hamlin was booted: one plus one equals two.

Hamlin would have denied punishing Lincoln for his humiliation. And perhaps it *was* a coincidence that Hamlin, who'd banned liquor from the Senate, had a bottle of brandy on hand to buck up his successor on Inaugural day. Andrew Johnson, who was feverish, took a sip too many and launched into the tirade that earned him the sobriquet "sot." Had Lincoln's new favorite been slipped a mickey?

If John Wilkes Booth had acted nine months earlier, the dark man of Maine might have ended a triumphant giant instead of a fulminating footnote.

iv.

The career of Franklin Pierce makes us want to look away. It was all wrong—the man, the times, the result. Hollywood-handsome, Frank Pierce had the sheen of a winner. Affable and gracious, he charmed. But he was deviled by misfortune. Whatever could go wrong did, and then some. He died an embittered drunk.

In the beginning all was sunshine. His father was a Revolutionary War hero, veteran of Bunker Hill, Saratoga, Valley Forge, one of New Hampshire's leading citizens and a man of means. Frank was the cute kid brother in a big family, petted and adored. Everything came easy to "this beautiful boy, with blue eyes, light curling hair, and a serene expression of face," as his college roommate (and bosom friend) Nathaniel Hawthorne put it in a fawning campaign biography. Frank was elected to the state legislature when he was 25, to Congress when he was 29, to the Senate when he was 32, its youngest member. He was always up for a party. "I have been leading, I need not say, a very agreeable life," he wrote home from Washington.

Oh, to be Franklin Pierce! But then . . . he married. What was it, we wonder, Frank saw in Jane Appleton, a small, frail, shy, gloomy woman? Frank was affable, bibulous: Jane wanted him to stay home and sober up. Jane wanted Frank out of politics, and more than once in his career he acceded to her wish. They quarreled. Then their children started dying: their first, Franklin, in infancy; their second, Frank, at four; and their last, Bennie, in a railroad wreck, decapitated before his parents' eyes, two months before his father's Inauguration. Bennie was 11. Jane saw Bennie's death as God's way of clearing the President-elect's desk. Her bitterness coils through the centuries like electrical smoke: Hawthorne himself could not have envisioned a more brooding character. Jane's first two years in the White House she remained upstairs, writing letters to Bennie. Imagine coming home to that after a rough day at the office.

And rough they were.

Pierce had not sought the Presidency and didn't know what to do with it. He was nominated on the 49th ballot of a punch-drunk convention as a compromise, a "dark horse." The nation was optimistic when he began his term, deluding itself that the Compromise of 1850 had closed the slavery debate. "I fervently hope that the question is at rest," Pierce said in his Inaugural address, "and that no sectional or ambitious or fanatical excitement may again threaten the durability of our institutions or obscure the light of our prosperity."

Pierce longed to please people, but he had no more success with the Union than with Jane. The Kansas-Nebraska Act not only failed to knit the states, it hastened their division. Could a confident, percipient President have forestalled Civil War? Maybe not. But waffling, temporizing, conciliating Frank Pierce was the worst man for the job.

He wanted to be renominated but his party wouldn't hear of it. Retired, he took his wife to Europe to restore her spirits, but to no avail. Back home, he enraged his neighbors with his support of slave-owners. On the day after Gettysburg, he gave a speech denouncing the Civil War and was almost lynched.

When Jane died in 1863, Pierce resumed drinking. "After the White House," he said, "what is there to do but drink?" Other failed Presidents had at least their earlier successes to look back on, an ascent from obscurity, say, or military triumphs. Pierce's victories were handed to him. His rapid rise in

New Hampshire politics was his father's doing. His nomination to the Presidency was a fluke. Any time poor Frank tried anything on his own—choose a wife, lead a brigade, chart a course for the country—it turned out badly. His bad luck is almost spooky. He was eager for action in the Mexican War, then his horse bucked, startled by gunburst, tossing Pierce forward. His pommel pummeled his groin, causing him to faint, which gave him a reputation for cowardice. (One is reminded of the ridicule heaped on Gerald Ford, probably our most athletic President, when he stumbled before the cameras.) In 1864, Pierce brought his old pal Hawthorne to the White Mountains to repair his health; Hawthorne died in his arms.

"So what did he see in her?"

"You wonder," my docent pauses. Her name is Chips—"Everybody calls me Chips"—Holden, an attractive older lady with a limp (last year she broke her ankle), who has devoted 20 years to this house. They call the house (inaccurately) the Pierce Manse ("manse" signifies a minister's dwelling—but then, wasn't Hawthorne's *Mosses from the Old Manse* being penned at this moment, some of it, perhaps, in these very rooms?).

This house was occupied by the Pierces from 1842 to 1848. Their son Frankie died here, in a room upstairs. Their son Bennie was born here. It was the only house the Pierces ever owned. In 1966 it was slated for demolition. Neighbors raised the money to move it to its present site in Concord, New Hampshire, down the road from the statehouse and the Pierces' graves.

A yolk-yellow autumn afternoon sun makes the drawn shades glow. We are alone, Chips and I. Her telephone number was displayed on a card in the front door window, in faded ink. The house was open only by appointment after Labor Day, she told me, but no matter, she'd be there presently if I could wait. I spread open a canvas chair and read in the warmth. I read about the Democrats' convention of 1852, how the leading candidates—Cass of Michigan, Buchanan of Pennsylvania, Marcy of New York, and Douglas of Ohio—stubbornly blocked one another, opening the way for a barely known former Senator from a tiny state. I read about Pierce's Vice President, William King of Alabama, our only President or Vice President to be sworn in abroad (he was in Cuba, hoping, vainly, to lick tuberculosis), our only Vice President never to marry, our only President or Vice President never to serve a day. I could not bring myself to read more about the Pierce family. It was too sad.

The advantage of forgotten Presidents is that nobody comes to see them. Nearly a dozen times this summer I have stood alone or with only a docent in a President's home and listened to the silence—at Buchanan's in Lancaster, Garfield's in Mentor, Hayes's in Fremont, the elder Harrison's in Vincennes, his grandson's in Indianapolis, Harding's in Marion, van Buren's in Kinderhook, Polk's in Columbia, Taft's in Cincinnati, Coolidge's in Plymouth Notch. Here, now, in Concord, holding still, I could feel the Pierces, their hopes and fears and sorrows in the walls and chairs. Modern and popular Presidents we "present"—with movies and exhibits and guarded (I mean, guided) tours. We are herded through a script, like a ride at Disney World. Groups through Lincoln's home in Springfield start every 12 minutes.

Celebrity and our nation's growth have lifted our popular Presidents from us, into an ether where they float, neither gods nor men. Here I can touch: hold in my hand the President's ivory-capped walking stick (shortened by a later, shorter relative), his tarnished shaving implements, the stovepipe hat he wore at his Inauguration (which his wife would not attend, still grieving for her sons). I could see the chairs where she sat—and sat—a sad depressive, her Franklin dead, just a baby, her Frank sick upstairs, her Bennie, oh, well enough for now, the picture of health, but weren't they all in this house pursued by some doom?

"I think it was her conversation that attracted Frank," Chips muses, holding a large teacup, Pierce's father's favorite. "She was intelligent. Frank felt comfortable in her company. And she was said to have been beautiful, though you can't see it from the photographs. Also, she was well-born—her father the president of Bowdoin, her brother a professor. And she had wonderful manners. Do you know it was she who began the tradition—sad as she was—of placing little bouquets at the ladies' places at White House dinners? That tradition continued for a long time. And it was her idea."

v.

By the rude bridge that arched the flood,
Their flag to April's breeze unfurled,
Here once the embattled farmers stood
And fired the shot heard round the world.

The words—Ralph Waldo Emerson's—grace the pediment. The statue—by Daniel Chester French, sculptor of the Lincoln Memorial—depicts a handsome young man, standing foursquare, one hand on his plough, the

179

other holding his musket, alert, yes, but no more heroic in posture than if he were out shooting rabbits or a pesky coon in his corn. This is not a military man, bent on martial glory. This is a volunteer, willing but not eager, called from his work to do a job that needs doing.

Across the field from the Minuteman statue, in Concord, Massachusetts, is a largish wooden house built by Emerson's grandfather, Reverend William Emerson. Reverend Emerson was Concord's pastor. On that fateful day, April 19, 1775, he stood with the Minutemen, while his anxious wife looked out her window to see if she could discern her husband through the smoke. (Reverend Emerson survived that famous skirmish only to succumb to typhoid the next year while serving at Fort Ticonderoga.) Sixty years later, in that same upstairs room, grandson Ralph Waldo wrote his first major work, "Nature," the foundation stone of American philosophy. A decade and a half later, Nathaniel Hawthorne used the same room to write his stories, *Mosses from the Old Manse*, the first American fiction that was more than fable or adventure. Hawthorne and his bride Sophia scratched sentiments in the windowpanes of this room: you can still read them. When Nathaniel and Sophia came to this house for their honeymoon, Henry David Thoreau planted them a garden, as a wedding gift.

We walk these few acres, the planks of the Old North Bridge, the wide floorboards of the Old Manse, with an awe almost vertiginous. The first battle of the Revolutionary War, the first American philosophy, the first American fiction! The author of America's most influential work of literature, *Walden,* planting pumpkins in the garden! What was it about Massachusetts' Concord?

There's a subset of historians determined to trace any flowering to its roots. They admit no miracles. A confluence of trends can be used to explain any event. The moment makes the man.

A rationalist, I too am interested in causes. In King Lear's words, "Nothing comes of nothing." The moment, at least, must offer the opportunity for greatness. Lincoln, for example, would never have been "Lincoln" without the Civil War.

Emerson would never have been "Emerson" without six generations of forbears who had been preachers; or without a community as curious and serious and communitarian as Concord. Concord from the first was a passionately earnest and cerebral place, dedicated to puzzling out God's mysteries and addressing the world's ills.

Thinking made Concord a hotbed of Revolutionary sentiment. That made them a natural weapons cache, after the British occupied Boston.

The weapons attracted the British to Concord, which led to the first shots of the war. Thinking gave rise to an Emerson, whose disciple was Thoreau, whose admirer was Hawthorne, and so on. Reformers bred reformers, writers writers, until Concord became, for a few dazzling decades, America's Athens.

Explanations can be advanced but they are never enough. Just as nature, by inexplicable accident, mutates, generating a new gene, for well or ill, so humanity spawns "sports," freaks, glorious or hideous or sometimes both, who, by any calculation, must be rated impossible. You can cite all the preconditions for a Socrates or Jesus or Shakespeare or Mozart or Thoreau, but you cannot predict them. The soil may be receptive but still you need the seed. And the seed comes from—where?

I know nothing of God. All religions seem to me shelters from the storm of doubts. Those who profess unreasoning faith have traded in eyes for ease. I wish them comfort. Who am I to judge?

I'd like to believe in some proffered god; it'd make life simpler. But neither can I believe in no God. Reason is a thrilling road to nowhere. A leads to B leads to C and so on, but then what? The world is too well made to imagine it makerless.

America is as much a wonder as any masterpiece of art. It seems impossible that a handful of ragtag soldiers could wrest their freedom from the greatest power on earth. That first exchange in Concord should have ended in the hanging of those rebels—by any calculation! It seems impossible that a small group of mostly young men, inexperienced in nation-making, could craft a new form of government that would not only endure but triumph over all other forms ever devised. It seems impossible that this flimsy enterprise could have been guided down the rock-strewn river of time without shipwreck. Impossible, impossible, impossible. Yet here we are.

So, yes, there is a Providence—that is, a Foreseer, one who discerns a future and steers us somehow toward it. And yes, he—she—it—whatever this entity may be—is, to this traveler at least, inaudible, so I must make my own way. And yes, I am free to fritter my being on meaningless work or obliviating play—the Foreseer has granted me that freedom—but could such waste gladden my heart?

My conclusion—to me it seems inescapable—is to make the most of my time, to use my life as if I were being observed by—whomever—call him Foreseer, call him Father, call him God—doing my best to make Him proud. And to thank him for his presence in my world, made manifest in Concord—and in America—and in the veins of a leaf.

181

vi.

This is my fourth climb to the leafy summit of Sleepy Hollow Cemetery. I'm hoping for several more before I die.

Thoreau is my father. My birth father never asked me how I was, or who. He told me. My choice was to accept or reject. I was readying my rebellion when he died. I was 16. My clenched fist swung at air.

Thoreau is always asking me how I am—and who. He used to smile at my absorption with appearances and chide me for wasting my chance. He encouraged me to look at my life and say what I saw. He was wise and funny:

> The greater part of what my neighbors call good I believe in my soul to be bad, and if I repent of any thing, it is very likely to be my good behavior. What demon possessed me that I behaved so well?

We shared the disease of journal-keeping.

> Every man has to learn the points of compass again as often as he awakes, whether from sleep or any abstraction. Not till we are lost, in other words, not till we have lost the world do we begin to find ourselves.

His kidding deflated disappointments.

> You need not rest your reputation on the dinners you give.

He said it was OK to dream.

> I learned this, at least, by my experiment; that if one advances confidently in the direction of his dreams, and endeavors to live the life he has imagined, he will meet with a success unexpected in common hours.

I argued with him, as one should with a father. Why couldn't this extoller of life admit to the pain that drove him to Walden, his nervous collapse after his beloved brother's death? And what are we supposed to do about kids? And who'll bake the bread or mend the roads if everyone's studying the stars? And is loneliness really preferable to love? (Thoreau hated to be touched.)

No prescription is perfect. But Thoreau freed us spiritually as our Signers, 60 years before, had freed us politically. If we were enslaved to obligations or expectations, it was because we'd allowed it. Our new free state permitted a new free spirit. Sadness was not our fate but our fault.

Walden remains one of history's most exhilarating exhortations, right up there with the Declaration of Independence, the Gettysburg Address, and the Sermon on the Mount. Nothing new on your shelf is half as bold. Rinse your life in its intelligence and watch the crud flake off.

Thoreau issued me my passport to America. "Only that day dawns to which we are awake." His headstone is the perfect tribute. Here on the holy hill of the American intellect you'll find Emerson, Hawthorne, Louisa May Alcott (author of *Little Women*), her dad Bronson Alcott (father of Transcendentalism), Daniel Chester French (sculptor of the Lincoln Memorial and the Minuteman), reformers, abolitionists, Congressmen, eccentrics, Elizabeth Peabody (founder of the American Kindergarten movement), Anne Rainsford Bush (the first woman licensed to drive a car). Square foot for square foot here is more intellectual audacity and zeal to do good than in any graveyard in America, maybe the world. And what honor is bestowed on the most daring of these darers, the spiritual father of us all? Barely a foot high, out of unraked dirt, amid tree roots, pine cones, pebbles, his marker juts crookedly. "Henry" is all it says.

He'd have thought it fine.

vii.

It took me too long to find Henry Wilson not to write about him.

Henry Wilson is a name known to only a handful of Americans, all experts or buffs. How interesting or important could Henry Wilson be if I've never heard of him!

Very interesting, it turns out. And surprisingly important.

Grant's second Vice President, Henry Wilson was a member of our log-cabin club of leaders, men who rose from rural penury to the political heights without the advantages of birth, education, or connections. It's a small roster—Jackson, Fillmore, Richard Johnson, Andrew Johnson, Garfield, Barkley, and of course, Lincoln—and all are heroes, no matter their records in office. (The inaugurator of the club—William Henry Harrison, whose 1840 campaign celebrated his log cabin origins—was a phony. "Ole Tippecanoe" was an aristocratic Virginian, a child of privilege who went west.)

Henry Wilson was born in 1812 to a lazy, boozing New Hampshire laborer. Apprenticed at age 10 to a local farmer, he drudged involuntarily for the next 11 years. He received no education. Age 21, he fled, changing his name (he was born Jeremiah Jones Colbath) and settling in Natick, Massachusetts. He took up shoe-making. Four years later, at age 25, he had a hundred employees manufacturing brogans.

Henry was ambitious, with the implacable anger of a man born wronged. He went into politics—for recognition, sure, but also to make it easier for poor boys to rise. He worked to end imprisonment for debt, reduce the poll tax, enact a secret ballot and mechanic's lien law, legislate limits to alcohol consumption, and fund public schools. Having been a slave of sorts, he abominated slavery. An abolitionist to the bone, in the roiling decades before the founding of the Republicans in 1856, he bobbed from party to party, searching for one that could gain him office and attain his ends. We may sniff in retrospect—what an opportunist, switching from Whig to Free-Soiler to Know-Nothing to Republican in 16 years! But what *should* he have done? The established parties, then as now, dodged the divisive issues to maintain their majorities. Only so-called fanatical fringe movements had the guts not to pussyfoot. Slavery blocked America's future: a revolution was needed to remove it. Eventually, after some false starts, the revolutionary party was formed and four years later it prevailed. Astonishingly, this revolution was accomplished constitutionally. We never had to change our form of government. We never failed to elect our leaders democratically. Though our Civil War was terrible, we didn't have to start over, as most nations have, with a new form.

From his election to the United States Senate in 1855, Wilson was among its leaders. He chaired the Military Affairs Committee, where he worked to provide Lincoln with the manpower and materiel needed to conduct the war. He pressed for the Emancipation Proclamation and the thirteenth, fourteenth, and fifteenth amendments, and rejoiced in their passage. Sharing his fellow Radicals' view that Andrew Johnson was soft on the South, Wilson worked for the Tennessean's impeachment—a sad irony, since no two political leaders, one a tailor, the other a cobbler, rose from such similar backgrounds. Though tainted by the Credit Mobilier scandal, Wilson's poverty attested to his probity (he had to borrow money to buy a suit for his inauguration as Vice President in 1873). Ignored by President Grant, bypassed by the times, he devoted his Vice Presidency to finishing his massive memoirs. He died in office, in 1875, after several strokes.

There is no sign of Wilson in Natick's Old Dell Park Cemetery. Nor is there anyone to ask. Dusk deepening, I scan the weedy rows with diminishing hope. Natick is one of those down-at-the-heels New England mill towns that found new life in high-tech and the highway. The Mass Pike skewers it. Along the Pike are plopped those boxes people work in.

I really don't want to return to Natick tomorrow. Then an attractive young woman arrives in a bright red sports car to visit her grandfather. She doesn't know where Henry Wilson is, never heard of him, but points me to the house of the cemetery's former caretaker across the road. I knock uneasily. Robert Whitney is a frail, dignified gentleman. Widowed a year ago, his neat home reeks of emptiness. Though flustered at first, he claims to be grateful for my intrusion. "I was just sitting daydreaming," he murmurs.

It's been a number of years since Robert visited that part of the cemetery. His wife is buried here and he will be too, when he "comes to his reward." He isn't absolutely certain where Wilson "rests." He holds my arm for balance: dark is deepening and there are roots and ruts underfoot. Finally we come upon it, a weathered stone, hardly bigger than a shoebox. The inscription? "Henry Wilson." No dates, no word of his service, no flag, not even a flower.

viii.

It is raining in Foxboro, Massachusetts. Acorns rat-a-tat my roof. This campground is almost empty. The cyclone of Labor Day has whirled children back to school, their parents to work. Now there are only old people—and me.

I think, not to think. The Presidents protect me from my present. In a few days I will be home. I do not know what to expect—or what I want. I have been free this summer. Home, I wear my past like a heavy coat.

I am thinking of sons and fathers. John Quincy Adams (JQA) and John Fitzgerald Kennedy (JFK) were dutiful sons. They did their fathers' bidding. The elder Adams and Joseph Kennedy, Sr., both knew how to hold a grudge and get their own back. Determined men, each saw his son's election as vindication. The Presidency would repay the insult of John Adams's rejection (of our first five Presidents, he alone was denied a second term). It would answer those Protestants who sneered that an Irish Catholic was not good enough to be President.

JQA and JFK both retreated to books. Books are a place boys can hide from fierce fathers. When Johnny is studying, he cannot be catechized. "Leave him alone, can't you? He's *reading*."

185

JQA and JFK were both dapper, self-assured. Favored sons swagger. They are protected by a giant. The giant may die, but he survives in his son's consciousness. Favored sons seem brave, with their father's courage. They play their hands as if aces were available for the asking.

JQA and JFK were both audacious. Adams was the last President to insist that the job wasn't political. The idea of partisanship enraged him, as it had his father. One's loyalty was to nation, not faction. Some see such purity as nobility, others as folly. John Quincy Adams set forth an ambitious program for America—and no one listened. It's not concepts that convince but clout.

The Kennedys understood clout. An Irish immigrant alone might be despised and impotent but he was mighty in mass. John F. Kennedy's grandfather, "Sunny Fitz," could be elected Mayor of Boston while in jail—that's how little the individual mattered if he represented the tribe. When John Quincy Adams advocated a national astronomical observatory, he was laughed at: his head was in the clouds. When Kennedy pointed us to the moon, he was cheered because he had the votes.

Both JQA and JFK became President after a long stretch of peace and prosperity. (The Eisenhower years, like the Monroe years, might have been dubbed "the era of good feelings.") Both tried to rouse the nation from its complacent torpor to a higher, more stirring prospect. Adams, because he failed to understand politics, failed: his words were just words. Kennedy's cadences reeled us starward. It is astonishing how Kennedy's Inaugural Address still echoes—more powerfully than any Presidential oratory in the intervening decades.

Both JQA and JFK grew greater after their Presidencies. Adams, returned to Congress by his neighbors, could advocate the right without worrying how to achieve it. He could rant like a prophet about slavery. A prophet does not require partisans; he needs only truth.

JFK grew in the glow of martyrdom. No matter his mistakes, his promiscuity, the brevity of his tenure or meagerness of his attainments; no matter the evidence of sly deals and deceptions, he glows. That smile, those words, that wife! We have had many capable Presidents, but few luminous: Kennedy, Reagan, and the Roosevelts in the twentieth century; Lincoln, Jackson, Jefferson, and Washington before. It's a mystery—like beauty—what makes a Presidency glow. You can analyze the elements—the man, the moment, the message—but their sum does not explain.

John Quincy Adams's birthplace in Quincy, Massachusetts, and John Fitzgerald Kennedy's in Brookline are a few miles apart. The houses impress by their modesty. It is a recurring shock that our rulers rise from averageness. The houses are nice enough—comfortable, upper-middle-class dwellings of their day—but we'd expected more.

Royal dynasties are predicated on an ordained order. God makes kings, kings princes, princes lords, lords serfs, and so forth. In America, anything can happen. Rich become poor, poor rich, the obscure famous, the mighty mites—in an eyeblink. The diceyness of destiny makes Americans edgy, as de Tocqueville noted a century and a half ago. Success, even if it comes, can't be counted on.

John Adams and Joseph Kennedy, Sr., envisioned dynasties, and raised their sons accordingly. It seemed for a time as if their dreams might be realized. But then bad things started happening. Of John Quincy Adams's three sons, one was an alcoholic, one a suicide, and the third, Charles Francis Adams, while distinguished in public service, felt a piker by comparison to his forbears. Charles Francis's son, Henry, by writing memorable books, may prove the most durable of the clan; even so, a sour wistfulness wafts through his prose, as if he were but the shadow of a shadow of a noble house.

The almost macabre decline of the Kennedy clan is too familiar to recall. Assassins' bullets, deadly frolics, accidents, drowned airplanes—all the Furies, it seems, conspire to frustrate their promise.

In JQA and JFK I feel the mystery of history. It is with me this rainy night in Foxboro, as acorns rat-a-tat—and I think of home.

187

*In a few days we will be seeing each other. While we've spoken—finally—
by phone, it's been timidly, lest a wrong word set us off. You've had it with
me. If months of absence on a whim isn't cause, what is? I've had it, too—
with what I left. Yet I'm coming home—and you say you're glad.*

*I should warn you: I've changed. Only how I have no idea. More and
more this whole notion of a self strikes me as a fairy tale to help us sleep.
We say, "I'm not myself today," "That's not like so-and-so," as if there's
some I-beam inside us we could locate by ripping up the floors. Clothes-
shoppers study mirrors: "I don't know. This just isn't me."*

*The road has taught me a lot. For one thing, I'm more relaxed. Shit
happens—but when you're nobody it's no big deal. I dent my van backing
up. So what, with no neighbors to take note? Drop a plate—who cares? I
can buy another for a buck.*

*So much of what bothers us—and costs us—is vanity. Out here there's
no one to keep up with. Sure, there's preening in an RV camp: the longer
people park, the more they gussy, with flowerpots and pinwheels and cartoon figurines and pennants and faux picket fences. Pride is a weed that
sprouts anywhere. But when you're on the go, never lighting longer than a
day or two, whose opinion matters? My neighbors can roll their eyes all they
like, I'm out of there.*

*It's amazing how frightened I was and never knew it. What else is a big
house with a manicured lawn and chintzes and antiques but a panic attack? Honor me for my stuff because the me behind it ain't so hot! People
drive gazillion-dollar cars, they insist, for the engineering. Please! They
drive them the way generals wear stars.*

*Most of my life, it turns out, I've spent chasing the respect of people I
don't respect. Worse, I looked down my nose at people I ought to have honored. When a friend told me he was writing poems, I pitied him—then in
secret scribbled a poem about it. How sick is that?*

*You might think I'm bummed by my waste of life. Oddly not. I find it
funny—how stupid I've been, thinking myself so smart. Also, I'm grateful to
have woken up in time—maybe—to do something about it. No road is bad
that leads to a good place. I have my chance. What more can I ask?*

Another thing that's different is my certainty. You remember the man you married—often in error, never in doubt? That comes of being a critic, editorialist, pundit, always rendering verdicts.

On the road I'm under no obligation to conclude. And you know what? Nothing's ever what it seems. The deeper I look, the less I know. Any student of American history knows, for example, that Hayes "stole" the election of 1876—it's in all the textbooks. Well, maybe not. Or that Harding was a bum. Or that Jefferson or Teddy Roosevelt were paragons. Or that our history—from Andy Jackson to the twentieth century—except for Lincoln— is dull. It never ends. That we've had an Indian Vice President—who knew? And (I'm pretty sure) a gay President—or two—and a gay Vice President. It's not just the history that's surprising. Everything is.

You might think a loss of certainty leads to loss of confidence. If I am not I and history isn't what we thought and religion is a fable, where do we find our bearings? You've got to believe in something, don't you, to know how to spend your span?

I have never been surer of myself or less sure of anything I thought. What I'm sure about isn't a fact or creed or code but a feeling. What I'm do- ing feels right. This waking in the morning—to seeing and saying—feels like why I was born. I can't explain it, justify it, defend it. It makes no sense. It just is.

How will these discoveries affect my behavior? I have no idea. In all like- lihood, I'll seem the same—grayer, maybe, more casual—but little changed. I'll be the same old Carll because that's what everybody expects. Why make a fuss?

And I will be the same old Carll. And as different from that predecessor as a son from his father. Whether this changed Carll and his inevitably changed wife get along is anybody's guess. I'm hopeful but wary—and more than a little shy. It would be nice, after all our time together, if we could make this work. We'll give it our all. But will we click?

History shows, in the end, we are none of us in charge. Chance rules. A bullet, a forgotten overcoat, a missed meeting change everything. Medioc- rity soars. Giants slip on banana peels. Tomorrow's never what we had in mind.

I used to know my future. I had my three-year, five-year, ten-year plan. Now the story of Carll is a mystery movie. I buy my popcorn and take a seat in the dark.

12
The Road Again

"You know—"

Her name was drowned in the festive gabble.

She was an historian, she said, an art historian. Her concentration was American stained glass. She had a fine, chiseled face, but nervous. She pronounced judgments with assurance.

"How many miles a gallon does your RV get?"

"Ten. So I'm told."

"That's terrible."

"Not the greatest," I smile determinedly.

"They should be banned."

"Banned?"

"They're destroying the environment."

My smile is growing strained. "They enable millions of Americans to travel—see their country—who couldn't otherwise—"

"That's nonsense."

I hesitate. Debates heat my brain. They lead to acrimony. The easy exchange of ideas is not an American talent. "Nothing personal" means "it's personal."

Hours after a debate, I'm still honing arguments. My failure to convince taunts me.

The room is crowded. It would be simple enough to slide away from this cockatrice. She probably wishes it too. Her anger brims.

It startles me how often I ignore my advice. I know what's in my interest and do the opposite. My behavior mocks my intelligence.

This woman means nothing to me. There is no animal attraction, no point of honor. To indulge in avoidable violence is unforgivable. And yet—

"Have you ever been in an RV?"

"No, but I know how—"

190

"You know nothing. You're talking through your hat. There are 20 million RVers out there who are every bit as decent and patriotic as you are. Before you condemn them, maybe you should meet one."

"No need to get—"

"Maybe you should stick to stained glass."

ii.

The van makes me a man. If I do not thaw the pipes and refill the propane and buy food and drinking water and plot my course, what then? RVs in snow, unsoftened by awnings and flowerpots, recall coffins. January is a Calvinist. Set in order thy life.

The gap between the Carll who visited this RV camp last June and my present self seems a chasm. Then I was running *to*, I claimed, not *from*.

Now I am indentured to a half-done job. I have seen too much, said too much, dreamed too much, not to keep on.

Growth surprises. We expect it in plants and children but not our selves. "Grown-up" implies completed, awaiting only fruition and decay. At 21, some uncle thumps us on the shoulder, bellowing, "Now you are a man!" Thirty years later I wonder, Will I ever be?

I began by taking a journey. Now my journey takes me. This book feels impossible, but if I do not finish it, who will I be?

A journey must be made to mean something. Tourists forget this, riffling snapshots: "We went here and then here and then here." "So what?" is the hardest question in the language.

The bear went over the mountain. So what?

The bear who began this journey was less than honest. Not in what he said, but in what he didn't. An explorer he called himself, not a refugee.

Was flight cowardly or brave? For 26 years my wife and I fought for the steering wheel of our marriage while the car lurched.

Were we happy? Frequently. Unhappy? Frequently. Well-matched? Too. We'd whack and bash past nightfall, rearming at sunrise.

Then one day I quit. The contest didn't seem worth it. My wife was flabbergasted. Competitors didn't quit. You fought till one or the other surrendered.

Where two are one, there can be no victory, only different faces of defeat. My wife had won—but she'd lost. I had lost too. Gingerly, we tiptoed back together. Our civility surprised us. There was another way, it seemed.

191

The truce lasted until a difference arose too deep for compromise, too essential to ignore. We did not fight—we had forsworn fighting—but neither did we talk.

Again I left. This time in an RV. I wasn't divorcing, I was writing a book, going *to*, not *from*. I almost believed it.

That is the story behind this story. But it is not the end. Time whispered during my absence, Was this what we really wanted? Divorce is easy in our throw-away culture. Sometimes it is best. But oh, the loss—of memory, history.

I could have stayed home this January. I found myself looking for reasons. I shattered Migrant's rear window, backing into my son's basketball hoop. An accident? The replacement window arrived—air-shipped, at unseemly cost—and was installed. My itinerary stared. Any man who stayed at this juncture would be one I couldn't respect. I'd miss her, I murmured at the door. To my surprise, I meant it.

iii.

End of day two, second leg. The road reasserts itself. I wake to write— no phones, faces, news, only coffee and sweet biscuit. I write—two hours, three, till spent; then run, shower, phone, plan. Then I'm off, nagging myself to remember my electrical umbilicus lest I rip it off the utility stalk— again. My destination is . . . how about Winterthur?

Winterthur, in Wilmington, Delaware, is the preserved home of Henry Francis du Pont (1880–1969), great-grandson of the French-born founder of the famous firm. Henry's father, Colonel Henry Algernon du Pont (1838–1926), according to the Winterthur brochure, was a "Gentleman farmer and U.S. Senator," in that order.

It's hard being a scion, willowy branch of a stout trunk. It's hard quarrying significance from redundancy.

Henry Francis, unsuited, we suppose, to be even a Senator, snagged his posterity by amassing a pile. He called his 175-room home an "American country estate," though it resembles less an English manor than a jumbled-up American hotel. He crammed these rooms with American artifacts— furniture, China, glass, silver, ceilings, floors, paintings, quilts, costume—a cornucopia of domestic aspiration—which back then could be bought cheap.

He was born, we sense, too late. The age of shameless American estates—of Newport and Stanford White and Richard Morris Hunt and brutal ostentation and barbaric profligacy—was a generation prior. That was the time when, as Henry Adams hissed, "the American wasted more money more recklessly than anyone ever did before; he spent more to less purpose than any extravagant court-aristocracy; he had no sense of relative values, and he knew not what to do with his money when he got it, except to make more or throw it away." After the first World War, the rich, sensing resentment, grew less flagrant, tucking their showplaces up long drives. They would still be grand, but now they sought an excuse. Henry Francis's treasures were not for himself—of course not!—they were for scholarship, education. This was philanthropy, not showing off.

What legions visit is worth visiting. We are what we applaud. The fascination of Winterthur—and the Breakers in Newport, Rhode Island, and Biltmore House in Asheville, North Carolina, and the Vanderbilt Mansion in Hyde Park, New York, and appalling San Simeon—is less history—these builders were mostly historical ciphers—than fashion. These are designer showcases, *Architectural Digests* you can stroll through, dreaming of chintzes.

iv.

The visitor's Washington is such a decent place: quiet, clean, maintained. Other American cities exhibit more fervor and flavor; exuberance, dilapidation. They are, for better or worse, what their natives made them. From high-rises to low-rent districts, opera houses to flophouses, they reflect their electorate. Washington, by contrast, was built not by natives but by a nation. It is a city made by committee. Superimposed on an improbable swamp, L'Enfant's plan is unnatural. We are unused to such control.

As it was born, so has the District of Columbia grown. None of the public buildings is what a locality—even a big one—would erect. They are whiter, costlier. A developer, intent on recouping his investment, would not pick such opulent materials, stretch corridors so wide or ceilings so high; or if he did, he would add stories and razzmatazz to entice tenants. The famous Metro—deep, quiet, and convenient, with its coffered ceilings— seems nicer than taxpayers would spring for.

The enforced squatness of the buildings—none taller than the Capitol— similarly reminds the visitor that the nation, not the neighborhood, is in charge. It's wonderful living among buildings so person-sized, but it's weird. Our democracy tends to pile higher and higher, till the towers touch the clouds and, like the World Trade Center, draw lightning.

It is not only the might of America that keeps Washington decent, but a ubiquity of awe. Here is the triumph of America made manifest. The distance from the assembly room in Philadelphia, where our founders described our intent, to today's monumental Washington, seems incalculable. Yet in less than two and a half centuries, we accomplished it—we, the ordinary men and women whose names are emblazoned on every street sign and whose headstones carpet the hills of Arlington; We—the People.

Surprisingly, Washington retains few of our Presidents and Vice Presidents. All (except Washington) lived here, but only Kennedy, Taft, Wilson, and Elbridge Gerry stayed. (Clinton—George, one of two Vice Presidents to span two Presidencies[27]—began his afterlife here, but was removed in 1908 to his native Kingston, New York.) They're sad, in a way, these hangers-on, as if they'd died on a business trip.

Only Taft we're happy for. Because Taft, of all our Presidents, was the happiest (and fattest). Taft stayed because he liked it here. His Presidency had been painful, after his patron Teddy Roosevelt, impatient with retirement, took to bashing him. But eventually Taft got the job he wanted. President Harding appointed him Chief Justice. From his Arlington hillside he can almost glimpse the court he presided over, a place unlike politics, where participants were genial and polite.

Kennedy's death still stings. The eternal flame—a novel and vivid memorial—flicks angrily in the January wind. I was 13 when it was lit. For the first time I was allowed to watch as much television as I wanted. Our housekeeper, Susie Brown, brought sandwiches to the TV room, wiping her tears. I learned the word caisson. I saw a man shot. I wondered what little John-John must be thinking, saluting so smartly, and how dark things must look behind Jackie's veil. For weeks, I played almost nothing on the piano but the Navy hymn.

Wilson's tomb, in a side-apse of the National Cathedral, feels mournful too. It's overlooked, awkward, absorbed into the soaring Gothic architecture. Wilson's words, carved in the wall's recess, are obscured by flags. His second wife, Edith, is buried in the crypt a floor below. (The first Mrs. Wilson, Ellen, who died in the White House, was sent home to Rome, Georgia.) As often in his career, brilliant but prickly Wilson finds himself friendless, with no place to welcome him home.

---

[27]George Clinton served under Jefferson and Madison; John Calhoun under John Quincy Adams and Jackson.

The Congressional Cemetery where Gerry can be found (if you look hard), at the run-down eastern end of Pennsylvania Avenue, is not listed in any guides. As slums go, Washington's seem pleasanter than most, but even America cannot keep all of its capital in tourist trim. Poor Gerry, who served briefly as Madison's Vice President before dying, gets the bummest rap of any of the men who've led us. A stand-up member of that brilliant patriot generation, Gerry risked his life at Concord and Lexington, signed the Declaration of Independence, worked diligently as a delegate to the Constitutional Convention, served his friend John Adams as ambassador, was elected to all sorts of offices in Massachusetts, including Governor, thought and wrote tirelessly about the shape of this new nation, and what's he remembered for? A verb, derived from a partisan political cartoon that depicted Gerry as a salamander, redrawing election districts for his political benefit. Not notably corrupt, Gerry hardly invented this tactic, but as the Gerry in gerrymandering he must spend eternity as a byword for sleaze.

I happened on the Tomb of the Unknown Soldier in time for the changing of the guard. This puffed-up performance cries out for Gilbert and Sullivan. Three frowning ramrod-erect soldiers click heels, shoulder rifles and exchange places at a dream-slow pace. The sergeant adjures onlookers to remain silent "due to the solemnness of the occasion." Remembering the informality of generals like Taylor, Grant, and Ike, I almost chuckled. Nothing could be less American than such jackbooted posturing. The free-spirited Minuteman, portrayed at Concord's North Bridge, is the American type: summoned from his fields and restless to return to them.

One day, with DNA testing, there will be no more unknown soldiers. All will be named, no matter what remains. Even so, the message of this vista will resonate: the pristine dome of the Capitol, the Lincoln and Washington monuments, the orderly streets and clean white buildings; and in the foreground, that simple sepulcher of souls "known only to God," to recall the cost.

v.

A typo to end all typos:
President Wilson, whose wife had died in 1914, was courting Edith Galt, a widow. The capital was abuzz. That morning's report in the *Washington Post* was meant to read, "The President spent the evening *entertaining* Mrs. Galt." What appeared was, "The President spent the evening *entering* Mrs. Galt."

vi.

What if—

That "if" whistles like a bullet. And the lithe, dark-curled matinee idol vaults from the bunting-draped box onto the startled stage. Does he shout *"Sic Semper Tyrannis"* or have those lines been supplied by our mythologizing instinct? (History's not certain.) He twists his leg (clumsy for an actor), then limps off into eternal obloquy, perpetrator of the worst crime ever committed against America, our public enemy number one.

Terror jitters prohibit backpacks from Ford's Theater and there's no place to check one. With Migrant an hour away, near the last stop on the Metro, this poses a dilemma. Where in the capitol does one park a backpack? I try a hotel check room. In my dripping poncho I'm not their type. I try a restaurant. No, they eye me, customers only. I feel like an Arab. I feel *for* the Arabs. To be suspected—and blameless—riles. Because I'm wearing a poncho and want to rest a backpack? Is that all it takes to be despised? Where is FDR when we need him (quoting William James), "We have nothing to fear but fear itself"!

I don't really need to see Ford's Theater. I've seen it in pictures—indelibly in Ken Burns's reconstruction of that drastic night in *The Civil War*. There's no new news to be gleaned here; my shoes are sopped; my throat tickles. If the theater had been shut, I'd have skipped it without regret. Wilson, Kennedy, JFK, Taft, and poor old Elbridge Gerry are whom I've come for.

Tell me I can't, though, and I must. In a sidewalk hotdog stand, a pretty Asian immigrant—Vietnamese, I'm guessing—huddles against the sleet, awaiting her occasional customer. Could I leave my backpack with her for 20 minutes?

She looks at me with handsome dark eyes—then grins. "What if you a terrorist?"

The two ineradicable blots on America are our treatment of Native Americans and African-Americans. If the gravity of a betrayal is measured by the numbers betrayed, Reconstruction is our deepest shame.

Reconstruction, not slavery, we must repent. The abomination of slavery was not an American innovation. Only a handful of far-out visionaries, mid-nineteenth century, endorsed the equality of races. If you think you'd have been one of them, you're flattering yourself.

196

Reconstruction—making good on our promise of equal citizenship for the freed Negro—*was* an American initiative. We said we would, we began to, we kindled hopes, then welshed on the deal. It was too hard restoring the Union, we were sick of war. The Radicals' plan to enforce cultural transformation by military occupation would have failed. Guns rarely change minds. Our abandonment of the freed slave to the embittered vengeance of his former masters was worse.

What if—! If John Wilkes Booth had missed his cue; if the President had not given his regular bodyguard the night off; if, when Ulysses and Julia Grant sent their regrets, the war-weary Lincolns had decided to catch *Our American Cousin* some other night, might we have kept our promise to the freedmen and re-knit the nation? Would Lincoln have been able to enforce a new order in the South, "with malice toward none and charity toward all"? That Andrew Johnson failed is no surprise. Maybe only Lincoln, with his newfound political capital and uncanny wisdom, could have pulled it off.

The impact of individuals on history is a debate as old as history. Do leaders shape their times or times their leaders? Are we destiny's puppets or responsible for our results?

Like any worthwhile question, this has no answer. But gazing up at the President's box from among the jacket-shakers (we are all drenched), it's hard to suppress a spasm of loathing for the dashing Booth.

"You enjoy the theater?" Her dark eyes are still laughing.
"Please," I offer her five dollars.
"No, no," she shakes her head.
"Please."
"I did nothing."
"How much are the hotdogs?"
"Two dollars."
"I'll take three."

vii.

I'd never spit on a grave. Manners matter. And while I don't believe God's watching, what if I'm wrong?

For Spiro Agnew I'd risk it. Agnew spat on me—spews of alliterative bile. I was 18, trying to understand the world. I didn't feel responsible for the nation's wrangles—over Vietnam, black power, dope, hair, sex, etc.—but somehow I and my schoolmates were being blamed. We were pointy-headed liberals, educated by "an effete corps of impudent snobs," unpatriotic faggots. ("I didn't raise my son to be a daughter," declared the Vice President, to cheers.) Critics of administration policies were "nattering nabobs of negativism." (Patrick Buchanan, Agnew's speechwriter, was a master of zippy invective.) Agnew called one reporter "a fat Jap." Students at eastern universities he dubbed "Radiclibs," whatever that meant.

Being hated clarified my allegiance. I never had to think through global communism or black nationalism or drugs. What Agnew supported, I opposed. The enemy of my enemy was my friend.

Nixon could have chosen a nicer running-mate. Either Ronald Reagan or Nelson Rockefeller would probably have accepted in 1968. But Nixon wanted a Doberman pinscher, who'd make him look pettable by comparison. Agnew energized blue collar resentment, enabling Tricky Dick to eke by Happy Hubert. It was darkness versus light, and darkness won.

Both Nixon and Agnew got the exits they deserved.[28] But our spirit suffered. As high as JFK had elevated politics in my young eyes, Nixon and Agnew debased it. Politics was for punks and crooks. Government service was a soulless game. Though every President after Nixon ran on a promise of restoring luster to the Oval Office, campaigns grew continually less civil, sincere, substantive.

Timomium, Maryland, is one of those graceless sprouted-up suburbs where souls seem more warehoused than housed. Dulaney Valley Memorial Gardens is its dispose-all. No headstones are permitted on the treeless hills, only flat brown plaques, each with a circular indent to screw a vase in. Plaques come in small, medium, or large. Epitaphs cost extra.

The office receptionist sat behind a sliding glass window. The man ahead of me—a haunted nervous character about my age—was complaining that his parents' plaques had been cracked by the backhoe for the second time in three years. "You've got to watch graves all the time," he whispered darkly.

Dulaney Valley's brochure extols its advantages. There's a Children of Liberty Memorial, American Eagles Memorial, Fallen Heroes Memorial, Good

---

[28]While Agnew never pleaded guilty, he eventually repaid to the state of Maryland the $268,482 he claimed not to have taken in bribes.

Shepherd Feature, Eternal Light Feature, Abbey Garden Turf-Top Crypts, Dulaney Pet Heaven. Special events include "Fallen Heroes Day," which "commemorates the members of Maryland's public safety community who have lost their lives in the line of duty." Mother's Day and Memorial Day present floral buying opportunities. "Twenty-five soldiers and marines from Maryland who died in Vietnam are buried within the Circle of the Immortals." "The marble for our reproduction of Michelangelo's 'La Pieta' was taken from the same quarry in Carrarra where the sculptor found the marble for the original."

No mention is made of the Vice President. The lady behind the glass buzzed a young man to escort me. The young man scrutinized a map, shook his head, disappeared into an office, then returned with another map, more detailed. The Agnew plaque is about 20 yards to the left of The Last Supper Feature, which replicates da Vinci's fresco in marble. Agnew's plaque is the small size, 12 by 18 inches or so. The inscription reads:

AGNEW

Spiro T.

1918–1996

Elinor L.

1921–

The indent, which I mistook at first for a religious symbol, was cracked.

The young man asked if there was anything else he could assist me with. No, I thanked him. A bitter January wind drilled through my parka. I snapped a picture, climbed into my van, and drove. Schubert was playing, his eighth symphony.

I had not spit.

13
Virginia

i.

The visitor to America in January should not miss the Super Bowl. Whether or not it's amusing, it's amusing.

The place to watch is on TV. In person, the Super Bowl is a confab of big shots. The true Super Bowl is the one available to all, that pals collect around with their Buds and wings and chips.

I pop my Bud and nosh my wings and chips. A whistling wind shudders Migrant's flanks. I'm alone but not lonely. I've been invited to two nearby Super Bowl parties. (The Super Bowl's getting to be like Thanksgiving, a day on which Samaritans see no one's stranded.)

I've used my satellite TV half a dozen times in five months. I dread to calculate cost per usage. I installed my TV in case loneliness got the better of me. Or in case of another 9/11.

The surprise of the Super Bowl is its monotony. Action on the field, in the sportscasters' booth, in the ads, during the half-time show is all alike: exploding, shrieking, blazing: a three-hour fireworks display. Whether the product being pitched is a car, a soft drink, a movie, chewing gum, sneakers, online classifieds, or football, some one or thing is getting beaten or blown up. The TV personalities don't sit and talk: they pace and scream, as if pursued. Female pop stars at halftime are dressed dominatrix-style, in black leather and silver chains, while their male backups writhe over their guitars like Nibelungen amidst sparks and smoke. Graphics hurtle. An on-field injury is a welcome breather: cameras don't twirl for once; sportscasters murmur.

Delight depends on variety, pacing. Symphonies that endure alternate between major and minor, fast and slow, loud and quiet. Too much of the same induces numbness, like ice cream for every course.

Our diversions reflect us. Our jobs we must put up with. Pastimes we choose.

The population reflected by the Super Bowl broadcast is stupefied, dazed as a brained hog. Too many explosions have deafened us to all but yelling. We are incapable of sustained attention. Calm conversation is out of the question. We no longer notice what we're shown. Bombs exploding are no big deal.

I turn from my TV depressed. Our technological ingenuity is a marvel, but is this all we've done with it? Has our genius contrived a culture in which there is no room for complexity, silence, awe?

Long-time grade school teachers note the shortening of attention spans over the decades. Restlessness overtakes kids more readily. Words no longer instruct; audio-visuals are required. The response to intellectual challenge is to shy away, demand that the channel be changed. "This is boring," the uneasy student decrees.

(I've read that our President hates the word "nuance.")

The day after the Super Bowl I visited Mount Vernon. It was freezing and a weekday, so Washington's home was as empty as it gets. You could feel the quiet of the place, the learning that derives from reading and letter-writing and cultivating new plants and the cawing of geese amidst the ice. On the path to the wharf, past Washington's tomb, I was startled by a squirrel in the leaves.

America, almost alone among the countries of earth, was not an inadvertent result but the product of deep thought: a notion, then a nation. Long quiet hours with Thucydides, Montesquieu, Gibbon, and Addison informed our Founders' debates.

Freedom of thought is, of all, the most valuable. But we cannot exercise it if we don't know how. One cannot meditate amidst riot. Ideas take longer than 60 seconds to germinate.

Our modern American stupidity is a shame. It may also be a peril. Stupid people do stupid things.

ii.

Tombs talk. This is not mysticism. Listen. The shape of the marker, its condition, epitaph, statuary (if any); planting and maintenance, placement, locality, all confess.

Compare the two leaders of the Confederacy: General Robert E. Lee's Memorial Chapel at Washington and Lee University in Lexington, Virginia, and President Jefferson Davis's grave in Richmond, Virginia's, Hollywood Cemetery (Hollywood, for the holly trees). The statue of Lee ranks with Daniel Chester French's Lincoln as a masterpiece of consolation. An inch longer than life-size, Lee is depicted napping on his cot during a battle. His uniform is neat. He is calm. The reassuring form, of bright white Vermont marble, is theatrically framed at the chapel's front. Downstairs, in an elegant small museum, hang portraits of Lee's and his wife's ancestors, including George and Martha Washington. Lee's decades in the American army and his five years as president of Washington College are celebrated as much as his leadership of the Confederacy. The message is clear: a great American from a family of great Americans performed his duty honorably and now rests. Winning or losing is not the measure of greatness: honor is. No man can alter fate, but he can determine how he meets it. There is no war in Lee's Chapel: there hardly ever was one, only an honorable disagreement honorably settled, after which we embrace and move on.

The Lee Memorial Chapel is in the center of the handsome, porticoed, prosperous Washington and Lee University campus (Lee's name was added to Washington's in honor of his service to the school). Attractive students amble the crisscrossing paths, thinking of tomorrow. For them, the past is the past, almost quaint.

Lee truly rests (as does Traveler, his beloved horse, just outside the chapel). Jefferson Davis's tomb claims "He rests," but don't believe it. Davis stands upright on a high bluff, overlooking his late nation's capital and the foaming stone-studded James River. He is skinny as an anorexic, tense, defiant, delicate jaw elevated, sleepless, vowing beneath his breath that independence will *yet* be achieved. His is the spirit of the unvanquished—bitter, unbowed—an embodiment of the fantastic certainty that led to secession in the first place.

Hollywood Cemetery also houses Presidents Monroe and Tyler. It is hemmed by city, like many once-rural city graveyards. The day I visited some florid men in too-tight Confederate uniforms were firing an antique cannon from beside Davis's grave. Their pickups sported Confederate decals. They cheered when the cannon roared. Spotting my New York plates, one gunner elbowed his companion, who nodded. New York to them was not Wall Street or Broadway or the twin towers, it was what was wrong. I grazed a headstone backing up. A word could lead to words. For these reenactors, the past was still the future. The war was still on.

iii.

It may be my Clara Barton streak, but overlooked leaders tempt me more than our stars. Lincoln, Washington, the Roosevelts, Jefferson, Kennedy spawn industries. Ditto, Jackson, Grant, the elder Adams. Their facts have been combed, debate lines about their legacies have been drawn. Academic societies convene around them, with by-laws, minutes, web sites. The suffix "-iana," tacked to their surnames, means something. My voice can only swell a chorus.

But with Harding, the junior Harrison, Hoover, Pierce? These reputations could use a hand.

John Tyler makes it hard. He bristles at sympathy. His Roman nostrils flare dismissively. His pose, alone of the official Presidential portraits, looks away. He has no patience for politics—or for history, which assigns him his low rank. He did what he thought right (sniff), helped his fledgling nation through a rough patch (sniff), solidified the authority of the Executive branch (sniff), merits thanks (sniff). That no one cottoned to him, that he got little done, that he's our only President who died as a citizen of another nation (the Confederacy), well, that's the cost of principles (sniff), which must be borne.

Our first accidental President, succeeding to the office after William Henry Harrison died of long-windedness, Tyler could have accepted his position as titular and let Congress rule. Congress would have liked that. The Constitution states the duties of the President "would devolve upon the Vice President" if the President left office. Did that mean the Vice President would *become* President, or only Acting President? Opinions differed, depending (as ever) on self-interest.

John Tyler slammed the door on this uncertainty. He was President—not "His Accidency," as lampoonists styled him, not Acting anything—but President, sworn in, as empowered as if he had been the people's choice. The United States, thanks to his decisiveness, would never be leaderless in such crises.[29]

Thank you, President Tyler! But oh, couldn't you have lightened up? Did you have to alienate your partisans as well as your opponents with your stubborn hauteur?

---

[29]We've had nine so far.

He is almost too proud to want to help. Leave him in history's ditch! But then, one word—a tart aside—makes me cotton to the guy.

Nobody could stand Tyler at the end of his term. Exasperated relations with Congress made him impotent as Chief Executive. His unpopularity appalled his fellow Whigs and delighted the Democrats.

Dismissed as an irrelevancy, diminished by the hoopla over President-elect Polk (a Democrat), President Tyler decided to host an outgoing gala, a defiant sumptuous affair. During it he was heard to remark: "Who can say now I'm a President without a party?"

iv.

When our kids were small they liked a book called *Where's Waldo?* Waldo was an engaging imp whom the author buried in teeming illustrations. The game was spotting Waldo in the throng. "There he is!" eager fingers stabbed. "There! No, there!"

Today's grown-ups play history the same way. We scan the mob for faces to latch on to: "There he is! No, there!" The flow of history is dim to us without these familiars. The evolution of ideas, systems, or states must be illuminated by personalities, or not at all.

1808 to 1824 was an important period in the growth of our republic but darn if we can recall what happened. There was a war—at least, a sort of war—the White House was burned—General Jackson won the battle of New Orleans—but what else?

The problem is "Where's James?" We know the names—Madison, Monroe. Each has an essential document linked to him—the Constitution, the Monroe Doctrine. But we can't for the life of us conjure an image. They have no stories somehow, no personalities: no flamboyant excesses or salacious secrets: no arch-enemies or fatal defects. You could never make them a miniseries.

Perhaps their most intriguing attribute is their invisibility. Where are they hiding? We are whizzes in America at inflating nonentities into celebrities. Yet two legitimately famous Americans—they were Presidents, after all, and not dopes—we can't coax out of the shadows.

Our perplexity would have puzzled James and James. Well-bred gentlemen of the eighteenth century were not expected to be distinct. One strove toward the common ideal: perfect manners, perfect syntax, perfect appearance. What transpired in private was nobody's business. Conformity, not peculiarity, elicited applause.

The confessional impulse is so rampant nowadays it's hard to conceive of a time when indiscretion was repugnant. Everybody's a "unique individual" with a sob story. Win an Olympic race and next thing you know your heart is breaking over a kid sister's leukemia. We unzipper our souls at the click of a mini-cam. People who don't are considered strange.

The word "personality," before the nineteenth century, meant being human, as opposed to being an animal or thing. Rousseau and the Romantics were the first to glorify the individual. Once we started looking at ourselves we couldn't stop. Confessional poetry, the novel, psychiatry, biography peered deeper and deeper into our wriggling innards. We were all sickos down deep and the sickest were those who didn't think so.

James and James saw themselves as public servants. They weren't outlandish romantics like their mentor Jefferson, whose contradictions and charm will keep tongues wagging till the end of time. Jefferson had "personality," in our modern sense. James and James, while Jefferson's juniors (by seven and fifteen years), were more old-fashioned. Madison was a brilliant mind in a miniscule body. (At 5'4" and a hundred pounds he was our smallest President, and almost pathologically shy.) Monroe was a middling mind in a handsome body—an amiable fellow, by all accounts, who worked hard. Neither wished to appear eccentric or superior. Near their lives' ends they burned their personal correspondence, frustrating gossipy posterity. Were they hiding shameful secrets? Who doesn't? (Madison, according to his principal biographer, suffered from epileptoid hysteria, psychosomatic seizures resembling epilepsy, during which you black out. What TV's tragedy-mongers might have made of that!)

The absence of photographs further protects James and James from our prying. (John Quincy Adams was the first President to be photographed.) Painted portraits interpret. The subject appears as he prefers. Madison and Monroe sit bland as bread (except for one dashing late image of Monroe, by Thomas Sully, which is misleading). Photographs give us the man as he was—the creases, the eyes. (How much of our empathy for Lincoln, we wonder, is attributable to the sad gaze in Matthew Brady's photographs?)

Not having to campaign also insulated James and James. Political campaigns, which began with Andrew Jackson, force candidates define themselves. James and James were anointed President. They accepted the assignment; they did not run.

Sometimes you can find the man in his remains. The preserved homes of Buchanan, Hayes, Garfield, Benjamin Harrison, Harding, Coolidge, both Roosevelts, and Truman reek of them. George Washington is ubiquitous in Mount Vernon; Jefferson overflows Monticello. The Adamses' houses in Quincy, along with their voluminous correspondence, offer clear keys to their characters.

Here again, James and James vanish. I had hopes of finding Madison at Montpelier, his Virginia plantation, but the ill-maintained mansion is a sorry hodge-podge (some lesser du Ponts elephantized the original, so that little of the Madisons survives). Ashland-Highland, Monroe's farm next to Monticello, was altered unrecognizably; and while Monroe owned the place for 26 years, he lived there for only a few.

I drove to my campground irritable. I felt thwarted. Even these men's tombs were afterthoughts, reflective of the funerary fashions of a later generation. Reagan also hid his private self—only, in Reagan's biographer's judgment, there was not much private self to hide. All I would know of James and James was what they meant me to: their deeds, their portraits, the objects that survived their families' bankruptcies (our planter Presidents, except Washington, were bumbling businessmen), the words they had not burned. James and James would not be psychologized, dramatized, sentimentalized. They would be loyal and devoted husbands, kindly masters to their slaves (though they never freed them), diligent, patriotic, upright, selfless: in short, model public servants. If that wasn't enough for posterity, well, that was posterity's problem.

v.

Why can I never predict what I'll remember? After Monticello it's not the gardens or calendar clock or dumbwaiter or polygraph or greenhouses or exotic artifacts. Neither is it the delicate Palladian architecture nor the long views over Virginia's hills. I do not forget these things—few houses on earth are less forgettable—but what returns to me in my dreams is Jefferson's bed.

Crammed in an alcove between his study and bedroom it feels built for one. Another person might fit there, for a quick encounter, but not live there. Jefferson, among his scientific instruments and books and inventions and musings, lives alone.

The house was stuffed—with grandchildren, visitors, slaves. The handsome parlor hummed with family and friends reading, chatting, playing games. Often the big dinner table wasn't big enough. No Presidential home is more gregarious, less austere. But for all the burble and bustle, the strollers on the lawns, the laughter upstairs, Jefferson—for long hours at day's start and end—was by himself.

His curiosity was insatiable. He's our brainiest President. Philosopher, politician, diplomat, educator, architect, inventor, paleontologist, archaeologist, horticulturalist, linguist, musician, plantation squire, the breadth of his interests recalls Leonardo's. John F. Kennedy's wry tribute to his predecessor at a gathering of Nobel laureates still makes us smile: "I think this is the most extraordinary collection of talent and of human knowledge that has ever been gathered together at the White House—with the possible exception of when Thomas Jefferson dined alone."

We shake our heads, incredulous. He's not one man, he's 10. Twenty thousand of his letters have been preserved. There are the books he wrote, the drawings he rendered, the measurements he recorded, the catalogues he collated—not to mention his careers as legislator, governor, ambassador, Secretary of State, Vice President, President, and university founder. Where did he find the time?

He was too busy to brood. Yet we feel him brooding. He misses Martha, whom he called Patty. She had been so slight,[30] smart, accomplished, vivacious, frail. She had understood him. Their marriage he described as "ten years of unchecquered happiness." She was 33 when she died; he was 39. The next 44 years he lived alone.

Loss isolates. So does intelligence. The Man of Mind might like to lose himself, become one of the boys, remarry maybe, but it's hard. To be one of the boys you have to shout Right on! and mean it. Jefferson, one senses, especially after losing Patty, found himself on the periphery of the fun.

People frustrated him. Right solutions were obvious. But so often others didn't see it his way. They misunderstood, took off on wild goose chases, refused to listen to reason. He felt like saying to hell with them.

He did say to hell with them in the final months of his Presidency. The Man of Mind had decided that he would force the British and the French to respect America's rights by forbidding them to trade with us. He would punish their pocketbooks and in no time they'd cry uncle.

Many people thought the Embargo Act was a bad idea. Jefferson's astute Secretary of the Treasury Albert Gallatin cautioned against it. "As to the

---

[30]She weighed practically nothing and stood five feet next to Jefferson's six-two.

hope that it may . . . induce England to treat us better," he wrote to Jefferson shortly after the bill had become law, "I think (it) is entirely groundless . . . government prohibitions do always more mischief than had been calculated; and it is not without hesitation that a statesman should hazard to regulate the concerns of individuals as if he could do better than themselves."

Gallatin was right. The pocketbooks that got punished were American, not British, and the Americans didn't like it. They turned on Jefferson, so Jefferson turned on them. Fed up with being President he retired prematurely to Monticello, leaving others to run the country. Three days before the official end of his term, Congress repealed the controversial Embargo Act—a sharp rebuke.

Jefferson, like many Men of Mind, was as impractical as he was brilliant. He was born rich and died deep in debt. His actions frequently failed to jibe with his assertions. The decrier of slavery failed to free his own slaves or acknowledge his mulatto offspring. In his view anyone who called him a hypocrite would have misunderstood. Men of Mind always know why they're right, appearances notwithstanding.

Jefferson dictated his epitaph, insisting that "not one word more" be inscribed.

HERE WAS BURIED THOMAS JEFFERSON

AUTHOR OF THE DECLARATION OF AMERICAN INDEPENDENCE

OF THE STATUTE OF VIRGINIA FOR RELIGIOUS FREEDOM

AND FATHER OF THE UNIVERSITY OF VIRGINIA

No mention of the Presidency. I snapped his obelisk in a blurring snow.

vi.

It is past four. I am in Williamsburg, Virginia, trudging west on the Duke of Gloucester Street from the College of William and Mary to the old colonial capitol.

Why this gloom?

Moods turn tyrannical when you have no obligations to distract you. I am not, I'd say, moody. You wouldn't find me, if we met, veering alarmingly from ebullience to despair. People who impose their moods annoy me. It's as selfish to sulk in public as it is to fart.

Still, moods, whether or not we exhibit them, churn in us ceaselessly as tides. One moment we are hopeful, the next despairing, for no obvious cause. I observe my moods with an explorer's curiosity. Is this shift rational or physiological? Have I happened on some truth or am I hungry?

Deepening my dismay this cool Sunday is my distance from relief. It'll be two foot-sore hours before I'm parked and can pour a glass of wine.

Stuck with my sadness, I try to extricate myself with an explanation. I look around. Something is bothering me about America's—or maybe the world's—top "history tourism destination," but what?

Colonial Williamsburg is to history tourism what Kellogg's is to breakfast cereal. For one in my line, eager to alert neighbors to our past, grumbling about Williamsburg seems churlish. These visitors, at least, aren't wasting their brains on sitcoms or video games. What happened here mattered.

I rejoice in the existence of Williamsburg. Really. But what comes over me this February afternoon—if it's not hunger or fatigue—is a sense of loss. Strolling from restored to recreated to new buildings in a "colonial style," from "historical" shops and eateries with "authentic" merchandise and menus and clerks in period garb to the predictable pricey boutiques you find on any fashionable avenue, it's unclear where history ends and hustling begins. The true fate of the Duke of Gloucester Street, if John and Abby Rockefeller hadn't intervened to rescue it, would be as a slum or mall or condo complex. A precious chunk of our past would have been crushed beneath the boot of time. And yet, inexorably, by making this past palatable and popular, we distort it, wresting memory into a theme park, narrowing the gap between history and Disney.

We also crowd out the individual. Williamsburg guests are not participants, as the brochure brags, but spectators, subjected to the show, told what to think. "This is how it was," we are assured by costumed docents (or are they cast members?), straining to smile as they recite. "But this is not how it was!" I feel like shouting. "This is a fantasy of how it was, conceived by 'interpreters' to ingratiate crowds. The actual authentic is buried beneath this seductive pleasantness. History is not this easy. It is not this nice."

The young woman playing cook in the Palace kitchen that afternoon was in an unscripted funk. Ask her about the dough she was rolling or the rabbit wrapped in bacon on her elaborate spit, and spit—very nearly—was what you got. Startled visitors hurried to the next exhibit. I lingered, curious.

Whatever was bugging her—her boss, her paycheck, her period: who knows?—she was doing her best to advertise her distress. Her surliness I found oddly reassuring. It, at least, was true.

vii.

I-64 is the superhighway of American history. Jamestown, where it all began, Williamsburg, Yorktown, where freedom was won, Richmond, the capital of the Confederacy, Charlottesville, Appomattox, dangle from this necklace. Washington, Jefferson, Patrick Henry, John Marshall, Madison, Monroe, Tyler, the Harrisons, Jefferson Davis, Lee, Grant, Stonewall Jackson, Lincoln, Woodrow Wilson all traveled this road. The Revolution was fought here, and the Civil War.

I wonder what I'm doing—at Mount Vernon and Williamsburg and at all the museums and battlefields and monuments and parks and gift shops and libraries and roadside markers I've visited these months. I've been looking, yes, but for what? I am no scholar. My attention skitters like a leaf before the wind.

There is too much history to master. Information is infinite. It's not proficiency I've come for, but risk; not then, but now. Only through encounters do we encounter our self.

History measures us. There's a telling moment in the play *Waiting for Godot*, when Vladimir asks Estragon, "You're not comparing yourself to Christ!" and Estragon answers, "All my life I've compared myself to Christ." It's ridiculous to compare ourselves to the great figures of the past. But only by such comparisons do we learn and grow. How do I stack up against Washington or Jefferson or Grant or Lee? How do our times differ? What do they teach us? What might we teach them?

viii.

Something stings. Then again. A scattering on the pavement of rubber bands.

I look up. A giggle and two heads disappear in a window.

"Least it's better 'an 'em whackin' off," shrugs the man I've stopped to ask directions of.

* * *

It's 40 minutes till the next house tour, so I stroll to the river. The James. Berkeley Plantation. Birthplace of William Henry Harrison.

Harrison's father Benjamin was a Signer of the Declaration of Independence, Governor of Virginia, and rich. William Henry's campaign relocated his birth to a log cabin.

Harrison's handlers also transplanted him from the Tidewater to the western territories so they wouldn't have two Virginians on the ticket. (His Vice President, John Tyler's, plantation, Sherwood Forest, closed to the public, is a few miles down the road.)

In its bid to be most "historic," Berkeley awards itself three firsts. Here, on December 4, 1619, the "first official Thanksgiving" was celebrated by arriving Englishmen ("despite what you may have been told," declares my docent darkly). Here, in 1621–1622, bourbon was first distilled by "Master George Thorpe, Episcopal Preacher," bless him. And here, on a bored steamy night in 1862, encamped with General McLellan's 140,000-man Army of the Potomac, Brigadier General Daniel Butterfield whistled "Taps." (I've run into Butterfield before. His statue stands in a park outside Grant's Tomb in New York City. The Parks Department plaque reads, "General Daniel Butterfield (1867–1941)." In view of his service in the Civil War, these dates make him a prodigy.)

Berkeley's walls have witnessed more history than almost any in America. Benedict Arnold raided Berkeley during the Revolution, hoping to capture its owner. Our first 10 Presidents spent time here. Washington was a close friend. Jefferson made remodeling suggestions. William Henry Harrison wrote his inaugural address here—the longest ever, delivered in cold wet weather, which led to Harrison's pneumonia and death. Lincoln visited his army here twice in the long frustrating summer of 1862. The Harrison dynasty, which began here, extended through two Presidents and two Congressmen, a legacy rivaled only by the Adams and Bush families.

Had Berkeley been located in New England or the Midwest, it might have become a shrine. Instead, it fell into ruin, along with the planter society it represented. It wasn't until after the Great War that Americans discovered they had a past worth preserving. Saving the old was a new idea.

Wealth can be measured different ways. Among America's treasures is its past. The quantity and quality of our American inheritance defy imagining:

211

thousands of places and buildings preserved and maintained for the pleasure of all. I have visited hundreds in recent months and not one has failed to better me.

The past is a luxury few nations can afford. Destitute nations, like China during the Cultural Revolution or Afghanistan under the Taliban, may erase splendid pasts, aggrieved by the comparison. The presence of the past enriches the present. It entertains, instructs, admonishes, encourages. It makes us wiser, humbler, more reverent. It makes our stories more interesting.

In Berkeley's dining room, there's a gentleman's desk with 12 small drawers for his monthly receipts, four larger drawers for his quarterly, and two still larger for his semiannual documents. There are also discreet compartments for his wig, gold coins, and false teeth. Connecting Berkeley's cook house to the manor (eighteenth-century kitchens were often in outbuildings to protect from fire) is a tunnel. Because slaves carrying the warm food could not be observed as they passed through the tunnel, they were required to whistle, to prove they weren't nibbling. The tunnel was known, unapologetically, as "the whistling tunnel." In a dim glass case in Berkeley's cellar are recovered Civil War bullets with teeth marks on them. Soldiers "bit the bullet" during amputations without anesthetic.

ix.

Phrases revealed:

"Sleep tight"—on a rope bed, that needs to be tightened.

"Range"—cast iron cook stoves supplied a *range* of temperatures, unlike the hearth.

Two about rodents:

"The mouse ran up the clock" because the clock's works were lubricated with tasty animal fat.

A "drowned rat" was a common sight. The rat was trapped, then the trap submerged in a water barrel to finish the business.

Three from Yorktown:

"Lock, stock, and barrel" are the components of a musket.

"Half-cocked" is the position in which a musket won't shoot.

When the powder sparks but the bullet doesn't fire, there's "a flash in the pan."

X.

A between day. But the road forbids emptiness. Even with nothing to do, you can't do nothing.

Henry Adams quotes Pascal: " 'I have often said that all the troubles of man come from his not knowing how to sit still.' Mere restlessness forces action. 'So passes the whole of life. We combat obstacles in order to get repose, and, when got, the repose is insupportable; for we think either of the troubles we have, or of those that threaten us; and even if we felt safe on every side, *ennui* would of its own accord spring up from the depths of the heart where it is rooted by nature, and would fill the mind with its venom.' "

This is half true: we go *from*. But we go *to* too. Away from futility and toward discovery. Yes, we are meaningless, yes, our works and loves will vanish into dust, but oh, what we can encounter in the interim!

Take yesterday. It was a Saturday. I woke uncertain where I was. I raised the shade by my bed, tried to reconstruct. Yes: Dixie Caverns Campground in Salem, Virginia. But it wasn't the caverns I'd come for, not even for the famous Wedding Bell stalactite, beneath whose lacy tracery, according to the brochure, "dozens of couples have been united in 'wetted' bliss." I'd come because Salem was a couple of hours south of Staunton, Woodrow Wilson's birthplace, which got me a couple of hours closer to the Carolinas.

I studied myself to assess how well I'd slept. We monitor ourselves continually, our pulse, our bumps, our aches, our looks, wondering why this soreness or that hardness, tonguing an abscess when no one's looking, secretly scratching a mysterious itch. It is sad when people stop inspecting themselves.

If I've slept well, I've a chance of writing well. If not, I must summon Reason to buck me up.

Happily, Somnus has befriended me. I light my burner, drain my bladder, warm my muffin, spoon coffee into the beaker, shelve last night's dishes, waken my laptop, listen for beep of microwave and whistle of kettle, pour from kettle to beaker, beaker to cup, clamber back into bed and I'm off. Where? Wherever! Any road leads to where you've never been.

Emptied of words, I plan my day. I check the map. Booker T. Washington's birthplace is near. Why not? I'll camp in . . . oh, how about the KOA in Enfield, North Carolina? My tattered campground directory says it's

"Open all yr."—as many aren't. It'll be a haul, but I like the book I'm listening to—McFeeley's biography of Grant. It'll be OK.

Now I dawdle, not to jog. I dislike jogging, but dislike not jogging more. I jog until I pant, sweat, and my fingertips tingle—a mile or two.

Jogging, I amuse myself by remembering what I've forgotten. I am always misplacing things in my mind. Practical obligations, in particular, are never where I left them. I think of the kids, my wife, friends, birthdays or anniversaries approaching, the names on road signs, the maintenance of lawns, the aspiration of stoops.

I am always glad to find Migrant again. What if I didn't? What if a fire broke out in my absence or she'd been hijacked? Love grows from dependency. Migrant, for the present, is my protection. She cares for me, so I for her.

One of the things I remember wanting to look up is how in blazes Woodrow Wilson, an academic, got elected President of the United States only two years after getting more or less ousted as President of Princeton. Nowadays academic attainment would blight, not promote, a candidacy. Candidates labor not to seem too brainy (most don't have to labor much).

Turns out (everywhere you look, a surprise), Wilson's ascendancy was triply accidental. He quit the Presidency of Princeton after alienating faculty and trustees with his reforming zeal. The New Jersey bosses recruited him to run for Governor because they thought he'd be pliant and when he wasn't he became the darling of reform-minded Democrats. Back then, to win a Presidential nomination, you needed the support of two-thirds of the delegates. Champ Clark of Missouri, long-term Speaker of the House, had 556 votes, 11 more than a majority. Not since 1844 had the winner of a majority been denied the nomination. But William Jennings Bryan, the Democrat's great pooh-bah, was iffy on Clark. The convention deadlocked. Wilson was within minutes of throwing in the towel, but then one thing happened and another, and Teddy Roosevelt, restless out of the limelight, split the Republican vote by running as a Bull Moose, and the Democrat sailed to easy victory with 42 percent of the popular vote. The inevitable in retrospect—Wilson the Great Reformer—was a fluke.

We flatter ourselves with the idea of destiny—God has a plan—but everything is accident. That is the wonder, the glory, the comedy. Why am I—why are we—here now? Because, because, because. But there is no because. Champ Clark, by rights, should have been President. John Tyler, Millard Fillmore, Andrew Johnson, Chester Arthur, Teddy Roosevelt, Calvin

Coolidge, Harry Truman, Lyndon Johnson, and Gerald Ford should never have been President. My father, by my age, shouldn't have been dead. It makes no sense. But does anything? That I am making my way across back roads on a dark February night toward a place I've never heard of for reasons not quite clear, whistling Confederate battle tunes, is nuts! But so it is.

14
South to Georgia

i.

Raindrops crack like pellets on Migrant's tin roof. No lights out my window. No other campers this off-season. What if my heart—

The Outer Banks, that narrow necklace of islands off the North Carolina coast, is a land of lore. Here, on Roanoke Island, the first English colony was planted by swashbuckling Sir Walter Raleigh, in 1585, only to vanish into myth. Here Virginia Dare, the first English child born in America, became the first missing child.[31] Here on the dunes of Kitty Hawk, a mere century ago, Wilbur and Orville Wright accomplished the dream of Icarus. Legend whispers of pirate treasure buried in the sand. Corroded smokestacks and boilers and mast-tips poking out of the water recall the more than 2,000 ships sunk in these shallows. The rapscallion settlers of Nags Head, we're told, tied lanterns on their horses' necks and rode them along the night shore to lure seamen onto the reefs.

The thrill of the dangerous, the exotic. Who'd be so stupid to build his house on this sand spit which one day the sea must erase?

The answer, of course, is everybody. In our beach-lust, we stack homes— four stories tall, six deep—against the ocean. Nature is no deterrent. The spit's single through-road (sometimes six lanes wide) is jostled by the chain stores and eateries of any seaside resort. I imagine the bronzed flesh and forced smiles of August. In February, at least, one is not obliged to exuberate.

ii.

Past dawn. Sky vivid blue. A furtive squirrel scoots across a branch. A portly blue jay alights and fusses.

---

[31]People who disappear never die. They drift in the imagination, crying out. If Virginia's face appeared on a milk carton—"Have you seen me?"—it would hardly surprise.

I am in Williamston, North Carolina, west of Albemarle Sound. It is poor in these parts: endless soggy fields flecked with old cotton; rusting trailer homes down pitted drives.

I should have reached Williamston before dark, but as usual I'd miscalculated. Mariah, my navigatrix, seems never to have visited here. Key in Ed's Grocery Road, Dan Peele Road, Bear Grass Road, Rodgers School Road and she comes up blank.

Finally, a Samaritan at a gas station leads me to Green Acres. He says he's headed that way but I'm not convinced.

I'd settled on Green Acres after seeing their ad in my tattered Woodall's. Having sold print ads for a quarter century, I know which have been sweated over. The Greene Family, owners, offer a web site, an e-mail address, local and toll-free numbers, two swimming pools, par-3 golf, boating and fishing, mini-golf, shuffleboard, volleyball, and, my favorite, a "climate-controlled clubhouse." This was no franchise—a KOA or Yogi Bear Jellystone, out of a kit. For 35 years, the Greene Family has been inventing, refining, discovering, improving, reinvesting, welcoming, and tending their guests. There are some 16,000 RV camps in North America, hard subsistence livings most of them. Many have a forlorn air, their owners' early hopes drubbed by results. Starting a business is scary—with bank payments, personnel, weather, all that can go wrong. Tight margins turn mishaps into deficits, meaning no new car this year, no helping out the kids. We salaam before the captains of industry but for my money the heroes of American business are the hundreds of thousands of owner-operators who risk their all and love what they have made.

The way I travel, where I park doesn't matter much. My room is the same every night. All Migrant needs are a plug, a spigot, and a drain. Still, I can sense beyond my shades and it affects me. Attention to detail points to confidence in the future. Confidence is contagious. So is despair. Two weeks ago, outside Richmond, a hulking female with a crew cut hounded me out of an empty campground when I stayed past check-out time. In response to a request to exchange nickels and pennies for three paper dollars, she replied that was not a service she offered. So much of what I've seen has vanished from memory, but her picture lingers.

Past seven, Mrs. Greene is still busy at her business. A hearty, affable lady, she moves with the easy assurance of one who knows every aspect of her enterprise and has seen it all. It's still not too late, she suggests, for my wife to join the aerobics class in the clubhouse. I watch her red marker trail across the site map. Payphone and modem are here—behind the fireplace.

Propane tanks here. My slot here. Anything I might want or need call this number—she circles it—day or night.

The electrical outlet and spigot and sewer opening, while not new, are well-maintained. The sky, after a long rain, is full of stars. I sleep like a child.

iii.

Pinehurst, North Carolina. No vans out my window, only tall pines, tan sand, red needles, a dumpster, a picnic bench. The birds' counterpoint is intricate. Branches hang motionless. Clouds hide the sun, enfeebling shadows.

I study the faces in the photograph: four men, age 20 or so, standing shoulder to shoulder, staring stilly forward. Each has signed his name beneath his image: Edwin Hill, Carl Speck, R. E. Theizer, C. J. Cunningham. The Lyons Studio in Charleston, West Virginia, took the picture. Suits, hairstyles, neckwear reflect 1900, maybe 1910.

I found this foursome in a flea-market in Salem, Virginia. A half price sale was in effect. If the picture had cost 20 dollars, I would not have bought it. Such a price would suggest that the dealer considered this object desirable. Four dollars, marked down to two, meant these men were dumpster-bound. Presumably, three other copies had been made by the Lyons Studio, but did they survive? Might this be all that remained of Messrs. Hill, Speck, Theizer, and Cunningham, and their friendship?

They are ranked by height. Hill, on the left, has the burly frame of a football player. Football players were college heroes in 1900, which may explain Hill's complacency. Cunningham, on the right, has the lithe build of a coxswain, and a wary, scrappy glance. Speck, next to Hill, is the Oscar Wilde of the lot. He alone wears a wing-tip collar. His smile is ironic and superior. Theizer has the mild forgiving face of a minister or family physician. Not for him the jostling energy of this new century.

The gazes of all are determined, confident. 1900 was a good time to be a white American male. There was no end of work, and little to fear. Women knew their place. The psychoses and uncertainties of the twentieth century had yet to sprout.

What became of these men, I wonder. Was their optimism confirmed? Did they find their satisfaction? Did they fly in airplanes? Did they remain friends?

Such a picture could not have been taken in my lifetime. We were never so easy in conventional clothes. We were never so sure. Destinies

218

were apparent in 1900; a man mattered—to his family, neighbors, nation. My generation—and my children's—had to invent our significance. We had to "find ourselves"—a phrase Messrs. Hill, Speck, Theizer, and Cunningham would have puzzled at.

The photographer at Lyons Studio—Mr. Lyons, presumably—was expert at fixing the gazes of his subjects, so they stare. I squirm. My enterprise strikes them as unmanly. A man does things that can be explained. If he writes, it's a history or essay, something of use.

I plead with their gazes not to judge me yet. I turn their faces to the wall.

iv.

I am in the parking lot outside North Carolina's old state capitol. It is a sunny afternoon. I have lunched with a friend, strolled the Capitol's halls with its usual portraits. (Portraits I can identify gladden me. Portraits I can't have the opposite effect. These were big men in their hour. They were hung in the Capitol. And now?)

I'm not sure what I'm thinking. When I'm not thinking is when I'm thinking. In school we are taught to think in a straight line. State your thesis, marshal your arguments, restate your thesis. It's useful training. Make your case and advance your cause. Leaders are lucid.

Like many small boys I wanted to be a leader. I'd tell mom's friends I was going to be President. (Ladies believed me more than men.) Later, after my dad died, I wanted to be a preacher for the same reason. I did not want to help people, I wanted them to help me—by looking up.

The statue of George Washington in the center of the Capitol's rotunda may be his silliest depiction. In the decade after the War of 1812, Americans were feeling their oats. It was the period historians label "The Era of Good Feelings." We were big and growing and free, we'd licked the Brits, our democracy was a wonder, what could go wrong? North Carolinians wanted to demonstrate their prestige by commissioning the world's greatest sculptor to depict the world's greatest Citizen.

Venetian Antonio Canova was a genius. His genius was making marble resemble resilient female flesh. Flesh and frolicking was what interested Venetians then. Long lapsed from their glory, why not party? Canova's sculptures thrilled Venetians. The faces were pretty and impersonal, but the bodies—wow. His statue of Pauline Bonaparte (now at the Borghese

Gallery in Rome) I have stared at slack-jawed as long as the guards permitted.

When we think of George Washington, flesh is not what comes to mind. The faces on the dollar bill, in Gilbert Stuart's portraits, on looming Mount Rushmore are not cuddly. It's hard to imagine George tickling Martha in the hay.

Canova and Washington were a mismatch. What the Venetian made of the American was an ancient Roman. That way he got to show toes, thighs, biceps, arms, neck, even midriff and pecs, beneath toga and sandals. (The Father of our Country, in case you were wondering, was buff.) The face, which bears no relation to other Washingtons, is a refined dandy's. Manicured fingers hold a stylus as an artist holds a paintbrush. (Canova might have used himself as model.) With this Commander-in-Chief we'd have won the Revolution—if cannon-balls were powder-puffs.

Rugged North Carolinians were appalled by what they'd bought. But as with anything we've paid a lot for and can't get rid of, they came to claim it as a prize. It is the toast of Raleigh, blazoned in brochures. A visitor happening on this statue unawares blinks incredulous.

I was thinking of George Washington and Canova and Pauline Bonaparte and my friend at lunch and what North Carolina owed to toxic tobacco (anything named Duke, for starters) and a forlorn local museum I'd driven past and how to exit this parking lot. Getting in had been no problem. There was no gate or sign, plenty of spaces. (Migrant occupies at least two, but more make it easier.) At the far corner there seemed to be a toll booth. There'd been no information about a toll but what could it amount to?

I inched toward the booth, languid, dreamy, serene. Deep anonymity was still new to me, and sweet.

The attendant seemed startled as I lowered my window to pay. There wasn't much traffic mid-afternoon. Perhaps she'd been dozing.

I'd prepared my apologetic smile. I didn't have a ticket. There'd been no sign. I thought this parking was free. How much, if anything, did I owe?

The lady's eyes widened. And suddenly, boom, she was keeling over backward. "What the—!" she screamed.

Since 9/11, big bangs mean the worst. *This is it*, we can't help thinking—especially at government sites.

I clambered from my cab. Apparently RVs were not expected in this parking lot. The overhang from the tollbooth was lower than my truck. The flimsy prefab unit had toppled like a bowling pin.

The attendant was brushing herself off. "Man—" she exclaimed, but neither of us knew what to say next. It was funny but it wasn't. This was a good joke, one of those nutty things that happen, only it wasn't.

The police took their time. The sergeant frowned solemnly. Destruction of government property. I protested. If there'd been a sign I would never have entered—maybe the state of North Carolina owed *me* for damages. (A strip of aluminum molding had torn off.)

Bureaucratic justice is not swift. The days when, after a mishap, the parties settled it between them and went their ways are bygone if they ever were. Bump a fender now and you get summonses, counterclaims, insurance adjustors, whiplash, and lawyers' fees.

I insisted that the sergeant include my comment on his report. (He was dubious.) I shoved my yellow copy into my document folder and drove to Andrew Johnson's purported birth shack. Andrew Johnson, age 16, escaped from North Carolina for the west and freedom. I knew the feeling.

v.

US-1. Heading south to South Carolina. February.

If seeing is your business, avoid the Interstates. Interstates mislead, like brochures. No life flanks them—the land is too valuable—only the splashy logos of mass providers.

US-1, notwithstanding its grand name, snakes through miles of mereness: dilapidating homes; dirt yards spiky with junk; old tires, wheel-less trucks; trash-flecked fields; burnt-out buildings; listless youths with skewed teeth and accents as slurred as their hopes. Each home, though, has its satellite dish. One tilts from a toppling porch.

I describe the scene to a friend, who has risen from modest beginnings to eye-popping wealth.

"Are you suggesting socialism?"

"I'm describing, not suggesting."

"Every system fails some. The question is which fails fewest."

"But this is America."

"Which means these folks at least have the *chance* to rise. If they only had the—"

"Don't." One of his favorite words is *gumption.*

"It's true. They could get a job at McDonald's—or Wal-Mart—go to college. Good colleges kill for kids like these, from nowhere zip codes. Demonstrates *diversity.*"

I think of my friend in his paneled study, leaning back, sneaker on desk edge (it is Saturday), phone steadied by his chin. He is paring his fingernails. Mine I gnaw, without thinking.

He'd be easy to ridicule—the Capitalist—but it wouldn't be fair. He's a good man. He gives. His children love him. He is faithful to his wife. He defends America like a sweetheart.

His deficiency is sympathy. He can shrug off lives as rounding errors. These lost boys along US-1—more supplied with stuff, perhaps, than their pioneer forbears, but bereft of hope—he can eye without remorse. Is it his fault they don't have—gumption? You can't have freedom to win without freedom to lose! The energy, the excitement—the genius—of America is the chance to *do better.* If everybody does better, nobody does. Somebody's got to come in last!

I can feel his frustration mounting. What's wrong with his logic, he demands!

"Nothing," I give up. "This is not about logic."

vi.

The bright new sanctuary of Columbia's First Baptist Church is a soundstage. Sight lines converge not on a cross or altar, but on the resplendent pulpit and behind it, the preacher's throne. Ranked behind the preacher, a choir of hundreds, their pressed robes and beaming faces dimly visible; hidden in an orchestra pit, the dozen or more musicians who'll accompany them. Hymns are numbers. Occasionally the congregation is urged to join in, while cameras pan, but the stars of this show are the talent—the paid singers and, of course, the preacher. Lighting is theatrical: brightening and dimming, widening, then narrowing to a spot.

I was welcomed effusively by ushers neat as cake-top bridegrooms. I looked a sight, having breasted four blocks of pelting rain (Washington, D.C., 300 miles north, was shoveling two feet of snow). My dress—

windbreaker, sweater, polo shirt, soaked khakis, and tousled hair—contrasted unfavorably with the thousand or more in their Sunday best.

The only black faces were three women deep among the choir. Segregation is not unusual in congregations, where we seek the solace of our kind. But since the Columbia First Baptist Church is where, in 1860, the secession movement officially began, I'd have thought, in 2003, some effort would be made to suggest progress.

The first order of business, as in many sects these days, was to turn to those nearest and declare affection. Such instant intimacy embarrasses me. How can you love someone you don't know?

Dr. Wendell R. Estep, Pastor and preacher, walks among the princes of earth, as he reminds his listeners not once, but twice. I'm not sure why, for my spiritual well-being, I needed to know that Dr. Estep has been "lucky enough to be personally acquainted" with five Presidents, or why his entry to the annual White House prayer breakfast (at which he seems a fixture) was eased by his being "the guest of Senator Graham." Dr. Estep is of the school of polite televangelists: he dresses like a CEO and eschews the fulminations of less chiseled preachers. While his theology remains exclusive (he prays that "his Jewish brethren" might save themselves by coming to Jesus), his veneer is nonconfrontational. He is a friend to all mankind—as long as they see things his way.

Dr. Estep's topic was how to justify irrational faith in a scientific age. It's interesting to observe preachers dancing around the conundrum: If their God is the one and only, how come only a sliver of humanity realizes it? Couldn't God, if He's so powerful, be more persuasive?

Dr. Estep, while no matinee idol, is an experienced performer, raising and lowering his voice, frowning and smiling, gesturing legibly, approaching and distancing himself from the lectern as if it were a dance partner. The houselights are dimmed to his penumbra. The point of his sermon is, plus or minus, the point of every sermon, thousands each week: "You're OK but could be better—You're loved, notwithstanding the evidence—Hurray for the home team."

After his sermon, Dr. Estep invites those so moved to come to Jesus right there and then. No one takes him up. At the door, he thanks me for coming with the glassy cordiality of a practiced politician.

I sit silent in Migrant, soaked and stunned. Faith has a weird effect on me. I admire belief, respect its utility. The idea that we matter, that we're meant and appreciated, may better our behavior and ease our trek. Who cares whether God made man or vice versa: we need one another. It is good to pray and praise.

I admire belief—and fear it. With credulity comes cruelty. Hurray for the home team and to hell with the rest. Dr. Estep's pity for those not sold on his Jesus spooks me.

Turning right on Gervais (Columbia's name for US-1), I pass South Carolina's statehouse, my thoughts drifting. A bright flag snapping in the rain rouses me like a shout. Here was what the national fuss had been about: this conspicuous display of the Confederate stars-and-bars at the state Capitol. The population of South Carolina, before the Civil War, was nearly 60 percent Negro. Since the planters of South Carolina had the most to lose by abolition, they were understandably the most fervent for secession. Economics shaped their ideology. Intelligent men like Vice President (later, Senator) John C. Calhoun turned rabid. They could not allow themselves to see slaves as humans because they could not afford it.

The flagrant presence of this flag suggests that some South Carolinians are still fighting that war.

That is the problem with faith.

vii.

3:00 a.m. My least favorite hour. I have slept enough to be wakeful but not enough to be spry. It is too late—or early—for a pill. Having peed, I switch off the light: I will sleep, dammit! But the covers bunch. My back itches.

I give up, power my laptop. If I'm going to think, let it be about something.

Yesterday returns, to my sorrow. It's not what happened, which is bad enough, but what might have, which is unthinkable. "Near miss," "close brush," "dodged a bullet," we shrug, masking dread.

It was four in the afternoon. I'd been driving since one. It was wet, cold. Why weather warps my moods is beyond me. I'm not a farmer or a snowblower distributor, whose fate is written in the sky. Have I been brainwashed by weathercasters who decorate the sun with a smiley face and the cloud with a scowl? Or is some primal instinct at work, which I share with chipmunks and fleas?

Bruckner was playing on the radio. Bruckner is no good to drive to. His music is ecstatic, weird, as if he were going eyeball to eyeball with the

Almighty. He's better after a drink. But Bruckner was what the radio had on and my brain was dull, so what the hell.

Local road 176 parallels I-26 from Columbia to Charleston. Local roads are not necessarily fascinating but at least you see something. On an Interstate all that changes are the exit names. On local roads you see boarded-up houses and upstart churches ("Sign is broken," declared one, "Come Inside for Message") and bicyclists doing wheelies and a middle-aged woman berating her wheelchair-bound mom.

This intersection, in the middle of nowhere, was incompetently designed. After a stop sign—not a light—you had to cross four lanes. Worse, the four lanes intersected at a bias, not a perpendicular. Hard enough in a car to see what's whizzing at you from two directions, but in a truck like Migrant there's a blind spot on the passenger side, which neither flat nor convex rearview mirror compensates for.

I knew what to do. Take the safe right turn, then, when I could see clearly, double back. There was no reason not to. I was in no rush and alone, far from home, I am cautious.

So why didn't I? I had nothing to gain by rashness, not even a thrill. The thought flickered that this was stupid. Yet I did it, gunning Migrant across four lanes, holding my breath.

Thud, screech, tinkle of glass, silence. I pulled over, all pulse. We've been trained in America, at the instant of an accident, to turn litigators. It's always somebody else's fault—the other driver, the highway engineer, maybe the manufacturer of Migrant. Greedy eyes glint after a collision, calculating.

I didn't feel like blaming. This is vanity in me, not nobility. Truth-tellers are rarities in this shirking hour. Was I man enough?

My victim gave me leave. She was standing by her bashed car, stunned but unharmed. She had a sense of humor: "That gave me a scare." She was new to the neighborhood, a young mother on her way to pick up her daughter from an aunt's. We examined her car tracks in the mud. She had sheered a lamppost, knocking off her side mirror, denting her door. Three inches nearer to the post and she might have been dead.

We exchanged information. When I apologized, she replied, embarrassed, "That's OK." I wondered she wasn't angry. I would be. Hurt, I'd want to hurt back. She accepted things. Bad things happen. But thank God, nothing really bad. Not this time.

Back on the road, my hands shook. I was furious. One heedless moment and I could have wrecked how many lives? "After such knowledge," groaned T. S. Eliot, "what forgiveness?" I saw the daughter, the husband, a mother maybe, huddled around a gray grave.

viii.

The visitor to old Charleston feels the poignancy of Pompeii. Here was a vital vivid city stricken, mid-strut, by a catastrophe. Of the four leading colonial cities, the other three—New York, Boston, and Philadelphia—kept growing. The bigger they've grown, the harder it is to disinter their pasts. Charleston's glory was buried beneath the suffocating ash of the Civil War. Their proud citizenry believed themselves America's great city, now and to come. The day they fled before General Sherman, who thankfully spared the place, their future became their past.

Unlike Williamsburg and its imitators, old Charleston is not a reconstruction, a prettified re-vision of how things might have been. There is none of the ersatz theatrical about its 50 or so preserved blocks, the morticious daubing of a Disney. The buildings have been polished and repaired; they are, for the most part, owned and occupied by rich folks with an antiquarian bent. Mercedes park where carriages used to. Tucked in period-appropriate cabinets you'll find DVD players and computer cables. But nothing new and contemptuous has been added, nothing that insults its heritage.

Strolling the painstakingly preserved waterfront, with little flat fatal Fort Sumter floating in the bay, I felt this fine, February afternoon as if I were not in America at all, or in Europe quite, but in some Shangri-la, to which we no longer hold the key. This was America, yes, the steady parade of joggers were American, the language was American, pleasantly accented, but the ways were foreign. The architecture, especially: something about these high handsome brick and stone homes with their tall windows facing the sea—the porches, as we Northerners call them, or in local vernacular, the verandahs. They were two, three stories tall, and half as wide as the homes to which they were attached. They were not just entranceways or places to sit when you chose to socialize: they were living rooms, essential spaces any resident had to pass through in the ordinary course. You could not have lived in these houses without appearing on their verandahs; and once you appeared, you were in public view, your conversation might be overheard on the street, your interlocutor noted, your dress and aspect open to neighborly inspection. It was as if you and your neighbors were living under a single roof. If you were absent from your verandah, neighbors would wonder.

I dislike being seen. Even from those I love I sometimes hide. Eyebeams turn me into an actor. I am easy in Migrant, free. No one knows who I am.

Charleston was making me claustrophobic. I could feel those eyes. They observed my crumpled trousers, my untrimmed hair, my eccentric zigzagging. They wondered what I was up to. Was I casing their homes? Was I *criticizing*?

Where all live as one, conformity turns tyrannical. Eccentricity, with its implicit rebuke, offends. The more we see of others, the more we want them to console us by imitation. Parents grin when their children mimic them.

The solidarity and conviviality of Charleston are splendid, even today. Two gents in St. Philip's churchyard, where John C. Calhoun is buried, are measuring a tended patch of grass for an additional perfect planting. They are dressed in ties and tweed jackets. The volunteers in the gift shop wear perfect modest dresses, smell of sweet fragrance, and address me with impeccable politeness. Manners matter here. The war may have been lost, but not the honor of fine behavior. A different code prevails than in the uncouth North. It is understood, not expressed. It is enforced by eyes.

I suppress a sigh for this gentler, lovelier time. How distant from the trudging ugliness of Wal-Mart! Is there anything in contemporary American life one could characterize as gracious? We are bludgeoned with crudeness, obviousness, come-ons, sledge-hammer art. We are thumped on the back by oafs. Tasteless glop is heaped in shapeless mounds. Who knows the name of his neighbor, much less his neighbors' grandparents? "Tradition," like so many sterling words, has been filched by Madison Avenue. Products concocted in a laboratory are extolled as "traditional" (and "natural" and "fresh").

Oh, it was fine then. One can feel the finesse. But one can feel, too, the fatality of such conformity. Who in Charleston could risk telling his neighbors that their defense of slavery was mad? Who could admit that, in their desperation to maintain their pleasant society, they were blinding themselves to the crimes on which it was built? One can understand, even sympathize, with pre-war Charlestonians' dilemma. Acknowledge the Negroes' humanity and in a majoritarian culture, sooner or later, they'd have to bend to their will. To survive, the ruling class had to invent a theory to justify its ascendancy. As Americans, they could not

227

repudiate the assertion "that all men are created equal." So they found a way to convince themselves that slaves were not men. Panic made their foremost political thinker, Vice President and Senator John C. Calhoun,[32] slavery's most rabid apologist.

Such was the force of their verandahs. Charlestonians nodded in agreement while, in the cold north, reform debates raged. Northern thinkers sat alone by their fires and arrived at new convictions that they tumbled onto their neighbors like burning coals. Thoreau, Emerson, William Lloyd Garrison, Horace Mann, the teetotalers and prison reformers and women's suffrage and public education advocates—none were dissuaded from calling their neighbors knaves. Accusation became a popular pastime. It is no surprise that in 1856, Congressman Preston Brooks of South Carolina answered Massachusetts's Senator Charles Sumner's vitriolic attack on his uncle, Senator Butler, with a debilitating caning in the Senate chamber. Both were right, by their lights. Any well-bred Southerner knew such rude words were not to be uttered. Sumner might be a Senator but he was no gentleman! To Brooks, honor meant caning; to Sumner it meant candor, calling wrong by its name.

ix.

The man in the Laundromat just sat. His wife had brought a book to read while the clothes bobbed behind the glass portals. It was she who had placed the clothes in the washer and would, unaided, remove them to the dryer. The man just sat. It was not that he was unwell or unfit; he seemed about my age, not yet debilitated by emphysema or a tired heart. He did not seem sad or preoccupied or enmeshed in thought. His expression was placid. His eyes studied some middle distance. I supposed from the hour and the couple's dress that they were early retirees, heading south in pursuit of warmth. Wednesdays were laundry day. The wife did the work, apparently without complaint, in the Laundromat and elsewhere. The man probably had a few prescribed chores—"man's work," like hooking the car to the motor home. But mostly he just sat, gazing into nothing, while his days ticked.

---

[32]Fiery Calhoun is our only national leader to quit his job over a matter of principle. President Jackson believed in a strong Federal government. Calhoun, his Vice President, advocated states' rights. Rather than be party to policies he opposed, Calhoun resigned as Vice President to become Senator.

I kept sneaking glances, while folding my hot shirts and socks, to see if he'd snap out of it. I make a game of my cleaning days, a contest against the clock. This Laundromat was conveniently located by a do-it-yourself truck wash. The self-consciousness of Charleston had made me notice how Migrant looked after three rainy weeks. I could play tic-tac-toe in the grime.

My plan was to load my laundry in the washing machine, swab Migrant inside and out, and be done when my dryer was. People who abandon their clothes in the machines are viewed as infidels by Laundromat regulars. Leaving your clothes unattended means they don't matter to you. Occupying a machine when its cycle is finished indicates indifference to other patrons. Laundromat protocol calls for sitting while your clothes revolve. Reading, watching TV, playing cards, or conversing are permissible, but not decamping.

Waiting is hard for me. I hear the clock's tick. In no time I'm thinking of my father, dead by this age. A pall of futility descends. I am superfluous. We all come to nothing, why bother trying? I must divert my attention to avoid such mewling. Not doing I am done for.

With an apologetic shrug, I dart from washing machine to car wash, sudsing and scrubbing and dowsing myself in the spray from the power-wash. You can't imagine the pleasure of cleaning your car if you haven't tried it. She fairly beams with gratitude.

All this time—88 minutes, to be exact, to both wash and dry—the man just sat. He was practicing Zen, you say? I promise you, he wasn't. Zen demands concentration—on nothingness, granted, but that's not nothing. This man was not concentrating on anything. He was just sitting there. The sands of his life were dropping through the hourglass and it did not bother him.

My months on the road have taught me efficiency in laundry-folding. I find ways to reduce my time. My career best is 12 minutes for a full load. I suppose I look odd to other Laundromat patrons, rushing this way.

Shouldering out the glass door, my still-toasty armload steadied by my chin, I cast a backward glance. Yes, he is still there. His wife is folding now, but the man just sits. I'm not sure why this strikes me, but it does.

x.

A roadside bromide: "Aspire to inspire before you expire."

A T-shirt zinger: "Give a man an inch and he thinks he's a ruler."

xi.

Charleston exudes History with a capital H. Poor Savannah, Georgia, pants for some.

History-capitalized differs from history-lower case. Every town and body has the latter, that is, a story whose tentacles extend into time. We all go back to Adam and Eve, more or less, and following that trail may be the best "free entertainment value" ever offered.

History-capitalized is history folks will buy tickets to. History doesn't draw like theme parks or sporting events; George Washington ain't no Mickey Mouse. But big-h-history spares many a middling American town the ignominy of featurelessness. Forlorn zip codes proclaim themselves "the home of" some name they hope you recall. A threadbare burg outside Raleigh revels in the nativity of actress Ava Gardner. I passed her museum without stopping.

Neither James Oglethorpe, Savannah's idealistic founder, nor Juliette Gordon Low, mother of the Girl Scouts, nor Flannery O'Connor, eloquent though she was, is a household name. The battles waged in Savannah don't make it into the top 10 of either the Revolution or the Civil War. The Savannah History Museum, despite delving deep into the attic of inconsequence, can't fill its space. When a city museum devotes permanent exhibits to a forgotten recording artist and a once-popular garden statuary sculptor, you know they're straining.

Savannah's riverfront, too, resists the so-called renewal that has transformed many a derelict wharf or factory into a tourist trap. The cute-i-fication of outmoded industrial spaces is a contemporary contagion. Seedy slums become "historic districts," where yawning costumed clerks hawk local gimcrack.

Savannah is so famished for fame it embraces its notoriety as the setting for a creepy best-seller. This is the Paris Hilton effect—exulting in name-recognition, no matter for what. In an earlier era, *Midnight in the Garden of Good and Evil*, a nonfiction book about some very sleazy Savannahians, would have been denounced as calumny. Town fathers might have challenged its author to a duel. Now there are *Midnight* tours (Deluxe Minibus Tour B on the Gray Line) and author John Berendt is regaled as a savior.

America-the-competitive turns cities into winners and losers as if they were movie stars or show-dogs. Is there a category not spangled by a top-10 list? Rating is entertainment. It forces debate. But it wounds, too. "Loser" is a peculiarly American genus.

230

Savannah exhibits some of the rancor of an also-ran. You can almost hear the Garden Club beautifiers muttering anti-Charleston imprecations under their breath. It's not fair, they protest; Savannah has a lot going for it! And they're right; it does. Oglethorpe's ingenious town plan grouped houses around squares, many of which have been restored to elegance. Old trees dripping Spanish moss make even prosaic streets atmospheric. Seediness—moral and physical—can entice, as *Midnight*'s popularity proves.

Depression is contagious. I wanted to thump Savannah on the back and assure it this is not its fault. Cities, no less than men, swagger, attributing their triumph to character—gumption, verve, values, some *je ne sais quoi*— but really it is all luck. First, there's the luck of geography—are you placed to be a transportation node, defensible, temperate, fertile, scenic? Then there's the luck of politics—were you named a capital, did your side win the war? Then there's the luck of commerce—what would Battle Creek, Michigan, be without Kellogg's or Orlando, Florida, without the Mouse? After the fact, what happened seems inevitable, because after the fact, it is. Before the fact, chance rules. One man wins the lottery, another plummets in a plane. Go figure.

Savannah shares its airport with a brand-new winner of a town. Hilton Head's good luck is golf—water enough to keep its proliferating courses green, weather warm enough to play year round, and a bumper crop of re- tirees who enjoy the game. Hilton Head is such a draw that clubs start call- ing themselves Hilton Head 20 miles from city limits.

I have friends in Hilton Head, but I wanted to see what a stranger might, which it turns out is almost nothing. Hilton Head doesn't welcome strangers. It's a community of gated communities. Several roads dead-end in gate- houses, to Migrant's chagrin (Migrant U-turns as gracefully as her owner pirouettes). You can't see in. You can't see the shore. There is no architec- ture. Residents of Hilton Head live in units, not houses. It is all unspeakably pleasant—no poor people, no danger, no disturbing variety, no history.

I fled.

xii.

Where am I? Oh yes—Georgia, south of Atlanta, near Plains and Ander- sonville. Outside my window, gray tree-trunks rise soldier-straight. The ground is red with pine needles.

231

I am in a hurry now, promised home in 34 days, with Florida, Alabama, Mississippi, Louisiana, Texas, and Oklahoma yet to visit. My ignorance expands exponentially. The more I know, the less I know.

Yesterday, I took in Warm Springs. I'd tried earlier to visit Georgia's Capitol in Atlanta and Coca-Cola's exhibit across the street, but there was nowhere to park Migrant so I kept driving. I'd like to think about Coke, history's most famous product (it and, perhaps, the Cross), how it was born and spread, overcoming the barriers between men. I'd like to think of young Arabs and Africans inveighing against America while swigging Coke and of how our modern world, for better or worse, has been made in America. Kitty Hawk, Coke, Mickey Mouse, Big Mac, Tylenol, the light bulb, the PC: not even Rome imposed itself so indelibly. Is this the pax Americana or the pox Americana? A century hence will we look back fondly on these times?

Warm Springs I had to myself. In summer as many as 1,300 people a day visit, quite a crowd considering that Warm Springs is an hour from anywhere and there's no theme park or casino nearby. There's only one reason to come to Warm Springs: to see where FDR died. The shock of that moment was such that I remember it perfectly, though I was not yet born.

Historians for many decades have concurred that Washington, Lincoln, and FDR are our three greatest Presidents. Each seems somehow irreplaceable, an astonishing stroke of luck. Their moment needed them and they knew what their moment needed. On their strong shoulders, they carried America across a raging river that might have washed us away.

Their accomplishments were remarkable. But more mysterious is their aura, their glow, which still infuses our American air. Many Presidents are forgotten; others represent their time. But these three ascend out of their time into timelessness. They both were and are, each the embodiment of some virtue we like to think of as American.

No President was more joyous or confident than FDR. That smile, that ease, that exuding warmth! He governed a nation in continuous crisis, yet never for a moment betrayed doubt. Horrible things happened—Depression, World War, polio—but they seemed not to faze him. He was happy—and glad, genuinely glad, to see you, whoever you were. As his parents had loved and tended him, he would love and tend us. He was relaxed so we could relax. All would be well.

Warm Springs reflects FDR more completely than any other place. In Hyde Park, we feel the imposing presence of his mother and forbears.

Franklin is the good son. Campobello, the family's summer home in Canada, had belonged to FDR's father. But Warm Springs was all his. Here he was free to be himself.

And how happy that was. I wish I could be as happy for one day as FDR seemed to be every day. Grainy film footage shows Roosevelt at play—swimming with children in the hot springs pool; sitting cross-legged at a picnic, making faces, unembarrassed by his polio-shrunk shanks. Most affecting are the scenes from the annual Roosevelt Thanksgiving, at which he entertained polio-stricken children and the children of polio victims. What a photo-op, we might sneer. But it wasn't that at all. The President wasn't acting when he was kidding and smiling with the boys and girls beside him. He was enjoying himself—really. The most powerful man in the world was enjoying being goofy with a turkey drumstick.

The surprise of Warm Springs is its size. It's a cottage, a few small rooms, ordinarily furnished. The house Franklin made for himself was Everyman's. Here, not the lofty parlors of Hyde Park or the pompous corridors of the White House, was his soul's natural habitat. No pretence. No falseness. No spin. Roosevelt didn't have to pretend to be an ordinary guy; he was one, by inclination, despite his birth.

The day Roosevelt died, April 12, 1945, was the last day the cottage was used. Everything is as it was. You can see the chair he was sitting in, the unfinished portrait he was sitting for. There is reason for optimism this afternoon. Hitler's on the run. So are the Japs. Roosevelt is tired—he has worked hard—but happy, in his favorite place. He is making pleasant conversation, and—

It is 3:45 p.m. The President, unconscious, is carried to his plain bed in the room next door. I look at my watch. It is 3:45. I don't know what the weather was that April afternoon. This day it rained.

xiii.

I make my way from Georgia's rural emptiness to the jazzy brightness of the Interstate.

Nearing the Interstate, density increases. Stores get bigger. Strides quicken. Clothes become newer. Geography is destiny. The faster you can get to a place, the faster it will grow. Our first cities clustered around harbors. Then it was rivers, then railroad termini, now Interstates and airline hubs. Access brings success.

233

I breathe easier where the people are more numerous, prosperous. Stopping at a dilapidated package store in the midst of nowhere I'd felt two young men's eyes. They slouched, with the restive languor of the un-employed. Migrant, in their sight, might have been a Rolls Royce, with this odd middle-aged white guy, apparently on his own, hopping out and pur-chasing a half-gallon of Jack Daniel's—a half-gallon!—as if the cost were nothing. The patrons of this store bought pints, which they swigged going out the glass door.

I wondered how I would have felt, were our roles reversed. The nerve of this hotshot in a white van with his full wallet just to arrive here, so easy and sure of himself! He probably thinks it's easy finding work in this fly-blown burg, that it's laziness or orneriness that keeps us here cooling our heels. Well, it's not easy—not to find work you can feel good about!

The Interstate's familiar signs winked in the dark like flowers. Is it my imagination or are the stalks for these signs stretching ever higher like Jack's beans? Exxon and Holiday Inn and Kentucky Fried and Dairy Queen seem more and more to rival the moon.

At night I prefer the Interstate. There's nothing to see after sundown and here there's less chance of getting lost. I can muse in the familiar roar. All I need to remember is my exit number.

The combination of the National POW Museum in Andersonville and the Jimmy Carter National Historic Site in Plains was too much for one day. I'm a slow traveler, given my druthers. Six hours of reflecting to one of seeing is about the right ratio, only at that rate I'd never get home.

The National POW Museum, which salutes the prisoners of all our wars, is a fine example of that new American genre, the pain memorial. Until the last quarter of the twentieth century, memorials were created to delight and stir. The moral of the story was triumphal: deaths redounded to our glory. Beginning, I think, with the Holocaust museums, we began to memorialize what we'd hitherto labored to forget. Now we are regularly reminded of human loathsomeness—toward slaves, Jews, sweat-shop laborers, women, Asian-Americans, victims of all stripes. Designers hone their exhibits so they slice into our guts.

The pain of the prisoners of war and their survivors, their desperation and courage and patriotism, made me grope for the exit. The crowded ranks of little headstones in the nearby national cemetery, foot-wide stones set a few inches apart, belied any notion of a private eternity.

Jimmy Carter's Plains preaches a different sermon, but preach, it does. That was Carter's strength—and weakness: he could not resist improving us.

Leaders who chide invite resentment. We want our President to be one of us, not better. Jimmy Carter is a pulpit-addict. He must demonstrate by his aggressive modesty the right way to be. The displays of Plains—his and Rosalynn's modest high school, now converted to a modest museum; his 1976 campaign headquarters, an abandoned train depot; the modest Baptist church where he still conducts Sunday school; brother Billy's rusting gas station; his modest boyhood farm, plainly presented; his and Rosalynn's modest home one can glimpse past the Secret Service barriers—shout in a whisper: walk humbly in the Lord, revere, respect, love. It is a good, good message, from a good, good man. Yet I find myself recoiling from his perfection. The pious make me nervous. They can't be as good as they seem or if they are, there's something wrong with them. Or maybe there's something wrong with me.

Curiously, Carter's greatest contribution to our democracy is one he does not celebrate at either his Atlanta Presidential Library or Plains Historic Site. He was the first to demonstrate that anybody by his own exertion could make his way to the White House. All 38 prior Presidents had been promoted either by prominence or party. Carter, an obscure one-term Governor of Georgia, was barely a blip on the national screen when he first took his message to Iowa. No boss boosted him. He won because ordinary folks preferred him. That's the power of television—a candidate can rocket from nonentity to celebrity in months. Bill Clinton, from even smaller Arkansas, followed Carter's playbook. So will others.

Carter's rise and the POWs' endurance exhibit a hardihood, a heroism, that make me feel like a creampuff by comparison. What a laggard I am—how lazy and self-indulgent! We Americans avoid exertion. Ease and convenience are our ideals, not hardship and sacrifice. A padded recliner with a vibrate option is our dream throne. Only it turns out hardship is healthier—for body and soul. Hoeing makes you stronger. Getting whacked by weather makes you modest. Shared struggle introduces you to neighbors from whom—amazingly!—you may learn a lot.

Rumbling down I-75—a road which, in the night, might be any other I— I wonder at the relentless convenience—and sameness—of our America. All my needs—food, fuel, shelter, sundries—might be satisfied in minutes by a recognizable vendor at a popular cost. We possess, most of us, enough of everything except privation, the pang that breeds determination. Our paradox is that, more than any people before, we've fulfilled our desires, yet we find, in Gertrude Stein's resonant phrase, "there is no there there." We long to long, ache to ache. Our pioneers and heroes, who had so much less than we, shame us by how much more they became.

15
Florida

i.

There is something about Florida. Even the office towers look as if they could be carted off in an afternoon. Roads are littered with retirement communities, each with its architectural theme and tired name. There are Spanish Mission, and New England Colonial, and Chateau, and Western, and Pennsylvania Dutch, and Contemporary to choose from; but the layouts are alike—and the brochures. A handsome bronzed couple is smiling on a golf course. This photo must be available from a catalogue; I've noticed the same couple smiling more than once.

Many come to Florida, not many from. It's the fastest growing state, but is anybody born here? Not even Florida's Governor came from Florida. Other states have accents—what's Florida's? Floridians speak like New Yorkers, Chicagoans, Kansans, Alabamians. Retirees come here not to live but live out. They come to where the sun shines so their kids might want to visit. They come to where the landscapes don't recall.

There's a light-heartedness about Florida that feels heavy. It begins at the Georgia line. Georgia takes itself seriously: its peaches, pecans, hospitality, Coke, industry, the confederate flag. Atlanta, with the Jimmy Carter Library and Dr. Martin Luther King, Jr., Memorial down the road from each other, is a city of heft, grief, history. To be a Georgian means something: one must locate oneself on the map of time. To be a Floridian means . . . oh, what the hell. Vacationers and retirees leave seriousness back home. Florida is for fun. Why think?

Enter Florida and up pop those flimsy citrus/tourist/souvenir shops with orange roofs and exclamatory graphics that look like nowhere else. They're jokes that everyone's in on, silly wares for silly wayfarers. What are you thinking, buying a baby alligator? Or a sack of grapefruit you couldn't eat in a year?

An entire wall of one shop is devoted to ha-ha plaques. Some are funny, but there's a querulousness about the humor, a resentment barely disguised:

I didn't
realize when
I married
Mr. Right
that his first
name was
Always.

* * *

MENU FOR TODAY
CHOICE OF TWO
TAKE IT OR LEAVE IT

* * *

YOU'RE GROWING OLDER . . .

"WHEN" . . .

Everything Hurts and What Doesn't
Hurt Doesn't Work

You Feel Like The Day After But
You Haven't Been Anywhere
The Night Before

You Sit in a Rocking Chair and Can't
Get It Going

Your Back Goes Out More
Than You Do

237

* * *

CAUTION
Men at Work
Women work all the time—
Men have to put up signs when they work.

* * *

Senior Citizen Serenity Prayer

God Grant Me The Serenity
To Forget The People I Never Liked Anyway
The Good Fortune To Run Into The Ones I Do
And The Eyesight To Tell The Difference

Who buys such plaques? Do they hang them? Do they laugh at the jokes
again and again and again?

ii.

Just my luck, it's Bikers' Week in Orange City. In Sunburst RV Park, bikers convene at all hours. Americans, bereft of conventional community,
turn conveners. We join what historian Daniel Boorstin calls "consumption
communities" to belong.

Bikers are no different from golfers or stamp-collectors or tennis players
or horse-breeders or any other sub-society. Our enthusiasms make no
sense, by definition. Jesus or a flag or a team or a pastime—we gather
round them, to be less alone.

Every sub-society has its ways, offensive to nonmembers. The offense
may be a barred door or pitying condescension or exclusive secrets or rau-
cous rituals. The offense is necessary to separate initiates from nonbeliev-
ers. The more we are opposed, the closer we cling.

Bikers' offenses are tattoos, scary hair, ominous outfits, and noise. Their
polished pistons shatter quiet like jackhammers. At 2:00 a.m. I bolt up,
thinking myself attacked. But it is only the bikers, who keep pulling in at
unpredictable intervals.

Now it is dawn and the bikes crackle and snort, making prose impossible.
Do they think about the people they're bothering? Probably—dimly—and it

makes them smile. In their daily lives, they may feel like nobody special. Helmeted and astride they zoom.

iii.

Being one, I was able to wangle a seat at the Hoop-Dee-Doo. Singles at the Hoop-Dee-Doo are rarer than Zimbabweans. Families of four, eight, a dozen or more, book their Hoop-Dee-Doo tickets months in advance. At a $49.01 per guest (including tax and gratuities), this is as much as most of the four-hundred-plus at each of the three nightly sittings ever pay to be fed and entertained. $49.01 times, say, six, added to all the other charges they've incurred since checking into the compound—hotel or campsite, theme park admission, breakfast, lunch, an ice cream or drink, the inevitable Mouse-ears—makes a Disney World vacation their patrons' biggest discretionary expense. This Hoop-Dee-Doo alone, if my daydreamy math is right, is a $20 million a year business, year after year, making it one of the most successful stage shows ever. Disney is to entertainment what Henry Ford was to cars and Sam Walton is to shopping. The sure road to wealth is the fealty of the majority. "Custom," "unique," "individual" aren't frequent boasts in Disney propaganda, and where they appear they mean their opposite. Our behavior at a Disney park, once we've entered the gates, is as predictable as a beetle's to an entomologist. Even that oddest of anomalies, a Single Male Guest, shows up point-something percent.

I'd been to the Hoop-Dee-Doo 15 years ago, with my wife and our three kids, and recalled the experience with my usual Disney mingle of delight and dread. I am not one who sniffs at popular success. It's an astonishing trick to melt millions—not just of Americans, but the world—into a single consumer, or "Guest," and contrive entertainments that keep us coming back. Disney treats us all as children, with protestations of affection, and sanitized silliness, and unhorrifying thrills, and sweets, and an illusion of license, and, above all, a guiding hand that directs with seeming gentleness but brooks no resistance. In Disney World, you do what you are told. There are so many choices and such pervasive pleasantness you happily obey, perhaps unaware of your subjection.

The menu at the Hoop-Dee-Doo is bread you slice for yourself, sweetened butter, dressing-drenched salad, fried chicken, spare ribs, baked beans, corn on the cob, and strawberry shortcake, presented in pewter buckets that are continually replenished. You wash down these "vittles" with water, milk, soft drinks, beer, wine, or coffee—all you can drink. The chefs (or food-"imagineers") aim at a five-year-old palate, while endeavoring not to affront the 50-year-old's. The beer and wine—a most un-Disneyish concession—relax the adults.

The family to my left on the balcony (or "the shelf") came from New Jersey; to the right, from Wisconsin. Both avoided eye contact. In Disney World you're supposed to have fun and conversation with strangers is unsettling. Only the sparkle-eyed eight-year-old at my right elbow snuck glances to make sure I was laughing and clapping and stomping and whistling and twirling my napkin on cue. If I wasn't, well, maybe he—and his family—and all of these folks were, uh, making fools of themselves. Those wouldn't have been his words, but they'd have been his fears. At eight, we're still trying to see the world for ourselves.

The object of Disney entertainment is audience capitulation. Disney is to entertainment what Ulysses Grant was to war. The wonder is so dazzling, the jollity so insistent, the music so swelling, the stimulation so constant, who has strength to resist? You are never asked at Disney, as at an historic site, "Do you have any questions?" Questions might disrupt the down-to-the-second timing, lead to discussion, prompt thought. There is no Q-and-A in Disney World, only cue. Do as you're told, pahdna, and we'll git along jes fine, y'heuh?

The story line of Hoop-Dee-Doo is the visit of a troop of itinerant players to a Western frontier saloon circa 1880. Each of the six players is, as any Disney character must be, a cartoonishly legible type. There are the beau and belle romantic leads; the sturdy cowboy and his Annie Oakley; the giggling soubrette and amorous buffoon. They arrive "late," bursting through the swinging doors, and, to the accompaniment of banjo and honky-tonk piano, regale us relentlessly with sentimental songs, hilarious hijinks, stomping dances, bad puns, flatulence jokes, and no end of "audience participation." I put "audience participation" in quotes, because, in truth, involvement is involuntary. Suddenly a performer plops in one's lap or the spotlight discovers you. You're on stage, like it or not.

One of the Pioneer Hall Players' skits involves Davy Crockett. As it happens, I've been reading a book about David Crockett as I wend my way toward the Alamo, and the career of this failed-farmer-turned-politician-turned-martyr reveals much about our early decades. How and why did this mostly unexceptional, somewhat clownish accident of history achieve the status of legend?

The Hoop-Dee-Doo's Davy Crockett is a silly slapstick, a name from a TV theme song, who engages in horseplay with a grizzly "bar." While the

Alamo is alluded to, this Crockett apparently doesn't die there, but teams up with Annie Oakley in Buffalo Bill's Wild West show—a chronological leap.

I wondered idly, picking at my gloppy shortcake, woozy with oversweetened sangria, if the contrivers of this Hoop-Dee-Doo realized that a David Crockett once lived. Or if the imagineers who constructed the 42 all-too-lifelike mechanized mannequins in the Magic Kingdom's Hall of Presidents were aware these men ever ruled. All history had been flattened to a cartoon, an occasion for siphoning more treasure from the crowd. I could not stop staring at these 42 robots standing or seated amiably along the vast stage, nodding decorously when introduced by the invisible announcer. They are so serene together—John Adams and Jefferson, John Quincy Adams and Jackson, Benjamin Harrison and Cleveland, Teddy Roosevelt and Taft, Teddy Roosevelt and Wilson, the Bushes and Clinton—men who could not abide one another's presence are now at peace in this pastel Valhalla, where even the living are dead. This is history for more Americans than will ever read our Constitution: a reassuring bedtime story, where all our flaws, even naughty slavery, are rinsed away in the cool currents of time, and we the people are good and fortunate and blessed, and all is well, and all will be well, no matter the fact.

I end my Disney day dazed, disheartened, drunk, greeting poor Migrant in her overpriced Fort Wilderness camp slot with almost teary gratitude. Save me, o God, from such bovine stupefaction, such eagerness to trade in truth for ease. The looming chewing dinosaurs, the light shows, the vanishing ghosts in the haunted house, the ubiquitous mood-manipulative music, the happy Mickeys and Minnies and Donalds, the unending greetings of my keepers, Mark Twain shrunk to good ole Sam, poor Lincoln embalmed as a pious preacher, David Crockett flattened to goofiness, all idea of pain and sacrifice and jeopardy erased, our obligations as citizens reduced to paying up and doing as we're told . . . how can an America so grand, anguished, and various have been dwindled to a vision so clever, deceptive, and bland!

I admire success—but I refuse to acquiesce. I gun Migrant to the exit with grim intent.

iv.

What's wrong? A week now I've been out of sorts, my sleep jostled, my prose whiney.

241

Driving across Florida, from Orlando to Ocala, bleakness deepened till I feared I was going mad. Retirement community after retirement community, with their guarantees of bliss. Retirement is the vilest of America's innovations, born of industry's need to replace old cogs. The cog is replaced, whether worn or not. So what that still usable cogs are discarded? What counts is the efficiency of the system, not the fate of its components.

In earlier epochs, nature paced careers. You worked until you couldn't. You gave up tasks gradually, as strength ebbed. Even the old by the fire with their ear-trumpets and adages had a role. You were never cashiered, declared superfluous, consigned to cartons where your job was to die.

The amenities of these compounds cannot disguise their purpose. These are ghettos, whose inmates console themselves that it is they who are keeping out the world, not the other way around. What are kept out are irritants—the young, the hopeful, the wretched, the different—any who might disturb the communal faith. The discarded conspire in their enclaves to convince themselves they count, like 10-year-olds in a cave.

The RV parks where I stay aren't much different. In this season there are no young families, only not-yet-crippled couples shifting like insomniacs for a comfortable lie. Their itinerary is their purpose: that, their vans, and their dogs.

I yearn for home: for the energy and complexity of community; for children waiting for school buses and commuters rushing and the strife of ambition and pride. I miss the annoying "emergency," which yanks me, grumbling, from my words. I miss the anxiety with each day's news, the social "obligations" that are no such thing.

Freedom and bondage take their meaning from each other, as warm means nothing without cold. Man means something only in relation. This journey only counts if I make something of it. For you.

16
Alabama, Mississippi, Louisiana

i.

"So, are you having a good time?"

That question again. I know it is not meant to plague me. A good time is what travelers are supposed to have. But what does it mean? I think of beer ads, buff bodies rollicking. That *is* a good time, when time seems to vanish in the solvent of desire. Time alone—seeing, saying—does not vanish. It trudges, burdened with awareness. I watch the clock, the calendar, my years, the country's. What time remains? Are we making the most of it?

I had traveled from Montgomery to Selma, the reverse of the famous Civil Rights march. Alabama is a place of mystery to most Americans. Not many go there, except to Birmingham, one of those recent fresh-from-the-box cities, corporate and faceless. The countless miles logged by the American businessman might as well be a windowless corridor. Airport, taxi, chain motel, meeting room, chain motel, taxi, airport; business class: thoughts sunk in deals, screens, spreadsheets; no eyes for outdoors except to check traffic, weather.

Alabama, beyond the airport, Interstate, and Holiday Inn Express, comes as a shock. The poverty is numbing. One senses in pedestrians a third-world listlessness. Burned and collapsed buildings are left to rot. Holes gape in fences. Seedlings sprout from high school bleachers. Only the public buildings gleam—too big, too new, too white. As poor people over-dress their babies, poor states overbuild their offices. The spotless edifices clustered around the state capitol seem capacious enough to run a nation out of. But, at least on this February Wednesday there was no one there. No bustle, no urgency, though the legislature was in session and the courts sitting. A wrinkleless suit flanked by wrinkleless suits nodded to me in the corridor. He seemed ready to shake my hand, but I kept walking. Only later did I recognize the Governor.

The capitol in Montgomery was the scene of two angry seminal episodes in our history: the swearing-in of Jefferson Davis as President of the Confederacy and the terminus of the grim Civil Rights march in 1965. Dr. Martin Luther King, Jr.'s, first pulpit, the Dexter Avenue Baptist Church, where the Montgomery bus boycott began after Rosa Parks refused to surrender her seat to a white man, sits eloquently at the foot of the capitol's steps. One statue on the capitol grounds commemorates an Attorney General–elect who was assassinated. Another celebrates the gallantry of the Confederate war dead, in execrable verse. The second floor of the rotunda is dominated by portraits of two Governor Wallaces—George, the hate-monger, gunned down as he ran for President, and his wife, Lurleen, who died of cancer shortly after succeeding her husband. A celebratory mural in the dome shows General Jackson accepting the abject surrender of a Creek Indian chief.

Anger thickens crossing the river into Selma. Montgomery has government as an industry, but Selma has only its crumbling past. I was here to visit our most fleeting Vice President, William Rufus Devane King, one of Selma's founders. Tall and handsome, King shared lodgings in Washington with another tall and handsome bachelor Senator, James Buchanan. The two men loved one another: surviving correspondence and catty contemporary comment leave no doubt. It was presumed that by selecting King as Franklin Pierce's Vice President in 1852, Buchanan, who'd been denied the Presidential nomination that year, would be appeased. The private character of the handsome Senators' friendship can only be guessed.

Live Oak Cemetery with its old magnolias and cedars and live oaks dripping Spanish moss evokes an era before the War—the only War here that is called the War—when cotton-rich Selma bristled with hope. Greatness waited: how could it fail? The big churches and porticos and broad avenues and filigreed balconies and extravagant funerary sculptures blazon that bygone faith. Then came Sherman, and poverty, and the bitterness of Reconstruction, and the Klan, and the collapse of cotton prices, and the tussle between black and white for society's lowest rung. Prosperity lubricates brotherly love. It is easier not to hate when you do not hurt.

William King's mausoleum is sinking into gloom, its inscription scarcely legible in the deep shade. It is tended, one suspects, intermittently.

The door to City Hall was stuck: I had to yank it. The sidewalk outside was cracked. Weeds grew knee-high. The population shuffled. A few staggered, drunk.

Then my phone rang. "So, are you having a good time?"

244

ii.

I wake, still steamed about history's treatment of William King.

I first encountered this titillating tidbit six months ago, in Concord, New Hampshire, on a perfect fall afternoon, lounging in my collapsible chair outside the so-called Pierce Manse. I was waiting for my new friend Chips Holden to come with the key and the tour. I say "new friend," though we met for less than an hour, and all that elegant lady remembers of me, probably, is my van. Traveling alone can intensify casual encounters. Recollection drops like a stone in a still pond, raising ripples that spread to the shores.

I'd been reading about Pierce's Vice President to distract myself from Pierce's career. All our other Presidents, even Nixon, died in comfort and love, clothed in a certain veneration. Only Pierce died abject, bereft of wife and children, friendless in his hometown, alone. If Pierce had been a bad man, such retribution might seem fair; but Pierce was only weak—and unlucky.

William King is not a Vice President even the eagerest of history buffs spends time on. He is mostly memorable as the answer to two trivia questions: Who was the only President or Vice President inaugurated outside the United States? And, Which President or Vice President died without serving a day? Having contracted tuberculosis during the campaign of 1852, King sought relief in Cuba, where he was sworn in, returning home only to die.

Hardly worth a second look. But what's this?[33]

"About 1834, King met and developed a friendship with James Buchanan of Pennsylvania. The two men shared most political sentiments, and both remained lifelong bachelors. In time their relationship became more intimate, and by 1836 the two senators shared a residence in Washington. Soon the usual talk about King's traits as a 'southern gentleman' generated amusement from northerners and caused others to joke about the two and refer to them as 'the Siamese twins.'"

In 1834, Buchanan was 43, King 48. Both were tall and handsome with courtly manners.

Buchanan wanted to be President. Talk circulated about a Buchanan-King ticket. But "by early January 1844, defaming comments about the

---

[33]From Daniel Fate Brooks' essay on King in *Vice Presidents: A Biographical Dictionary* (Checkmark Books, 2001).

intimacy of King and Buchanan again circulated around Washington. Andrew Jackson, who favored his fellow Tennessean, James K. Polk, spoke of King as 'Miss Nancy,' while the Tennessean Aaron V. Brown, a former law partner of Polk, referred to King as 'Mrs. B.' and 'Buchanan's wife.'"

Brown wrote to Polk's wife, Sarah: "Mr. Buchanan looks gloomy and dissatisfied & so did his better half until a private flattery and a certain newspaper puff which you doubtless noticed, excited hopes that by getting a *divorce* she might set up again in the world to some tolerable advantage."

"Referring to King as 'Aunt Nancy,' Brown went on to say that he 'may now be seen everyday, triged [*sic*] out in her best clothes & smirking about in hopes of securing better terms than with her former companion.'"

Smiling, we shake our heads. Mud-slinging by political rivals, nothing more. But then, in May 1844, King, who'd been appointed Minister to France, writes Buchanan: "I am selfish enough to hope you will not be able to procure an associate who will cause you to feel no regret at our separation. For myself, I shall feel lonely in the midst of Paris, for there I shall have no friends with whom I can commune as with my own thoughts."

In 1852, Buchanan, still angling to be President, lost the nomination to Pierce. To secure Buchanan's support for the ticket, King was picked for Vice President. Buchanan pledged his "cordial support to Pierce & King; because they are the nominees of the convention & to the latter because I love and respect the man."

What's curious about this friendship is how Buchanan's chroniclers omit mentioning it. My guide at Wheatlands, Buchanan's elegant estate in Lancaster, Pennsylvania, regaled me at length with why Buchanan never married. She told me he was brokenhearted at the breakup of his engagement when he was 28, followed by his fiancée's apparent suicide. That may be the explanation—it plays well with the Garden Clubbers who comprise a goodly percentage of Wheatlands' callers. But isn't it possible (o horror) that Buchanan *preferred* the company of men? That the love of his life was not a willowy (and apparently unbalanced) heiress but a handsome Senator from Alabama?

History's silence is embarrassing—and perhaps misleading. That hard-bitten fulminator, General Jackson, who'd as soon shoot his adversaries as debate them, famously disliked the soft, temporizing Buchanan. When President Polk, whom Jackson promoted like a son, named Buchanan his Secretary of State, Jackson objected. "But General," Polk reacted, "you yourself appointed him minister to Russia in your first term." "Yes, I did," said Jackson. "It was as far as I could send him out of my sight, and where he could do the least harm. I would have sent him to the North Pole if we had kept a minister there!"

Calling King "Miss Nancy" may have indicated Jackson's contempt, nothing more.

But mightn't the intimacy of King and Buchanan have altered history? Assuredly, it made King Vice President (for two months). But mightn't the gossip have undermined Buchanan's chance in 1844? And mightn't it also have colored his attitude toward the South, when he finally became President, deepening his reluctance to oppose their demands? King, by then, had been dead four years. But mightn't a weak, aging, sentimental Buchanan have considered a Civil War akin to losing for a second time his best, best friend?

We see what we want. A gay President and Vice President? Not in my America! How much truth—and interest—do we drain from our histories to console ourselves?

iii.

Yesterday I was in Mobile. The name Mobile, contrary to expectation, has nothing to do with the art form invented by Alexander Calder or a brand of fuel. It's a Frenchification of an indigenous tribe, the Maubilian, or canoe paddlers, now vanished.

I often wonder why I'm in one town and not another: why Mobile and not, say, Pensacola or Pascagoula, with their seductive names. Places beckon like ladies of the night, dozens winking when there is only time for one.

I didn't know much about Mobile. I knew what Admiral Farragut said at the Battle of Mobile, in 1865, lofting himself into the ranks of the remembered. "Damn the torpedoes, full steam ahead!" doesn't seem, at first blush, a ticket to eternity; but History is, of all the Muses, the most capricious.

I didn't know much about Mobile, but Mobile, better than almost any city I've visited, told me her story. Narrative museums, whose purpose is not to exhibit admirable artifacts but to educate, are a new American species that has spectacularly propagated in the past few decades. These are three-dimensional storybooks, packed with pictures, graphics, film clips, objects, models, mannequins, music, sound effects, stage lighting, drawers to open, buttons to push, ballots to cast. They can be exciting or execrable, like any art form, truthful or false.

Mobile's, in the Museum of Mobile, housed in the old City Hall, is a delight. The ground floor exhibit carries you through Mobile's political history, from its prehistoric and Indian heritage to the arrival of the Spanish to its conquest by the French, then the English, then the Spanish, to its attachment to the United States after the War of 1812, slavery, the Civil War, carpetbagging, bankruptcy, racism, the Klan, ship-building, harbor-dredging, bridge-building, to today's more democratic order, economic revival, and the renewal of a derelict downtown. Upstairs, a second exhibit tells the story of Mobile's people, their pleasure in music and baseball and festivity (Mobile claims the first Mardi Gras); their tradition of calamities—by fire, hurricane, epidemic, accident; their pride in their achievements, including blockade-running, boat manufacture, music-making; and their celebration of local heroes, such as baseball's Hank Aaron, jazz's BB Jefferson, and Clinton's Labor Secretary, Alexis Herman. A third, smaller exhibit flaunts the absurdly flamboyant finery of Mardi Gras. The Mobile outside is an ugly tangle of elevated highways and harbor cranes and broken buildings and stenchy streets. Like many other cities, it has surrendered its precious waterfront to industry and transportation. But the Mobile inside is individual, various, resonant, the city beneath what one sees.

iv.

Awake in the woods outside Natchez, Mississippi. A terrible high-pitched scream, then nothing. Worries wriggle into my wakefulness. Four states remain and 20 days. That should be enough. Enough for what?

Tomorrow is my last day in that segment of America we call "the South."

"The South" is not a geographical designation. Florida, our southernmost state (except Hawaii) is "Florida," not "the South." Texas is "Texas," California "California," Arizona and New Mexico "the Southwest." Louisiana, with its exotic French aroma, is not quite "the South." Neither is Virginia wholly, nor Arkansas nor Tennessee nor North Carolina, though the Confederacy included them.

"The South" is an idea, a dream, an attitude, that may never have existed except in hindsight. It pulses most powerfully in those cotton-rich states—South Carolina, Georgia, Alabama, Mississippi—that the Civil War made poor. It conjures plantations and gentility and gallantry and female delicacy and dashing horsemanship and disdain for New England money-grubbing and John C. Calhoun and Jefferson Davis and Robert E. Lee. Margaret Mitchell imagined it in *Gone with the Wind*. Its mythological vastness haunts Faulkner's Yoknapatawpha. What was maddening about the South was its insistence on its moral superiority, combined with its obstinate blindness to the abomination on which it was built. The Southern belle was made possible by the Southern slave. Southern "honor" bought and sold flesh in the marketplace and subdued it with a lash.

We see "the South" in the memorials at Vicksburg, Mississippi. Hundreds of Union and Confederate soldiers hold their lines in bronze and marble, as if the siege continues. The images of Northern and Southern officers are similar: hirsute, stalwart, heroic. But in the Southern sculptures and rhetoric one senses a defiance, as if, in moral terms, it was the South, not the North, that won the War. It's the same iconography we find at Appomattox, where the victor, Grant, is grubby, gruff, while the vanquished, Lee, is elegant, unflinching.

We see "the South," too, leaving the Vicksburg park, and making our way along the designated "Scenic Route," to the riverbank. The scenes on this "Scenic Route" are boarded-up houses and businesses, with poor blacks meandering like survivors of a bombing. Was labeling this a "Scenic Route" another instance of obstinate blindness or a sick joke?

The shock of "the South"—what we call "the South"—is that the War hasn't stopped being fought and "the South" hasn't stopped losing it. I'm not talking about big new cities like Atlanta or Birmingham, where the idea of "ancestor" draws a blank. These cities have moved on: what happened between 1861 and 1865 is just a story. I'm talking about Columbia, where the Confederate flag still flies outside the capitol, and Charleston and Savannah and Montgomery and Selma and Mobile and Jackson and Vicksburg, where the rhetoric and atmosphere still bristle with defiance. I'm talking about the endless miles of scrofulous farms and rusting-out trailers and fallen-down and burnt-out buildings and the proliferating Confederate flags and decals and a sense, still, of resentment at being licked in an unfair fight. This unwholesome preoccupation with the past resembles post-traumatic stress disorder. OK, your dream of "the South" was crushed, but that was a century and a half ago! It's time to get over it.

"History," James Joyce's Stephen Dedalus observed, "is the nightmare from which I am trying to awake." Faulkner's Quentin Compson might have said the same. What's bewildering about the backward portions of today's South is that they're *not* trying to escape. On the contrary, they're still wallowing in their nightmare, yee-hi-ing with their rebel yells, replaying their loss.

Blame and regret spare us the obligation of accomplishment. "I can't—and it's not my fault" justifies acquiescence to defeat.

We all have reasons why we can't. But so? The glory of life is not yesterday's dream but tomorrow's. What makes a man—or nation—mighty is not pining but yearning.

To fly the Confederate flag today is not only a racist slur, it is a humiliation. The great men of the Confederacy would have been appalled at this century and a half of whimpering. The brave know when they're licked. They get up, brush themselves off, and move on.

v.

Itchy eyes, which means spring.

The memory of an old man wakes me. Eighty-six. He approached me while Migrant was paused at a plantation gate. Tickets were eight dollars and I had only a 10, which caused confusion. The old man had noticed I was from New York. His granddaughter was going to school in New York, college, and she was from right here, Natchez, imagine that—big scholarship, which college he couldn't remember, he was eighty-six, after all, but one of the real prestige ones. The old man's baseball cap was inscribed with the name of a Pearl Harbor division, so I changed the subject. No, he hadn't been at Pearl Harbor, this was just a souvenir, but he'd served on transport ships in the Pacific, you always think of soldiers fighting, but somebody's got to carry over the tanks and the vehicles and . . .

Finally the gatekeeper returned with my change and I broke away. The old man would have sailed along forever before the gale of memory. It felt ungenerous, depriving him of his audience, but tours were on the hour, and if I missed this one, I'd have to skip seeing the house.

Maybe it was guilt that planted him in my sleep. Or maybe kinship. Was what I'm doing every morning—snagging some passerby and bending his ear—so different from this old man? That you, cherished reader, are prospective, not present, free to break from my spiel without offense, makes our connection more convenient. But the old man and I are propelled by the same need, not to die with so many stories.

Story and history are children of the same parent, the Greek word for knowing. A *histor*, in ancient Greece, was a man who knew a lot, a wise man, a judge. The Greeks understood that wisdom was not just mastery of facts or a talent for calculation, but an ability to narrate, connect.

We've lost the knack for storytelling in today's America. Conversation is mostly an exchange of facts and sentiments. We do not transmit to our children ancestral lore or teach them to beguile us with accounts of their time. TV shows and video games involve us in narratives, but they are somebody else's, not our own. The story most relevant to us, most surprising and available, we, curiously, ignore. "Americans," notes Daniel Boorstin in his invaluable trilogy, *The Americans*, "have tended to lose their sense of history. The American considers every moment a new climax, and he is so often told that every event is 'historic' that he loses his appetite for history."

Losing our history, our story, we forget why we matter. Facts and sentiments only matter in context, as part of a tale. Absent a story, I am just another creature.

My story keeps me going. Everywhere I look there is more to discover—about my past, my people, my place. That I am here, now, doing what I'm doing, seeing what I'm seeing, saying what I'm saying, amazes me. Everything connects—me to Baton Rouge to James K. Polk to my microwaved Krispy Kreme doughnut (highly recommended) to the old man at the gate. Everything pulses with mysterious significance—because it is part of the story.

This is not solipsism. Interest in one's story does not mean admiration. Only fools admire themselves. Our story is who we are, where we are, and most importantly, why. I am my father's son, my grandfather's grandson, my children's father, an American, a New Yorker, a consequence, and thus consequential. Whatever I make of my time says something about my time and all that led here. Without George Washington, Thomas Jefferson, Andrew Jackson, Abraham Lincoln, Calvin Coolidge, and the rest, there would be no Carll, not *this* Carll. They made me, as I, by remembering, make them.

My story also shows me how to behave. I want to play my part to applause. I want to make my father proud of me, and my father's father, and my children. I want to look good in your eyes. Were it not for all those eyes, I can't say who I'd be.

I do not mistake my stature. I am no mighty personage whose voice moves multitudes. I will not leave monuments to be gawked at. If I'm lucky, my words may be enjoyed by a few.

That my role is not a starring one does not excuse me from giving it my all. That's the fun of life: doing well, better. Greatness is beyond our control, but not what we make of what we've got.

251

All this seems obvious to me, almost too obvious to set down. Yet we live in an age when few can tell their stories, where they are and why. We watch stupid shows on TV. We ceaselessly cater to our sensations. All we know of America is a few highlights and celebrities. We care for our children, our friends, our comfort, little else. We seek to fill the time, not fulfill it.

This is a waste and a shame. We are capable of more. Our history glows with heroes who dared greatly. The chapter we're writing now, for all its quantifiable marvels, feels tepid, selfish, dull.

In my decades as a newspaper editor, I'd hound young reporters for "the story." They'd attend a town board meeting and return with facts: this happened, then this, then this. "But what's the story?" I'd say. "Why should readers care? Why do you want them to know? Facts mean nothing until you connect them to lives."

A century ago, when the son of a farmer sat to his meal, his plate was full of histories. He knew where the butter came from and how it was made. He'd sowed the potatoes and dug them. He knew where the water rose from to boil into tea and the wood to fuel the fire. His meat may have been an old friend.

He knew where he stood in the cycle of being and why he mattered. He likely knew where he stood in the story of America, how his father's father came across sea or mountain. He had many fewer gadgets and conveniences than we have today, but he was rich with consequence.

Today we don't know where things come from. We push buttons and things happen for reasons too intricate to fathom. Food comes from the supermarket, not the soil. How our father's father came to this land is a concern for antiquarians. We know everything about a baseball team or skateboarding or a Conan the Barbarian video game and nothing about ourselves.

It need not be. History is everywhere and available. Find your story and you will find your purpose. You need only look.

vi.

It's worth visiting Baton Rouge just to see the state capitol, which they call the new. The old capitol is worth seeing, too: now a carefully restored museum, it recalls the greedy grandeur of a get-rich-quicker post–Civil War America. Vaulting faux-bois arches and moldings and balusters trimmed with gleaming gold, surmounted by a gloriously garish skylight, return us to the Eden of American avarice, when capitalism, never more vicious or efficient, could do no wrong. The miraculous markets, left undisturbed, would hoist all to gladness; or if it failed to, those newly elevated would reside far enough above the masses to avoid their stench.

As the old capitol extols the promise of capitalism, the new capitol, built in 1932 by the irrepressible Huey Long, exults in its defeat. Here, from one of the smaller, poorer states in the Union, beset by poverty, graft, and fatalism, rises the largest and grandest of the state headquarters, a capitol building rivaled only by the nation's. Little is wood here, that humble material, but rather glass and metal and stone—limestone and marble—rising 450 feet and 34 floors. Jefferson's republican dome, symbolizing the virtuousness of a free people, has become a soaring skyscraper. In New York and Chicago, early skyscrapers were soon joined by others, so skylines became corporate shouting matches. But in Baton Rouge, Huey's monument is still framed by clouds, like the cathedral towers of Chartres or Rouen.

One approaches with awe—even today, when moon voyages are routine and such scale is no big deal. Imagine the effect on its first viewers, Long's passionate poor white followers, who'd never seen a building of more than, say, a dozen stories, and might not own a car. Mounting the football-field-wide steps to the front doors one feels uneasily like a pilgrim to the Aracoeli or a Roman at an imperial audience. The grandeur inside is even more imposing: ceilings taller than two barns, of exotic colored marbles, and polished metals. Officials in the two great legislative chambers are swallowed by the architecture. They'd have seemed small, even to nonentity, when they stood to speak.

Public architecture is a manifesto. Whatever a people constructs declares its aspiration. A public building is less constrained by budget or marketplace than other buildings. If a people choose to spend more, they are free to, up to their all. The greater the proportion of wealth invested in a public edifice, the greater the people's faith in the force it represents. Skimpy public buildings confess scant hope.

Long's capitol was an answer to the hopeless helplessness of his supporters. Business would not haul them out of their financial and emotional bog. Businessmen were thieves and liars. They lived on big plantations and only let vote those they fancied (which after the enactment of Louisiana's 1898 state constitution, wasn't blacks). Free enterprise, especially here in the Depression, meant freedom to starve.

What would save them was Government. Government would take the money from the John D. Rockefellers and share it with the poor. Government would make "every man a king." And if government did that without too much regard for individual liberties, what good had individual liberties ever done the poor, except to make them poorer? If Huey, "the Kingfisher," needed to become a dictator to accomplish these good things, why not? What good was freedom without a fair shake?

Like another poor angry young man who was rising to power in a poor angry nation across the sea, Huey Long, drunken on the dreams of his partisans and his own steaming oratory, trod over the rights of citizens with messianic assurance. Sadly for Germany, no one got past Hitler's thugs, as they did past Huey's. Huey Long did much for Louisiana: he restored pride, rekindled hope, and commenced great public works, which enabled his state to compete economically. He did much for America: his surging populist appeal emboldened FDR to adopt more aggressive Federal programs to repair our economy. Huey deserves to be remembered. But so, too, does Dr. Carl Austin Weiss, Huey's intelligent, sensitive assassin, who, for reasons still not wholly clear, rid America of this menace. Murder can be noble, history sometimes proves. The great German theologian, Dietrich Bonhoeffer, spent long anguished hours reconciling his adherence to God's law—"Thou shalt not kill"—with his complicity in a plot to assassinate Hitler. Bonhoeffer was right, as Shakespeare's Brutus was, as Dr. Weiss was, idealists all, who paid for their courage with their lives. Our American system works. But during the decade of the Thirties it came horrifyingly close to not working. How close, arguably thanks to Weiss, we'll never know.

The statue of Huey rises alone before his capitol, above his grave. It is, I believe, the largest statue of a governor in the country, smaller than all but a few statues of our most revered Presidents. Bas-reliefs on the pediment show poor folk reaching toward their savior, much as in some Emancipation memorials, freed slaves strain toward Lincoln. It is heroic, moving, scary.

Too often we treat our nation as eternal, a mountain we can kick and gouge, whose needs we can ignore. It is well sometimes to remember that the body politic is a body. It breathes, digests, grows sluggish or lively with the times. Infection can beset it which, untreated, spreads.

We must attend to those appalling blots on our landscape—the uneducated poor, the discarded old, the abject Indians, the hollow-eyed addicts—not out of charity, but self-interest. These are infections which can spread. As attentively as we attend to our own spots and aches and submit to tests and checkups, so should we care for our countrymen. Mortality awaits all. But it's good to defer it a while.

vii.

The French Quarter at dusk, even on a Lenten Wednesday, is a lurid dream. The narrow streets are cramped with hucksters and would-be merrymakers. Every small shop offers cheaper liquor, better gumbo, glitzy gimcrack, or a peek of flesh. Tourist faces purse with anxiety. Retired couples, long past such indulgence, arch eyebrows and shrug. Mothers tugging bug-eyed 10-year-olds think how to explain. I am conspicuous slogging alone, in sneakers, shorts, backpack, and dank windbreaker (it has been pouring all afternoon). A solitary in such society is variously importuned—a drink? a woman? a boy? A lean jittery black man inquires how I'm doing, then erupts, "Don't FUCK with me, you heuh, man? Don't FUCK with me!"

I dread nothing more than coercive jollity. How can anyone have what's called "a good time" on cue? The prospect of reeling besotted down some stale-smelling alley gives me hives. Companionship, for me, is the reward of company, coming to know another. How can you know anyone in a riot of gyrations and bellowed pleasantries? I find myself pulling back like a threatened snail. My smile becomes a portcullis.

At last, I slump onto my trolley seat with a relieved sigh. New Orleans, as no other big American city, jars the brain. Other cities have entertainment districts and precincts of willful exoticism. Other cities have wharves with their stenchy squalor and screeching gulls. Other cities have vivid histories to bait their touristic hooks. But no other American city has such a durable tradition of licentiousness.[34] The orgiastic exhibitionism of the *vieux quartiere* is not a Disney reproduction. They're doing now what they've been doing for nearly two centuries: showing strangers—from upriver or across the seas—a "bon temps," while they stop in New Orleans to let off steam and trade in flesh.

That New Orleans was the center of the American slave trade helps explain its wantonness. In the booming 1850s, as many as 300 slave traders made their livings in the city. A strong usable male slave might fetch $35,000 in today's coin, the equivalent of a low-end luxury car. Slaves were worth $5 billion to their Southern owners. Those who condemn the South for their allergy to Lincoln should ask themselves: How hard would *I* fight to protect $5 billion?

---

[34]The cost of Hurricane Katrina is incalculable: centuries of history washed away in a few hours.

Where human flesh is a financial asset, who can long maintain probity or delicacy? That life in nineteenth-century New Orleans was so often abbreviated—by yellow fever, cholera, scarlet fever, typhoid, malaria, and violence—further weakened resistance to indulgence. If death waits 'round the bend, why not live it up? Then there is the Frenchness of the Creole culture, which flummoxes most Americans.

American and French mix like milk and orange juice. Granted, the French rescued America in the Revolution, a favor we returned in World War II. Granted, the French gave us that lovely lady in New York harbor, symbolizing our shared devotion. Still, it's no go. Americans see the French as irresponsible, vain, snooty, untrustworthy, addicted to pleasure and appearances. The French see Americans as money-grubbing, moralistic, hypocritical, brutish, and style-less. French and Americans resent each other. The Americans can't understand why the French don't support our laudable desire to reform the world to our liking. The French, who imagine themselves superior to the Americans in every important respect, resent America's hegemony, which, candidly, they cannot fathom.

I have no French in me, which may be part of my problem. I am all English, Irish, German, moralistic, idealistic, New England, convinced life has some purpose and therefore, so do I. That this is improbable is only too probable. We are creatures no less than insects, whose only evident purpose is to propagate our kind and refurbish the soil. Why not live and be merry and wear silly hats and flail our limbs and drink to oblivion and melt into some nameless lover's loins? I can make that case. But I cannot succumb to it. Fun for me is seeing, not being seen; making, not making out.

A culture devoted to avoidance of life's questions, to losing oneself in a sensual stew, strikes me as desperate and sad. It's no fun having to have fun. It is also profligate of time. Ambling up Bourbon Street (up in New Orleans means upstream), not too fast (not to draw attention), I glance into shops and eyes—the tourists, the vendors, the indigenous threadbare street entertainers and predatory bums, the bemused police—recalling a time when exile from such delights would make me wince. Oh, how I longed to be swept up in this tidal wave of experience, to lose myself in lust and adventure and camaraderie and depravity and purported bliss, to be so busy feeling, daring, rollicking, I'd have no time to think. It would make life easier, less alone!

These days I observe such antics with the detachment of an anthropologist. I am glad to have seen and gladder to return home—to silence, recollection, reflection, syllables, you.

Tonight I'm in the Austin Lone Star RV Resort, just up the road from the Texas Capitol. I drove here yesterday from New Orleans, an endless rainy haul across a highway built on stilts. The weather this winter (you may enjoy hearing) has been record-awful—wet and cold. So much for my plan to "snowbird" in the South!

Texas is, of all the states, most aggressively itself. Early in our history, allegiance ran to one's state, then to the Republic. Thomas Jefferson, for example, saw himself as a Virginian first, then an American. The United States (until the Civil War) took a plural verb.

Texans still tend to be Texans first, Americans after. The United States annexed the sovereign (albeit short-lived) nation of Texas in 1848, but in Texas you get the feeling the annexation went the other way. "Remember the Alamo!" is a battle-cry associated with the war for Texas independence. Roadside anti-litter signs echo the refrain: "Don't mess with Texas!" they threaten.

If I'm sounding grouchy, it's because I am. The partiers in the next slot keep erupting in guffaws. Such discourtesy is unusual for an RV camp, whose denizens—both young families and blue-hairs—are more the early-to-bed-early-to-rise sort. This is congregate living. Proximity to neighbors teaches us to pipe down. (Thoreau could crow like Chanticleer because there was nobody within hearing.)

In two weeks now, I will be home—for good (odd phrase). Or maybe I should say, for better or for worse. The question of our marriage will be beyond postponing. Marriage, I guess, is always a voluntary association, but most of the time it doesn't feel like it. One is married and that's that, it's a fact of life, a given. Our marriage, we both know, is no longer a given. It's a choice each must make, or it's history. The great experiment of more than half our lives may be over. Even to type this—1,500 miles distant—makes me woozy.

For years I brooded, What went wrong? The road has showed me "What went wrong?" is the wrong question. Anything alive changes all the time. (Rocks may change too, but not at a pace we can detect.) Alteration is inevitable. Persons, plants, peoples can grow together—or apart. It just happens.

My journey has grown me—in all sorts of ways. (By the time I'm dead, maybe I'll be a grown-up!) Never have I mused so long on a single mystery. I knew, setting out, that there was no "meaning" to America, any more than there was a "meaning" to my self, but I wanted to know us both better, to feel, if this makes any sense, from my where, my who.

The more I muse the farther I drift from any Therefore. What happens happens—for a reason or no reason or the wrong reason. Destiny only appears in hindsight, when the facts can be herded into a story. What if some intelligence operative had gotten wind of the 9/11 plot before the planes were hijacked? What if my father, age 46, hadn't had that heart attack? What if you and I hadn't been seated next to each other at that Christmas party where we met (I only decided to go at the last minute)? What if, what if, what if. It all depends.

I do not know who I am, only who I've been (even that I'm not so sure about). I can't say why I want to get up in the morning—and see— except I do.

When we married a quarter century ago, I knew who I was. What I knew, it turns out, was pretty much what I'd been told. My definitions of Success and Duty were inherited. A well-schooled pup, I begged, fetched, rolled over, for bones.

Gradually, as I did more and more of the things I was supposed to, I began to wonder why. What difference was I making—really? The only times I felt fully myself, beyond doubt's tickle, was when I wrote. I could never argue that my writing made much difference, but it felt good—like a warm bed after a cold day, where, somehow, I belonged.

The more I knew, the less I knew—and the less I minded. The childish dream of figuring out Life, of settling into some satisfying certainty, was just that, childish. The Meaning of Life was a fairy tale. Life's meaning, if any, was being, nothing more.

If being is life's sole meaning, then one's mission is to be the best one can. For me that meant quitting all the things I didn't care about and concentrating on the one I did. What I wanted was—who knows what—a glimpse of something true, the waft of a tune. I decided to pursue a feeling, an inkling, a whim. It was insane. But I'd been sane long enough.

I thought of this a few weeks back visiting the Booker T. Washington National Monument in (well-named) Hardy, Virginia. Booker T. Washington National Monument is a big label for what amounts to the slave shack where the great black leader was born.

As often happens, I was the only guest and, with closing time approaching, the rangers shooed me down the snowy trail, to glance at the wind-pierced hovel and be gone. A glance was enough. (Remember that line from Gray's "Elegy"—"The short and simple annals of the poor"?)

Booker T. Washington is one of America's indisputable marvels. Up from Slavery, *his autobiography, makes one gape at his accomplishment. To begin with less than nothing—no father, no education, no prospects, no manners, not even a name (he picked "Washington" when he realized, on his first day of school, that "Booker" alone was an insufficient appellation for a boy who was free)—and to found a great school and be a guest at the White House makes most modern careers feel like goofing off. There were carrots that enticed Washington—literacy, respectability—but there was an even greater stick—the insult of his childhood. Freedom* to *shone in the light of freedom* from.

Washington's story recalls that of other American heroes—pilgrims, pioneers, reformers, capitalists, soldiers, artists—bounded by grimness to glory. In the halting English of Simon Rodia, the illiterate wizard of Watts Towers, "I had in my mind to do something big and I did." That is the genius of our American freedom—that souls can have something big in mind—and do them.

I have been lucky. Hunger, poverty, oppression never haunted me. From the smorgasbord of life, I could pick what appealed.

Good luck, though, can sometimes be bad. Comfort softens—me and America. Absent urgent need, meaning grows less vivid. When you're running for your life, your goal is obvious. But when you're ambling amiably, why run?

It is easier to be married to a man who knows his mind. I—or history—have played you a mean trick by transforming your husband into someone you hardly recognize. I, too, sometimes miss my old certitude: Here's where we're going and why, now shake a leg! It was simpler then.

Whether this new man will appeal to you or you to him, who knows? It'd be convenient—but convenience is weak glue. My job, the mission I imagine, is to make the most of my time. Together or apart, I have no idea.

17
Home

The George H. W. Bush Library and Museum, on the Texas A&M campus in College Station, is big, handsome, and modest, like the man it honors. It is proud, but not vain; expensive, but not gaudy. Except for the orientation film's characterization of the 41st President as "an American hero" (at which, one suspects, Bush squirms), the exhibits promote no outlandish claims for their subject or contort to rewrite history. Bush is neither an enigma, like his predecessor, nor a brilliant bad boy, like his successor. What we saw is what we got: a family man, affectionate, loyal, friendly, diligent, dutiful, decent, commonsensical, not stuck on himself, ready to laugh.

In short, a nice guy. Really. Taft, Harding, Ike, and Ford, in the twentieth century are the only other Presidents one might describe that way.

We like Bush even better in retirement than as President. He's looser now, abler to express his emotions and paternal pride. No matter one's politics, it was hard not to be moved by George W.'s embrace of his dad after taking the oath.

The museum succeeds in giving us a good feeling. We remember that patriotic surge after the Gulf War, how together we felt, and proud. Saddam was a right-sized villain: vile enough to be vivid, greedy enough to be scary, but not so giant we couldn't deck him with a few cuffs. The exhibits make no apology for the decision not to finish off Saddam. Liberating Kuwait was what our allies had signed on for; and Bush the first was nothing if not true to his word.

The museum is so agreeable it is only later, squinting in the hot sun, I wonder what's missing. He was a good man, Bush, but a good President? He wasn't a bad President, surely: none of the seedy shenanigans of Reagan's reign or the moral lapses of Clinton's. He never had to apologize to us or we for him. He stood tall. But what did he stand *for*?

"The vision thing." Bush's exasperated gripe during the 1988 campaign exposed his limitation. He didn't see the difference between leading and

260

managing. A manager takes care of business, deals with what comes. Bush was good at that. A leader points his people to some star and urges them toward it. Bush was a patriot. He was all for patriotism. But he was never able to picture for us what patriotism meant.

His rhetoric—what we remember of it—is not sentences, but staccato bursts: "thousand points of light," "the vision thing," "voodoo economics," "line in the sand." When a verb appears—"Read my lips—no new taxes"; "This shall not stand"—it negates, rather than promotes. Bush shied from the first-person pronoun. You don't tell your children what to do, he remarks in the orientation film, you show them.

Leaders tell their followers what to do. They use active verbs and the first person (singular or plural). They personify a vision. Listen to Lincoln: we, we, we ("we here highly resolve . . ."). Listen to the Roosevelts and Wilson and Kennedy and Reagan. Listen to Martin Luther King, Jr. ("I have a dream"). These men were not modest. They were not diffident. They led—by example, yes, but also by exhortation. They may not have been nice guys—egoists seldom are. But they lifted their people, like the prophets of old, to a new plane. They made us more than we were.

Values, Vision, Efficacy, and Effect—those criteria for Presidential greatness. Bush the first had as good values as any who's held that office. He got a fair amount done, especially in foreign affairs, and his victories—over Saddam, the Panamanian despot Manuel Noriega, and what remained of Communism—left the free world measurably improved. But he failed to apprehend his opportunity—to mount his bully pulpit and wing a message through time. For Presidents, the vision thing is the main thing. Great Presidents never leave office. Their words keep sounding in our thoughts.

ii.

Rivers in Texas's Hill Country aren't what a Yankee thinks of. Rivers in New York run deep and predictably in glacial granite troughs. They don't rise or sink suddenly. Their predictability makes them pretty. Many the long-ago house built close to the banks of the Hudson, unafraid.

Hill Country rivers run shallow. They may seem innocuous, a trickle you can hop across. Their beds and banks, though, bear witness to their fury when aroused. Twenty feet they may rise in a flash, bearing all before. Their unpredictability makes them unpretty. It is hard to love where we fear.

In the garage of Lyndon Johnson's ranch there are two of the white Lincoln convertibles he favored, an old fire truck, a chuck wagon for the barbecues he'd host under the live oaks along the Pedernales; and then there's this odd little turquoise vehicle, high on its wheels, that looks more like a toy than a car. Over the tour bus's PA system (you can only visit the ranch on a National Park Service bus), Joe Califano recalls his first ride in that peculiar car. LBJ had invited Califano to the ranch to recruit him as his Presidential chief of staff. LBJ drove, his secretary sat beside him, and Califano was squeezed into the barely existent back seat. They came to the sloping banks of a lake and the car started to roll. "The brakes!" the President paled. "I've lost the brakes!" The prospect of yet another Presidential death must have flashed through Califano's mind. The car splashed into the water and . . . floated. It was amphibious. That was the President's joke. Later, over dinner, the President told and retold the story, roaring with delight. "Why, Joe was more worried about saving himself than his President!"

Not since Andrew Jackson had there arrived a President so dominating, determined, and bent on bending the nation to his will. Both men were born in states from which Presidents had never hailed and, in the received opinion of their time, never would. Johnson's Texas seemed almost as crude a frontier in the mid-twentieth century as Jackson's Tennessee early in the nineteenth. Both men were born poor and carried into the echelons of power resentment at the elite. Both having come within a hair's breadth of death (by a bullet or a heart attack) were fearless. Both believed they represented a despised constituency, and they'd be damned if they let the big shots rob these little guys of their rights. Jackson declared war on Nicholas Biddle and the Bank of the United States and all liberal eastern snobs. Johnson declared war on poverty and racism and illiteracy (and all liberal eastern snobs). Both were big and intimidating and ruthless. Both made their associates, as well as their enemies, quake.

Our other driving Presidents derived their power from intellectual conviction (TR, Wilson, Truman, Reagan) or national peril (Lincoln and FDR). With Jackson and LBJ the fight to change America was personal. They were settling a score, determined that their hardships and pain would not be endured by those who followed.

Jackson's contribution was less legislative than attitudinal. He ripped the reins of government from the polite propertied classes and handed them to the white male majority. He elevated the President into the nation's sole leader, ready to brave any foe, be it Indians, the bank, nullifiers, the Supreme Court, or Congress. He made American government combative, not collegial; clubbing, not clubby.

Lyndon Johnson was as dominant a legislator as Jackson had been a general. Both knew how to persuade—with flattery before and a drawn sword behind. The photos of Majority Leader Johnson subjecting his fellow Senators to "the treatment," his face so close they had to bend backward not to be bitten, make us feel like surrendering from afar.

It remains a mystery why Johnson, having lost the Democratic nomination in 1960 to the younger and much less powerful Senator Kennedy, agreed to serve as his running mate. My hunch is that Johnson did the math. No man had hurtled so long and hard toward the Presidency, and now he was bypassed by this rich young pretty-boy. The Vice Presidency wasn't a bad place to round out a career, not bad at all for a poor Texan kid (only one Texan—"Cactus Jack" Garner—had made it that far before). With his scarred heart, Johnson wasn't likely to outlive Kennedy, and he didn't have any taste, if Kennedy won, for taking orders from or doing battle with the leader of his own party, as Senate Majority Leader. Besides, Vice Presidents did become Presidents—seven out of 35, 20 percent: long odds, granted, but his best.

Kennedy's assassination gave LBJ more power than any President since FDR. With a spate of laws rivaled only by the New Deal, Johnson placed the United States government on the side of its less advantaged citizens—the black, the poor, the young, the old, the consumer, the factory worker, breathers of air, drinkers of water, females. Only Vietnam flummoxed him, a war he hadn't started, didn't want, and couldn't figure out how to end. Steering a middle course between giving up and giving it our all was unwise, he sensed, but what was he supposed to do? On one wall of the towering Johnson Library (predictably, the tallest and most ostentatious of any built by a President who was still living), one finds Johnson musing that it's easier for a President to do what is right than to know what is right. Since no President was surer about domestic legislation, this seems to refer to Vietnam.

Johnson did more for America's disadvantaged than any President. He deserved their regard. Instead, he ended his Presidency reviled, amidst some of the deadliest race riots and most acrimonious protests in our history. America was wailing—over the bodies of soldiers and riot victims and Dr. Martin Luther King, Jr., and Bobby Kennedy. Government, which LBJ had worked to make the friend of the people, now seemed its enemy.

History will be kinder to LBJ than his moment. His changes to our society endure: the guarantees of civil rights, health insurance for the poor and old, equal pay for women, environmental protection, consumer protection, federal aid to education, and freedom of information are part our national fabric. While the pain of Vietnam recedes, the quandary remains: would fleeing Communism have made the world safer? Would unleashing our full military might have brought on wider war? Hindsight is a genius, but even at this remove it hesitates. Was Vietnam a war that we lost or a losing battle in a larger war—against Communism—which we won? Were our nearly 60,000 American dead in Vietnam a waste or an investment?

Texas is big: in territory, the biggest of the contiguous United States; in population, second and gaining. No state swaggers more, perhaps because it's one of two states that began as a sovereign nation,[35] perhaps because it was born from such hardihood and sacrifice.

Lyndon Johnson was a Texan born and bred: giant in size, determination, rage, patriotism, energy, generosity, vengeance, accomplishment. Psychiatrist Robert Coles describes him as "a restless, extravagantly self-centered, brutishly expansive, manipulative, teasing and sly man, but he was also genuinely passionately interested in making life easier and more honorable for millions of hard-pressed working-class men and women. His almost manic vitality was purposely, intelligently, compassionately used. He could turn mean and sour, but he . . . had more than himself and his place in history on his mind."

Traveling Texas's Hill Country from Austin to Johnson's boyhood home in Johnson City to his ranch and birthplace and grave in Stonewall, one senses the mastery of the man. One can hear him gasping, "The brakes! The brakes!" as his little turquoise aqua-car pitches into the water. One knows without being told that Joe Califano took the job. What choice did he have?

iii.

Treetops RV Park, between Fort Worth and Dallas, ten past eight. Rain dapples the brown puddles left by last night's storm.

The moment. I'd meant to write of something else—the Alamo, say, which I visited two days ago, or "Cactus Jack" Garner's grave in Uvalde (the last of my 65!),[36] or the Texas Book Depository, at whose window one

---

[35]Hawaii's the other.

[36]Ornery, crusty, self-assured, Garner didn't suffer fools gladly, particularly that damned fool in the White House, FDR. It was Garner who characterized the Vice Presidency as "not worth a bucket of warm piss." (Bowdlerizers sometimes substitute "spit" for "piss.")

can crouch, like Lee Harvey Oswald, awaiting that festive motorcade. It feels creepy watching sun-sharpened cars whiz past the fabled Grassy Knoll. But these deaths are old, a childhood scar. My new wonder is a drab checkpoint in a scrubby emptiness. Orange traffic cones, "Dead End," "Road Closed," leafless trees. Miles off, the town, a half-block of flaking stoops. Crawford, Texas. The Presidential ranch.

My grandparents' vacation home in Hobe Sound, Florida, was a few doors down from the Bushes'. I'd shake hands politely with the Senator and Mrs. Bush as they lunched under umbrellas with other Protestants. (Jews were not welcome at the Jupiter Island Club.) New York's Governor Harriman and Pennsylvania's Governor Scranton were also members.

Our families were friendly, not close. Jeb Bush and I attended the same "teen" dances. (I'd be dressed in yellow pants, a pink tie, and a madras jacket.) Our fathers, both pilots during the War, knew each other from Yale. (Everyone seemed to go to Yale.) My godfather preceded Poppy, as our 41st President was then known, as Yale's baseball captain.

In those days, Poppy was viewed as a "great guy" who hadn't hacked it quite, so ended up in Texas. He was "doing something in oil" and maybe "in politics"—there'd been a run for Congress that hadn't gone well. The apple, as one might expect, hadn't fallen far from the tree, but this apple seemed a pippin by comparison.

George W. Bush and I were raised similarly—same set, same epoch, same college, same religion. Similar outcome, one might have guessed. Yet watching him on TV or pausing to snap a picture of his ranch's gate, I feel as if one of us, or both, has been abducted.

It isn't the accent, the slurring and odd pronunciations. It isn't the divergence in destinies, which is predictable. It's God—how He barged into one of our lives and not the other.

The God of the Episcopalians, being a good Episcopalian, minds His manners, speaks when spoken to, avoids disputes in the name of calm, hesitates to confront. From my boyhood I recall only one conversation you could call theological, and that was on a deathbed. I'm pretty sure the Bush dinner table, in Midlands, Texas, or Kennebunkport, Maine, or Hobe Sound, Florida, didn't differ much.

God didn't say how to lead our lives. He hovered over us, yes—but the way a shade tree might or an umbrella. He made us better—more generous, more aware of our neighbors. He comforted us. But He never made us sure.

The God of the first President Bush was the one I recognized. He encouraged, sometimes scowled, but who we were, in the end, was up to us.

The God of the second President Bush is a more specific counselor. On a range of matters, He issues orders, not suggestions. Conclusions that differ are worse than wrong.

I never question faiths. I have seen God too—in the leaves at dusk—and dislike being told I haven't. I'm sure George W.'s God is the genuine article, no political convenience.

But where and when did these two find one another? Did God sneak quietly into his heart or erupt like a cop? How exact are God's directives? Does He leave a to-do list on the President's desk each morning or are His guidelines more general?

I am envious, I confess. It's simpler to follow orders. I have long longed for God to take an interest in my career. How pleasant to know, without hesitation, what to do and say!

I am glad Bush has his God. But I worry he wants to make Him mine. How can I argue with God? If God tells the President something, who am I to demur? But if a thing is right—unarguably, incontrovertibly—why doesn't God convince *me*?

There are all sorts of ways to run a nation. Theocracy is one. But the God of our Founders, while vivid, was absent from everyday events. We were to govern by our own best lights.

"When God is for us," says the prophet, "who can be against us?" The question is unanswerable. But if God keeps His revelations incomplete, if on this policy or that he informs only a minority of Americans, where does that leave the rest of us? God is no democrat. He punishes those who oppose Him. But the basis of our system is compromise, the uncomfortable result of men quarreling with men. Murkiness is our inconvenient birthright.

The nearest city to Crawford is Waco, Texas, where, on April 19, 1993, cult leader David Koresh and 74 of his adherents ended their lives in a prime time inferno. Some, maybe all, believed they were dying for their God.

iv.

A quarter of a century ago, a murderer who styled himself Son of Sam was stalking young women around New York City. Local network affiliates lengthened their broadcasts, covering little else. Tabloids shouted themselves hoarse. Victims' relatives willing to be interviewed repeated their recollections tirelessly, for camera and pen.

The effect was frightening. Fear *did* "grip the City"—caused not by Son of Sam, but the press. If the press reported the facts matter-of-factly, a dozen million New Yorkers would realize that Son of Sam, who murdered, as I recall, at a rate of about one a month for half a dozen months, posed them less risk than banana peels. The press, I harrumphed in my magazine column, should be charged with fomenting a riot.

The press—in the person of a well-known local newscaster—took offense at my accusation and invited me to debate on a Sunday morning talk show. Back then, I believed in the persuasive power of Reason, so I eagerly accepted. To prove how much news was being manufactured, I told how one victim's mother had been interviewed repeatedly, and each time her hairdo and outfit were more extravagant. This mourning mom seemed to see her daughter's murder as a star turn.

Television, of course, appeals not to Reason but Emotion. The local newscaster, realizing this, ignored my point and turned his soulful eyes into the camera. "It is not for us to criticize the parents of the dead," he seemed to blink back tears. Ingeniously, he had transformed me into an insensate brute. I wanted to hide.

I recalled this humiliation as I made my way through the Oklahoma City National Memorial, a vast tribute to the victims of the bombing of the Murrah Federal Building.

The Memorial is an affecting and elegant work of art: beautiful, original, and serene: three-dimensional story-telling of a high order. It is worth seeing. But was it, I could not help wondering, worth building? Do the 168 lives lost—and the efforts of rescuers and grief of survivors—merit this apotheosis?

I invited Washington and John Adams and Lincoln and Lewis and Clark and the hearty settlers of the Oklahoma territory to join me on my tour. What would they make of this massive and expensive wail? The cost of the Memorial exceeds our federal budget in the early years.

What we honor defines us. In our early years as a nation, there were few memorials: we were too busy building to recall. The Washington Monument was not completed until 86 years after Washington's death. Many of our early Presidents and Vice Presidents were buried without much ceremony. Some are hard to find.

Grieving is a luxury. It takes time and money. To grieve you need a roof over your head. The children need to have been fed.

The fashion of mourning took hold in the second half of the nineteenth century, when ladies idled by luxury needed something to do. They wept, and hid themselves in crepe, and wove wreaths and pendants out of the departed's hair. They ordered up ever-more-elaborate tombs and statues. Cherubic infants were a favorite.

Our public memorials grew too. Villages erected monuments for their war dead. The Civil War persisted half a century after Appomattox, in bronze and marble. Every officer above the rank of Major, it seems, was a hero.

The disaster memorial is a phenomenon of the last quarter of the twentieth century. The Holocaust and slavery were the first subjects. Their purpose was never to forget, to combat our understandable tendency to sweep shame and misfortune under the rug of history. Arthur Miller's play, *Death of a Salesman* (1949), democratized tragedy. You did not have to be noble or outstanding to be a hero. The sufferings of ordinary citizens, he suggested radically, could be tragic too.

By century's end, every accidental death was routinely described as "tragic." Dying became a noteworthy accomplishment. Sorrow-sharing generated community. The Oklahoma City Memorial "honors the victims, survivors, rescuers and all who were changed forever on April 19, 1995," explains the effusive brochure. "It encompasses the now-sacred soil where the Murrah Federal Building once stood, capturing and preserving forever the place and events that changed the world." Forever, forever, sacred—the lexicon of religion.

Washington and John Adams and Lincoln and Lewis and Clark and the settlers of the Oklahoma territory would have been startled, I think, by this exorbitance of grief. Everybody dies, for pity's sake. What mattered was what you made of your time—and in this, there was a hierarchy of achievement, with a few at the summit and the middling majority beneath. Life, not death, was the great adventure.

Exiting the Oklahoma Memorial Museum one is urged by a solemn attendant to have, "above all, a safe day." "No!" I felt my guts clench. Safe is the last thing I want. I want a dangerous day, a day that threatens and tests and risks my complacencies and presumptions and causes me to discover and explore. I want a day dedicated not to regret for the past but to gratitude for the future. I shy from the "comfort, peace and serenity" this memorial purports to offer. I want discomfort, strife, the excitement of exertion. Comfort, peace, and serenity are the blessings of death.

V.

"So what's been your biggest surprise?"

The question dangles—a conversational convenience. I use it often my-self.

My problem is everything surprises me. Nothing's what I thought. When I'm not surprised I'm surprised.

No two days on this journey have been alike, no two views. That is how I want to lead my life from now on, every day new.

Everything surprises—but not everything shocks. The shock for me— greater even than Wal-Mart or RV parks or Confederate flags or the suppura-tions of poverty—has been Indians. I prefer the descriptor "Indian." When a white man says "Native American," he's absolving himself. "My bad old for-bear said 'Indian,'" his revision suggests, "but *I* am enlightened."

What shocks me is how I'd crammed Indians into a demeaning caricature. From Tonto and kindergarten pageants onward, I'd shrunk Indians into a col-orful adornment, an American accent. With their feather headdresses, toma-hawks, war-whoops, and funny names, Indians made me feel good about myself. We honored Indians, didn't we? I was raised in a village named for Chief Kisco. I attended Cisqua and Rippowam Schools. I gagged down suc-cotash at Sunday lunches and snuck Eskimo pies. We named sports teams after Indians and smeared our faces with war-paint for pep rallies.

The musical comedy Injun from Cole Porter to Irving Berlin did not of-fend me—why should it? The Indian was amusing, nice to have around. Slavery was evil. Coming from Yankee stock, it was not *my* people who kept slaves. But America's treatment of Indians never troubled me. Sure, they lost the battle for the continent, but that's how history happens. Some win, some lose. You move on.

We were not always so callous. "The utmost good faith shall always be observed toward the Indians," asserted our founders in the Northwest Or-dinance (1787); "their lands and property shall never be taken from them without their consent; and in their property, rights, and liberty, they shall never be invaded or disturbed, unless in just and lawful wars authorized by congress; but laws founded in justice and humanity shall from time to time be made, for preventing wrongs being done to them, and for preserving peace and friendship with them." Chief Justice Marshall confirmed this as law in *Worcester vs. Georgia*: "The Indian nations had always been con-sidered as distinct, independent, political communities, retaining their original natural rights, as the undisputed possessors of the land, from time

269

immemorial. . . . The settled doctrine of the law of nations is, that a weaker power does not surrender its independence—its right to self-government—by associating with a stronger, and taking its protection. A weak state, in order to provide for its safety, may place itself under the protection of one more powerful, without stripping itself of the right of government, and ceasing to be a state."

Such a policy, we nod, did us proud. America was victorious but magnanimous. And what happened? Our ideals became inconvenient. We were running out of the free land we'd grown used to. The Indians, even where we'd herded them, held too much. And really, it wasn't theirs at all, was it? We'd given it to them, but now we needed it, so they should give it back. They weren't *doing* much with it anyway, just leaving it open. Americans knew what to do with land. We settled it, cleared the forests, surveyed, dug wells, laid roads. We *improved* it. If the Indians weren't going to do anything with their land, they might as well occupy acreage that wasn't worth as much. Way west, say, in the Prairie.

Jackson's Indian Removal Act of 1830 is unforgivable, so we forget it. A century and a half later, we'd be wringing our hands at Hitler's treatment of the Jews. How, we asked incredulously, could a civilized people tolerate such viciousness? The Trail of Tears was no different. We the People removed tribes from their legitimate homes and drove them to distant compounds, casually killing stragglers and objectors without a pretense of justice. We the People, who held "these truths to be self-evident, that all men are created equal, that they are endowed by their Creator with certain unalienable Rights, that among these are Life, Liberty and the pursuit of Happiness," toppled within a generation from high-mindedness to genocide. And why? Rapacity. We wanted what we'd given. So we stole it, removed the evidence, and concocted theories to justify our crime. We shrunk Indians into Injuns just as twentieth-century Germans shrunk Jews into crook-nosed caricatures. Either we belittled the Indians or we'd have to despise ourselves. What choice was there?

Modern theology and psychology labor mightily to alleviate guilt. Say sorry and the boo-boo will be all gone. It is easy, indeed, pleasurable, to revile others for what we label "inhumanity"—the Germans, say, or more recently, the Serbs or Hutus or Saddam Hussein. Americans, by contrast, are a good people, who should feel good, really good, about ourselves. That's what we're taught.

Ethnologists estimate that more than a million Indians occupied North America when the first European colonists arrived, with their measles, smallpox, horses, and guns. In the museum at Fort Smith, Arkansas—for generations the federal command post of the Indian Territory—there's an ingenious electronic map, which tracks Indian migration from 1780 to 1861. Push a button and observe the pinpoint clusters of blue, red, purple, and yellow lights gradually drain from Tennessee and Ohio and Mississippi and Florida and Georgia and the Carolinas and Delaware and Pennsylvania and New York and New England into what we today call Oklahoma. Soon the lands of the east are dark. But we are not done yet. Having fenced the Indians in their new barren land, we further decimate them with laws that outlaw their customs and guarantee their inebriation and dereliction, until in 1907, when Oklahoma gains statehood, they are outnumbered, powerless and despised in the place we've given them for their own.

This too is America, home of the free.

vi.

"I still believe in a place called Hope."

I was 41 when I heard those words. Embarrassing tears pressed into my eyes. I was ready to believe.

"Patriotism," growled Dr. Johnson, "is the last refuge of a scoundrel." It is sometimes. But patriotism can also be the last refuge of a dreamer.

Cynics, sifting the evidence, can identify a self-interested motive for every episode in our history. The Puritans were fleeing persecution, sailing from, not to. The Founding Fathers were protecting cash flow, not liberty. Southern "honor" masked the dishonor of slavery, just as "Manifest Destiny" distracted from the Indians underfoot. The boys at Gettysburg *had* to advance, since retreat would have brought disgrace. And on and on. Lofty ideals grease the gears of crass calculation. Leaders are liars, followers dupes.

Such sneerers are tough to debate. Humans, like any creatures, act self-interestedly. We also delude ourselves about our motives. We say we marry for love, for instance, when it can be demonstrated, in a majority of instances, that a marriage makes economic sense. We worship a particular God, we claim, omitting to mention that membership in *this* congregation promotes our career.

"The shining City on the Hill," "We hold these truths to be self-evident," "a government of the people, by the people, for the people," "Making the world safe for democracy"—such slogans, as the cynics see it, only ease

271

our consciences. That may be—but that's not how it feels. Possessed by belief, we are lifted up, as if by an eagle's talons, to a thrilling height. We're convinced we matter, that we're not just insects, born to buzz and replenish the dust. We admit our belief makes no sense—is absurd, really—but so? It is precious, dearer to us than life itself. Try filching it and I'll claw your eyes out.

I believe in America. I can't help it. I don't want to help it. I feel myself a soldier in a great army marching toward some tremendous destiny. I believe with my eyes open. I can see the pimples and pustules on my beloved. I can smell her sourness. But still I believe. Nothing like America has ever happened. How the shining city on the hill became this great experiment in self-government, then one nation, then the mightiest nation on earth, is so improbable it must be a miracle. How, in a mere two centuries, we amassed such power—to pierce the heavens and explode the atom and defeat diseases and build above the clouds and girdle the globe. . . . I rub my eyes. It's not possible! And yet, unless I'm dreaming, it seems to have occurred. Here we are: more powered and privileged than any people ever. What now?

The hopelessness of "a place called Hope" should not have surprised me. I snapped a picture of the block adjacent to the Clinton Center in the old railroad station. In this typical row of five brownstones, the upper stories are vacant, the windows whitewashed, only two of the five storefronts are occupied, the paint is peeling. Sidewalks buckle, making walking dicey. Weeds sprout. The occasional pedestrian ambles or slouches.

I understood suddenly why a prodigy like Clinton needed to escape such a trap. This was no place for ambition. Neither, for that matter, was Arkansas after a while. In Little Rock, I drifted through the corridors of the Capitol as legislators milled. The governorship, too, cramped a talent as bursting as Clinton's. Bill Clinton, like Jackson, the Roosevelts, LBJ, and Reagan, barreled into the Presidency. His personal urgency, somehow, could not be stopped. There was no diffidence or modesty about his appetite for the job. He *had* to be President, had to be, and would be, just see if he wouldn't.

The scale of Clinton's political talent is what makes the result of his Presidency so sad. Here was a man who could really transform a hopeless reality into a place called Hope. He could make us believe. And what did he do with this great gift? Much that was good. But then he plunged the nation into a cauldron of moral crud.

It was not just the blow jobs in the Oval Office. It was not just the lies before the camera and under oath. It was a pervasive impression that nothing that was said was true, that every soaring sentiment was a manipulation, that those of us who believed in America were somehow suckers. The Clintons claimed a right-wing conspiracy was ganging up against them. Maybe they were. But I wasn't one of them. I voted for the man twice. I was convinced that any person who entered that office would be elevated by it. That a President would insult the Republic by his conduct, then lie about it, then insist on keeping the office he'd besmirched made me despise myself for my credulity. That Bill Clinton was unfaithful to his wife was her business. That he was unfaithful to me—my America—was mine.

My friends laughed. Get over it, they said, they all do it. I couldn't. I didn't want to. If insulting America didn't matter, then America didn't matter, then I didn't matter. All faiths are fantasies—I know that. But without them, why bother being? America was my dream, my cause, my explanation. That my fellow citizens could shrug off this assault filled me with gloom. Even Nixon, deluded though he was, thought himself a patriot when he lied. Did Clinton believe his lechery and evasions would improve America?

Time cools. Yesterday's outrage dwindles to today's regret. After the distortions of his successor Clinton's evasions feel like fibs. The memory of Clinton's excellence, his generous tone, softens anger at his seamy conduct.

He had so much talent—why not a little restraint! That the fate of the world may be altered by a throb of lust makes you think.

vii.

Horror.

Thursday, east of Knoxville, Tennessee, in a camp where, oddly, nine months ago, my water hose was stolen, my computer balked at starting. I tried this and that, my pulse accelerating, then bumbled into a program that erased my hard drive. You would think, since writing's my business, I'd been backing up regularly; but in the rush of the last 60 days, I'd neglected maintenance, so the erasures included all my work (and photos).

I tend not to panic in a crisis. What is is: Now what? A voice at Dell Computer pointed me to a California company, Drivesavers, which, for a mid-sized fortune, might retrieve my data. The reassuring voice at Drivesavers was "95 percent certain" this could be accomplished, but he was a salesman. I located a Mailboxes, Etc., where I shipped and packed my disloyal

273

machine, and commenced my vigil. Ninety-five per cent is favorable odds, unless you're the one in twenty who does not make it through.

Until this morning, Saturday, I could not speak. I accelerated my motion to avoid thinking, like a patient awaiting a biopsy result. I made my way admiringly over the Great Smokey Mountains, on a feathery early spring day; then to Asheville, where I revisited George Vanderbilt's sad, nutty Biltmore Mansion, America's largest house. Graceland, Elvis Presley's famous home in Memphis, which I'd visited the day before, is sad too. Two strange, isolated men, elevated from their peers—one by wealth, the other by talent—secure themselves in extravagant dungeons, posting toadies at the gates for their protection. The palaces of Europe glow with a public purpose: their glories heartened subjects and alerted rivals. America's private palaces are meant to exalt individuals, not dignify communities. The Biltmore Mansion and Graceland each attract a million or more gawkers annually (who pay more than $30 per person for the privilege). The displays dazzle, as they were intended to. But there's also wonder, that so much stuff could result in so little joy. George Vanderbilt and Elvis Presley preside sadly over their absurd piles, despite the best efforts of docents to portray these proprietors as glad. Gladness does not hole up amid luxury and sycophants, bolting doors. Too much is proof of not enough.

That's what I was thinking when I wasn't following my poor bubble-wrapped computer, as it made its way in the cold hold of a FedEx jet to San Francisco and Drivesavers. Speechless, unable to face my grotesque irresponsibility, I departed Asheville at 12:30 a.m. and drove all night. I hated myself—hated—but what use howling? I could only go on, make the best of what I was, try to reform, even knowing it was hopeless. Again and again in my life I've made trouble for myself by omitting obvious precautions. It's not stupidity, but something worse: scorn of conventional restraints; bravado; a secret smugness. I relish the excitement of defiance. It's why I write.

Now it is five-thirty in Cherry Hill Campground in College Park, Maryland, the same park where I spent five or so days back in freezing January. Yesterday I visited the sad home of Wilson's dreary post-Presidential phase. All the nearly blind, paralyzed, and repudiated former President could do, it seems, was attend the vaudeville, which he managed 47 times in a single year. I wonder at the scantiness of my account of Wilson, one of the handful of leaders whose vision revised the world. Of Washington, too, I've said little—and Taylor and Truman and Ford and Tompkins and Clinton (George) and Dallas and Wheeler and Hobart and Garner and Mondale and Quayle. There's no end of telling! Only of time.

274

viii.

I wake among big-rigs.

Twice this year, making haste, I have slept not in a camp but at a highway truck stop. Migrant, who looms in a grocery store parking lot, is a pipsqueak here.

I doze more than sleep, listening to the roar and snort and shudder. How slight and silly Migrant must look to these truck drivers, like a weekend skiff to the captain of a tanker. Do they smile on me or sneer? They are engaged in work—transportation—useful and essential commerce—while I?

Exhaustion is the enemy of clarity. A soft sun is rising in the dew. I blink and shake my head, not to drift off. In less than a dozen hours I will be home. My journey will be done, defining me. I will be the man who oddly upped one May day and bought an RV to visit the graves and homes of the Presidents and Vice Presidents. In a few months, with luck, I will be the man who wrote this book.

And so? We Americans are avid for Therefores. What did you find? What freight are you hauling home? What's the bottom line?

I cannot see America, it is too vast and various. Yet it shines, like this sun behind the clouds, lighting all. America is a place not on the map but in the mind, a nation, yes, but more, a notion. It has existed from the first in our imagination—a city upon the hill; a government of the people, by the people; the last best hope of mankind. It is our dream.

America exists because we imagine that we the People were born to some exceptional role. Cease to see what America might be and it will vanish. Blink and it will be gone.

Sometimes America has burned hotly in our brains, like a lover's vision. Nothing mattered more. At other times, America has seemed no big deal or worse. Lovers' ardor cools—it must, for us to go on—but without the memory of that love, and the chance of it, why are we here? We belong to America and America to us. We must care and take care.

I do not haul any great freight of thought, to mark on a bill of lading and roll onto skids at the docks. I cannot, with assurance, claim a use for what I've done. But I know the doing has enlarged me, made me better somehow. Never have I felt more alive, more grateful to the men and women who gave me this chance, more in love with my time. To be glad in the morning may be the summit of accomplishment. My soul rises in thanks.

The exhilaration of the road, the entanglements of home. My wife and I had hoped to be happy, but it was hard. We will always be a part of one another but, for now at least, we live apart.

Migrant waits in my field, as my dog Hercules waits by my door, to see when we're going. Migrant worries if I still need her. We have taken two brief jaunts, for old time's sake. I'm tempted to get in and go—anywhere—but you can't just travel to no end. Or can you?

America continues, big as ever. Triple A forecasts its busiest summer in a decade. Tens of millions of Americans will set out in search of—they're not sure what—and return with—they can't quite say.

But they'll be glad they went.

P.S.

A plain narrow room, its window overlooking an airshaft. I am propped on a bed, books stacked beside me, steam wreathing from my cup, a laptop warm on my lap. The city's music is new. A jet exhales, a taxi honks, a two-by-four thuds (construction will start soon, with its saws and hammers), a spoon clinks, a pigeon coos. Holiday mornings, in the building opposite, a boy practices his drums. (It seems a boy.) His progress in his art is not promising. I wish him well.

Friends ask why I work on a bed, in a narrow room. Before my year in the van, I worked in a chair or at a desk. Now, each dawn, return is urgent—to narrowness, stacked books, phones unplugged, a window looking onto—nothing much. The room where I compose, my spiritual home, has become a van.

I did not know what I was looking for when I heaved myself into Migrant's cab that gray Sunday. Escape, yes. A change. By ejecting myself from my life maybe I'd find out who I was. Uniform and props packed away, was there a person beneath? I hoped to strike up an acquaintance, become friends.

I left desiccated, discouraged. I returned raring to live.

My marriage, despite our best efforts, was over. But there were new loves, new lives. I had no idea who I was going to be. I was eager to find out.

I got lucky. My time with the Presidents and Vice Presidents made me a believer in luck. There's no telling why Chester Arthur became President and Garret Hobart didn't. When the expected happens it's a surprise.

The story of my luck is for another time. Friends see the effect. "You've gotten so much nicer," said one.

America's spirits, meanwhile, darkened. The America I visited was post 9/11. Attacked, we believed in our idea. Our cause was just.

Five years later, we find ourselves mired in an ill-advised war we cannot win. Nations, once our admirers, despise us. Others mock.

Gloom prevails. The American idea seems outmoded, maybe pernicious. Our decline seems irreversible.

My time in America persuades me there's no predicting. The weight of a feather, a single soldier at Gettysburg, may tip history's scale.

My life is happy so my forecast is. The great self-correcting engine, constructed by those young men in steamy Philadelphia, may creak, but it works. Past crises called up the leaders we needed—Washington, Lincoln, FDR. It can happen again.

Feeling low, we question the specialness of America. A shining city on a hill? The last best hope of freedom? Are you nuts?

I don't believe God made America. Chance did, the chance of geography, nationality, timing, personality. Stir in our continent, our climate, our forbears, revolutions in thought, Lincoln, and for once, the alchemy of history yielded gold.

America may not be the greatest power in history. Such comparisons are pointless. The Egyptian, Assyrian, Greek, Roman, Ottoman, Venetian, and British empire each was a wonder in its way.

We have our blotches and humiliations. Our history is marred.

But in one respect we dazzle. In no dominant power have more people been more free.

Our freedom is political: nearly all can participate in choosing leaders. Our freedom is economic: prosperity has never been more widespread. Our freedom is racial, religious, sexual, after much strife. We can travel where we like, live where we like within our borders. The state pretty much leaves us alone if we keep the peace.

Most astonishingly, we can believe what we please. This came to me every morning in my van. I could say what I'd seen without fear of censors or the noose. No pledge was required, no salute, no Amen. Booed I might be, but not booted.

Whether so much freedom is healthful may be debated. Lots of people insist on a single truth. That is their freedom. America, by permitting exploration, encourages it. Come over the mountain, she calls to us, see what you can see.

This, to my mind, is America's greatest gift, which it is up to us to preserve.

Thanks

To Al, Becca, Betsy, Bill, Camille, Carmen, Catharine,
Dan, David, Diane, Eileen, Em, Fredi, George, Gordon,
Hadassah, Hillel, Howard, Jack, Janice, John, Judy, Junie,
Kathleen, Larry, Lizz, Lynn, Mark, Mary Ann, Misha,
Nick, Peter, Sean, Seema, Shel, Steve, Stone, Susan, Tom
and especially Jane—friends along the way